# Praise for *One Land, Two States*

"The Parallel States concept to resolve the Palestinian-Israeli conflict is the
most daring and intriguing new idea for a permanent peace that has come
along in two generations of failed negotiations. It deserves very serious
consideration by all interested parties, because in its entirety or in some of its
component elements it could spark a more productive new path to peace,
justice, and coexistence."

> Rami G. Khouri, Director, Issam Fares Institute for Public Policy and
> International Affairs, American University of Beirut, and syndicated
> columnist for Agence Global and the *Daily Star*

"You may call it fantasy, daydreaming, or utopia. But isn't this what Herzl
faced too? When those who are preoccupied with the conventional two-state
solution are being called obsessive, this book offers a new, fascinating,
innovative approach with different tools to solve the same old problem for
the same people. Wanted! Two brave leaders to take up the challenge."

> Arad Nir, Foreign Affairs Editor, Channel 2 News, Israel

"The Parallel States Project is a vision aimed at shattering the accepted
conventions regarding the political solution of the Israeli-Palestinian conflict.
What it is in fact is an attempt to square the circle. It will take the political
world, which has come up against one failure after another in its efforts to
advance peace among the peoples living in the Holy Land, some time to
digest the concept. Ultimately, there is quite a good chance that the idea of a
functional partition will trickle down to the peoples and their leaders and
offer the formula that will finally lead to conciliation and peace."

> Israel Harel, chairman and founder of Yesha Council, head of the
> Institute for Zionist Strategies, columnist for *Haaretz*, and participant
> in the Parallel States Project

# One Land, Two States

# One Land, Two States

*Israel and Palestine as Parallel States*

EDITED BY

## Mark LeVine and
## Mathias Mossberg

UNIVERSITY OF CALIFORNIA PRESS

*Berkeley · Los Angeles · London*

University of California Press, one of the most
distinguished university presses in the United States,
enriches lives around the world by advancing scholarship
in the humanities, social sciences, and natural sciences. Its
activities are supported by the UC Press Foundation and
by philanthropic contributions from individuals and
institutions. For more information, visit www.ucpress.edu.

University of California Press
Berkeley and Los Angeles, California

University of California Press, Ltd.
London, England

Library of Congress Cataloging-in-Publication Data

One land, two states : Israel and Palestine as parallel
states / edited by Mark LeVine and Mathias Mossberg.
    p.  cm.
Includes bibliographical references and index.
ISBN 978-0-520-27912-4 (cloth : alk. paper)
ISBN 978-0-520-27913-1 (pbk. : alk. paper)
ISBN 978-0-520-95840-1 (ebook)
    1. Arab-Israeli conflict—1993—Peace.  I. LeVine,
Mark, 1966–  II. Mossberg, Mathias.
DS119.76.O54  2014
956.9405′4—dc23

                                        2013040123

Manufactured in the United States of America
23  22  21  20  19  18  17  16  15  14
10  9  8  7  6  5  4  3  2  1

In keeping with a commitment to support
environmentally responsible and sustainable printing
practices, UC Press has printed this book on Natures
Natural, a fiber that contains 30% post-consumer waste
and meets the minimum requirements of ANSI/NISO
Z39.48–1992 (R 1997) (Permanence of Paper).

# Contents

# Illustrations

# Preface

MATHIAS MOSSBERG AND MARK LEVINE

This volume analyzes the possibility and feasibility of establishing two parallel states, Israel and Palestine, on the same territory, the land between the Mediterranean and the Jordan River. Two state structures exercising sovereignty over the same piece of land is an idea that has not previously been explored in the context of the Israeli-Palestinian conflict—or almost any other setting, for that matter. At the heart of such a political arrangement is the still-novel idea of states responding primarily to their citizens, and only secondarily to their territory. In such a scenario, state structures would be separate and independent, but would have to take each other into account in most if not all major policy decisions and their broader function. Sovereignty over the broader territory would be both divided and shared between the two governing authorities and the bodies politic they represent.

This study, and the project it grew out of, is a provocation against conventional thinking, against the Middle East peace process as we know it, and against the main actors in the region and outside. The aim is not to provoke for the sake of provoking, but to study new thoughts and ideas that can contribute to opening a way forward toward a truly "just and lasting peace" between Palestinians and Israelis. The study is also a provocation against established understandings of concepts such as sovereignty and state and against some of the most fundamental principles of international law the way we are accustomed to interpreting it.

As we write these lines, the peace process, which has now lasted for more than thirty years, has not yielded any results that can constitute a solid foundation for an end to conflict, or even building stones for such a foundation. Many observers have come to question whether there was ever any intention, at least on the part of some actors, to achieve results, or the peace process was instead meant to deflect interest and energy, not least the interest and energy of the international community, while the decisive action of the conflict was taking place on the ground and outside the limelight.

Our ideas are thus designed not merely as an alternative to the reality of deadlock and bleak prospects for progress that have for so long characterized the peace process. Even in the event that the process reaches fruition and produces a "final status agreement" that includes the creation of some sort of Palestinian state (as this book enters production, Israeli and Palestinian diplomats have just met for the first time in three years in Washington, D.C., ostensibly toward that end), we believe the conventional notions of dividing sovereignty territorially likely cannot support the long-term viability of either an independent and autonomous Palestinian state, or a healthy and productive relationship between two states divided so within the territory of historical Palestine/ Eretz Yisrael. A truly "just and lasting peace" between Jews and Palestinians—the only kind that can ensure security and development for both peoples—will require a new political architecture and even a new system of thought and interaction, one that ensures both the greatest possible autonomy and the fairest and most flexible level of integration and mutual support.

## PROVOKING THE EXPECTED

We anticipate that the concepts discussed in this book could enter into the already rich debates about the contents of metaconcepts such as sovereignty and territoriality, yet our main ambition is not to contribute to the development of theory in the areas we are engaging. On the contrary, this study is an attempt to focus on a specific conflict in all its particularities and to address this conflict in a new way that is specific to its histories and present dynamics. Nevertheless, we hope and believe that the ideas discussed here have the potential to be applied to other territorial conflicts—kin the Middle East and elsewhere—that remain unresolvable within the traditional, territorially grounded nation-state framework.

Our study is, further, a provocation against conventional thinking about conflict resolution in general, and as it has been practiced within the Israeli-Palestinian conflict in particular. The point of departure is that only by forcing ourselves to think outside the box can the present state of deadlock be addressed. There is no longer the possibility to remain inside the realm of the box; the box is broken.

Finally, this study is an effort to focus on visions. It's about looking beyond everyday politics and focusing on long-term perspectives, as well as how developments—or the lack thereof—in the Middle East region relate to emergent dynamics in the rest of the world. Across world today increasing numbers of people, from powerful politicians to ordinary citizens, understand the global future as one of integration and unification: enabling people to see their common interests and what unifies rather than divides them. Increased communication is bringing people closer together, and building bridges between them is also increasingly a global norm, if still far from reality. In all these respects the developments in Israel and Palestine run contrary to global trends. Israel and Palestine today are not about unification, communication, and building bridges, but about separation, division, and closures, building walls instead of bridges.

Only by challenging the established paradigms and looking at the basic elements from a new perspective can new ways forward be found that will bring the much-desired ends of peace, fairness, and justice for both peoples. Existing parameters have proved not only ineffective but counterproductive; existing terms have been emptied of their meanings and, in some cases, abused; and the peace process as such, to the extent there can be said to be one, has long since ceased to have any significance outside its solipsistic political and mainstream media framework.

In this context, the research before you is a provocation against the main actors in the region and the international community, all of whom continue to focus on a conventional territorial two-state solution, long after it has become evident that this is no longer a realistic option.

Even if "everything goes as expected" with the just-restarted peace talks (as U.S. Secretary of State John Kerry put it), there remains a serious case against optimism for the achievement of an agreement that could bring the conflict to a definitive close, even one that produces a "two-state solution" and an official "end of conflict" signed on to by leaders of both sides. There is unfortunately little reason to believe that the present stage of the negotiation process will succeed better than preceding efforts. There are no new substantive elements in the picture, and political realities on each side speak a clear language. And there seem to be definite limits to the scope of outside—American or European—involvement, as the tolerance for continued settlement expansion has demonstrated.

## NEW QUESTIONS, NEW SOLUTIONS?

That being said, a breakthrough would of course be welcome, even if the objective of this study would thereby appear to be made less relevant. Unfortunately, there seem to be limited prospects for such a development, and efforts to promote new thinking still look not only worthwhile but seem to be gaining ground in the debate, both within the region and internationally.

Even should there be a breakthrough and a territorial two-state solution be arrived at, prospects are slim that such an arrangement could lead to the end of claims and the end of conflict. It is more than likely that key issues—such as refugees, or the economic balance of power between the two states—would be far from resolved and that a great number of people would still be left without a vision for their future, leading them to look for other ways to promote their cause.

If our goal is to stimulate new thinking in a situation of deadlock, our primary means of doing so is to ask new questions rather than provide answers to dilemmas that have already been scrutinized unsuccessfully for decades. We make no pretense of offering a new "definitive" solution to a century-old conflict. But if by offering new modes of thinking and conceptualizing the future we can stimulate further new thinking, either about the present conflict or about others around the world, this study will have been worth the effort.

The present volume takes a broad approach and covers areas of international law, constitutional issues, central and local government functions and bodies, security structure and strategy, economic concerns, legal systems, religious environment, and more. The ambition, however, is not to build a model of a society based on the idea of parallel states, but rather to investigate the general feasibility of the basic idea as such, and try to identify and formulate the questions that such an approach would pose so that those closest to the conflict could take the idea and explore its feasibility further. We have therefore limited ourselves to less than half a dozen out of a much larger host of issues that could be addressed in relation to the concept of parallel states: mainly we focus on the divisibility of sovereignty and issues related to security, economic prospects, jurisdiction, and religion.

First among these arguments is a critique of the norm of indivisibility of sovereignty, and of how sovereignty is implemented through the exercise of political authority. Our belief is that the emergence of new dimensions and practices related to how states relate to each other and to their citizens, as well as to the role and importance of borders in these processes, is likely to be applicable to the Middle East, and more particularly to the Israeli-Palestinian conflict.

The feasibility of a territorial two-state solution started to be questioned many years ago (indeed, at least as far back as 1987, the year the first Intifada erupted). Many of the contributors to this book have been deeply engaged in peacemaking efforts at various levels and stages during the past thirty years, from highly secret channels both before and after the Oslo negotiations to "track II" meetings and academic conferences, where political and social taboos have, however gingerly, been broken. In dialogues between Israelis and Palestinians, other scenarios have been discussed for a number of years. The origins of the parallel states idea goes back to dialogues with a group of outstanding Israeli and Palestinian academics and experts, many with close ties to leaders on their respective sides, arranged by the New York–based European-American think tank the EastWest Institute in the years 2004–2006. Under the influence of these dialogues, articles were published in the international press and scholarly journals starting in 2006.

Against the background of the ideas introduced in these articles it was suggested to the Swedish Foreign Ministry in 2008 that it support an effort by the Center for Middle Eastern Studies at Lund University to elaborate on these ideas in cooperation with Israeli and Palestinian colleagues. This became the Parallel States Project (PSP), with the objective to stimulate discussion about new forms for coexistence between Israelis and Palestinians and to produce a research report on the topic of parallel states.

The project began in September 2008 and culminated with a major international conference titled "One Land—Two States: An Alternative Scenario for Israeli-Palestinian Accommodation" in October 2010 at Lund University. Subsequent meetings were held through 2013 to update and revise research and prepare the book for publication. In addition to initial support from the Swedish Foreign Ministry, the project and the conference were supported by the Swedish Research Council, the Riksbankens Jubileumsfond, and Lund University. The editors of this volume wish to express their gratitude to these institutions for their generous support, and to the Center for Middle Eastern Studies at Lund University and Director Leif Stenberg for hosting the project and for having the vision to continue to support the work that has made this volume possible. They also wish to thank all those Israeli, Palestinian, American, and Swedish experts who, in addition to the authors of the chapters in this volume, contributed generously their time and thoughts to the project. Special thanks also go to Charlotta Liljedahl, Mikaela Rönnerman, Yildiz Arslan, and Lina Eklund for their invaluable efforts and contributions, as well as to Jonna Pettersson, Rickard Lagervall, Vanja Mosbach, Anders Ackfeldt, Anna Hellgren, and Christina Rothman, all at Lund University, who in various ways contributed.

*Lund, Sweden, and Irvine, California, October 2013*

# Foreword

*Two States on One Land—Parallel States as
an Option for Israel and Palestine*

ÁLVARO DE SOTO

The two-state solution to the Israeli-Palestinian conflict is the long-undisputed doyenne of the global agenda—a magnificent flagship presiding over a fleet of elusive international causes. No *tour d'horizon* of world hot spots is complete without the ritual hand-wringing over this maddening diplomatic puzzle. It is so deeply entrenched on the agenda that it boasts its own collegial international steward, self-appointed but Security Council–endorsed, in the shape of the Middle East Quartet, formed in 2002, composed of Russia, the United States, the European Union, and the UN secretary-general.

Well into its seventh decade, the idea of a two-state solution lives doggedly on in the speeches and talking points of world leaders; in resolutions at the United Nations and other bodies; in the writings of academics, doctoral candidates, pundits, and bloggers; in statements by members of the Quartet; and in the careers of successive generations of diplomats and academics, all in one way or another players in the "Oslo process" launched on the White House lawn in 1993.

It would be crude to question the good faith of all those who keep the idea of a two-state solution alive; but may I suggest that the time has come to acknowledge that the emperor is not in actual fact wearing any clothes? That an alarming gash, reminiscent of the *Titanic*'s a century ago, has appeared along the magnificent flagship's hull? That the Quartet, which seemed like a good idea at the time, has sapped the "peace process" of energy and creativity?

There is little relief to be found in turning to the parties to the putative two-state solution. Israeli spokesmen tell us that three successive prime ministers have explicitly accepted the creation of a Palestinian state as part of such a solution and that they are ready to negotiate without preconditions. But in point of fact the first of the three, Ariel Sharon, showed little inclination to negotiate: the 2005 evacuation of Israeli settlers and soldiers from Gaza and a handful of outposts in the northern West Bank was essentially a unilateral move—a *fuite en avant* designed (as Sharon's chief adviser told *Haaretz)* to use "formaldehyde . . . so that there will not be a political process with the Palestinians."

His successor, Ehud Olmert, issued a lonely *cri de coeur* to the Jews of Israel, also through *Haaretz:* unless a Palestinian state, crucial to the survival of Israel, was created soon, they would find themselves in a minority governing over a majority of non-Jews, like the whites of South Africa under apartheid, at which point Israel would lose the vital support of U.S. Jews. It was a cry of alarm from a beleaguered prime minister fated to leave office before long who, scorning his past as a hard-line mayor of Jerusalem, desperately wanted to share his epiphany with the political class, who weren't listening: Israel is doomed—as a state both Jewish and democratic—unless it mends its ways.

Prime Minister Binyamin Netanyahu has declared his willingness to accept the creation of a Palestinian state, while plowing defiantly ahead with the building of settlements that consolidate Israel's hold on occupied Palestinian territory in a manner designed to ensure that such a Palestinian state, deprived of the attributes commonly associated with statehood, would be unacceptable to most Palestinians as well as unviable. Before moving the goalposts outright in early 2014 he had carefully enveloped his acceptance in conditions and caveats that made his strategy perfectly clear.

In point of fact, Netanyahu's offer of "negotiations without preconditions" comes with two preconditions, one explicit, the other implicit: the first, to Mahmoud Abbas, is that he should tear up his agreement to reunify with Hamas if he wants to make peace with Israel—as if an agreement that leaves Hamas out has even the slightest chance of sticking. Since 2005 Hamas has moved toward the mainstream, participating in elections in the Oslo framework, restraining attacks against Israel carried out mostly by others, and accepting a Palestinian state within the 1967 borders. The danger now is that Hamas will be outflanked by uncompromising extremists. Not satisfied with getting "yes" for an answer, however, Israel insists that Hamas must also renounce its dreamy aspiration to reclaim all of historical Palestine—a demand not matched by an offer that the prime minister's party will modify its own mirror-image platform, or that government members will withdraw from the caucus—the largest in the Knesset—whose goal is never to give up any part of Eretz Yisrael.

The implicit precondition consists of the requirement that, by not pressing to freeze Israeli settlements in occupied Palestinian territory, the Palestinians should in effect accept that settlements will continue to be approved and built—in other words, that they should learn to live with Israel's creation of facts on the ground. One wonders what is left to negotiate.

Palestinians can see their territory being eaten away merely by glancing up at the increasingly colonized hilltops in the West Bank. Is it any wonder that they have grown increasingly skeptical, if not cynical, about the prospects for a two-state solution? The Fatah-led leadership of the Palestine Liberation Organization (PLO), which went along with the "peace process" that was set in motion—if that's the term—in the Oslo accords, lost a lot of ground to Hamas, victorious in the last legislative elections in 2006 at least in part because of sentiment that the Fatah had caved in to Israel, with little to show for having done so. In the aftermath of that political tsunami, fratricidal fighting—encouraged from outside—came close to tearing the Palestinian national movement apart. Efforts at reunification between Fatah and Hamas have been frowned on rather than encouraged.

Abbas's bid for UN membership—a Hail Mary pass if ever there was one—has been dismissed on the grounds that statehood must emerge from negotiations with Israel—even though nobody conditioned Israel's membership on an Arab or Palestinian blessing. With his apocalyptic warnings about Iran, Netanyahu masterfully succeeded in using his March 2012 visit to Washington, D.C., to eclipse the Palestinian question from the agenda altogether. Is it any wonder that ten months later, in the Israeli elections of January 2013, for the first time ever the question of peace with the Palestinians was not a significant electoral issue? The metaphor of the Israeli peace movement's death seems inapt: rather, it seems to have quietly slunk off into some obscure corner, slowly bleeding from the thousand cuts it has suffered.

As the crisis in Syria descends to ever further depths of horror, there is reason to fear for future relations among the various groups who have cohabited in that country, however uneasily, for decades. Palestinian refugees there are understandably wary of their fate. The crisis has contributed further to the waning of the Palestinian question on the international community's agenda—even as some Palestinians celebrate the slightly hollow recognition of Palestine's statehood via UNESCO membership.

Palestinian unity, indeed the entire Palestinian national movement, is under serious strain. Relations between the two most powerful factions, Fatah and Hamas, have swung back and forth across the spectrum that ranges from enmity and fratricidal strife at one end to fraternal embrace and reconciliation at the other.

Among Palestinians—without distinction—the sentiment continues to grow that the Oslo process, during which settlements in occupied Palestinian territory have more than tripled and East Jerusalem is being relentlessly de-Palestinized, is little more than cover for continued Israeli control over the entire territory of the old Mandate for Palestine. One day the occasional mutterings in Ramallah that Oslo should be torn up and the Palestinian Authority, its crown jewel, should be scrapped so as to force Israel to face its responsibilities might move from empty threat to the new situation on the ground.

The inescapable reality is that, save for responsibilities of an essentially municipal nature delegated to the hyperbolically named Palestinian Authority in the Occupied Territory, almost fifty years after the start of the occupation, Israel remains de facto in control of the entirety of the land from the river to the sea, running the lives of the people who live there. As a practical matter, a one-state arrangement is arguably now in place.

In view of this bleak panorama, the fact that serious people with impeccable credentials are going back to the designing board and daring to think the unthinkable is to be welcomed. The Parallel States Project is just such an endeavor.

It is important to understand that the proponents of the Parallel States Project (PSP), of which this book is one expression—who don't necessarily share the views I have expressed above—do not reject a two-state solution. They are not likely to join me in intoning, in an exasperated crescendo, the immortal words of John Cleese in Monty Python's "Dead Parrot" sketch, substituting the two-state solution for the parrot: *"The two-state solution has passed on! It is no more! It has ceased to be! It's expired and gone to meet its maker! It's a stiff! Bereft of life, it rests in peace! Its metabolic processes are now history! It's off the twig! It's kicked the bucket; it's shuffled off its mortal coil, run down the curtain and joined the choir invisible!"*

Rather, the PSP stems from the premise that dares not speak its name: that an irreparable deadlock has overcome the two-state solution. The cold reality is that it is out of reach and is becoming more so as each day passes; that, absent a massive change of context, the prospects for its revival are nil. The PSP also takes at face value the rejection by both sides—leaders and people—of a one-state solution.

The international system is still built around the Westphalian concept of the state, but its armor has been pierced in recent years by globalization and a gradual transfer of sovereign state powers to multistate machinery, moving us toward further human integration—overall, a good thing. Yet at the same time, the international community's post–Cold War tolerance for the fragmentation of states along ethnic or sectarian lines has softened its outrage at the spectacle of a prominent member of the government of Israel advocating a form of ethnic cleansing.

If the conventional solutions to the conflict—one-state, two-state—are closed off and the continuation of the status quo is truly considered unacceptable, this book tells us, the whole approach to the problem may need to be reconsidered. The PSP does not propose a plan, however; it is a work in progress for the purpose of provoking academic and public debates. Maybe looking beyond the zero-sum two-state/one-state toolbox, far from iconoclastic, has become imperative. If the devil is in the principles, shouldn't we search for the angel in the details?

Some of the ideas floated in discussions of the PSP—shared political control of the land, Israelis and Palestinians living wherever they choose—will smack, to some, of a one-state solution in disguise, and to others of a two-state solution in drag. There is no doubt an echo of the notion that, as individuals, Israelis and Palestinians are capable of existing side by side, and willing to do so—as long as discriminatory elements are removed from the equation.

I recently learned that some of the great leaps of modern medicine were the result of breakthroughs achieved, not by researchers in medical laboratories, but by NASA physicists and aeronautical engineers. Cross-fertilization, even among disparate and ever more compartmentalized branches of science, can inspire creativity. There is much to celebrate in such triumphs of human ingenuity. So why shouldn't the work of the late Hans Monderman, a Dutch traffic engineer who may never have thought about the Israeli-Palestinian conflict, come to the mind of this writer—decidedly not a scientist? Monderman conducted successful experiments with the elimination of traffic signs and lights in cities, in his and nearby countries, on the simple and beautiful premise that people, left to use their judgment, can be relied on to act as intelligent beings, aware of their surroundings and considerate of others.

There are those who will scoff (leaving a trail, faint but unmistakable, of closet racism) at the notion of transliterating to the turbulent and volatile Middle East experimental models of behavior from midsize northern European cities. Yet one participant in the PSP, an avowed Zionist, has pointed out that hope is to be found where you would least expect to find it: in the writings of religio-nationalist writers. Although the religio-nationalist movements have positioned themselves, politically, on the extreme right, it turns out that a new religio-nationalist version of Zionism that is emerging might not be incompatible with the basic tenets of the PSP—because this new strain emphasizes the connection between the *individual,* rather than the state, and the land.

Few Middle East mavens set much store by the Israeli-Palestinian talks set in motion by U.S. Secretary of State John Kerry in 2013, even if they produce some sort of "framework agreement" toward final status negotiations. Fewer still will want to be blamed for their failure. If the talks do fail, I hope that the ideas in this book will ignite the spark of human genius.

# One Land—Two States?

*An Introduction to the Parallel States Concept*

MATHIAS MOSSBERG

The conflict between Palestinians and Israelis has now raged for the better part of a century. Israel was established as a state in 1948, but the origins of the conflict go back much further, at least to the first days of the Zionist movement. Some say the conflict was born more than three thousand years ago, when Moses espied the green strip of Jericho from Mount Nebo, on the other side of the Jordan River; or earlier still, when Abraham first passed through the land of Canaan and rested in Shechem, close to today's Nablus.

From the biblical period through the present day the land between the Mediterranean Sea and the Jordan River has been the site of innumerable conflicts over territory and the identities that have taken shape within it. As we go to press, prospects for peace between Israelis and Palestinians remain bleak despite yet another wave of U.S.-brokered diplomatic activity, primarily because a territorial division acceptable to both sides is not in sight. Israel continues to strengthen its presence across the West Bank, while remaining in control over many aspects of life in Gaza. Among increasing numbers of both Palestinians and Israelis the view is gaining ground that the time has run out for a traditional two-state solution—that is, a division of historic Palestine/Eretz Yisrael into two territorially distinct states.

If a two-state solution seems increasingly remote, a one-state solution remains unacceptable to the vast majority of Israelis for political and cultural as well as demographic reasons. A significant percentage of

Palestinians is similarly not ready to give up the long-sought-after dream of a sovereign Palestinian state. Facts on the ground have led to loss of hope, and the belief is widespread that the two-state solution is dead. There is a growing debate about alternatives, and this book is a contribution to that debate.

The fundamental question that this book poses is whether it is possible to envisage a new kind of two-state structure that could meet some of the basic demands and desires from both sides. Could a concept with two parallel state structures, both covering the whole territory, with one answering to Palestinians and one to Israelis regardless of where they live, be envisaged? Could such a concept contribute to unlocking positions on key issues and thus opening up a way forward?

The contributors to this volume explore different aspects of this vision of a Parallel States structure, one Israeli state and one Palestinian, both states covering the whole area between the Mediterranean and the Jordan River. In such a scenario, military, political, and economic barriers would be lifted, and a joint security and defense policy, a common and equitable economic policy, and joint and harmonized legislation would replace existing divisions. Such a structure would allow both for an independent Palestinian state and for Israel to be both Jewish and democratic at the same time. It would bring an end to occupation and would permit free movement over the whole area for both peoples, as well as providing a vision for an end of conflict.

This vision of two states on the same land is, of course, only a vision. It may be that it is far too remote from present realities ever to be implemented or seriously contemplated as such. But considering the present lack of movement and of ways out of the present deadlock and even of ideas, more imaginative scenarios may have to be reflected upon. It cannot be excluded that such a discussion might reveal elements of solutions not previously considered, and thus indicate other ways forward.

The international situation is constantly changing, not least in the Middle East, where the Arab uprisings have created a completely new situation across the region. Old truths are being questioned and new thoughts introduced, while long-stable balances of power, alignments of forces, and strategic principles and concepts have been challenged and even upended.

Today, neither sovereignty nor the role of the nation-state is what it was even a generation ago. Despite the ongoing political and ideological salience of the nation-state, in practice national sovereignty is now divided and circumscribed in unprecedented ways, while control of territory has lost its power to determine the shape, path, and speed of development or the broader well-being of peoples.

Developments in international law; the growth and proliferation of international institutions; and economic, technological, and political globalization have all contributed to creating more porous borders between states, as well as limiting a state's capacity to exercise indiscriminate power. The concept of power itself is gradually gaining both new content and new dimensions. The scope of military power is increasingly challenged and complemented by economic, technological, and political power, as well as the power of information. Economic and political power no longer flow mainly from control of land.

But the conflict between Israelis and Palestinians is like few others, stubbornly focused on control of land. Developments on the ground have in many ways gone too far to permit a workable territorial division of Palestinians and Israelis into distinct political entities. Physical and political obstacles continue to grow. Politically, the Israeli electorate is increasingly skeptical, not to say hostile, to a deal with the Palestinians built upon the principle of dividing the land (Pedazhur 2012). The thirst of the Israeli right to settle more and more land remains unquenched. Physically, the web of Israeli roads and settlements on the West Bank is forming a geological sediment on top of the existing Palestinian society, and politically the Israeli "matrix of control" is slowly making substantial and sustainable development impossible for the Palestinians (Halper 2008). In Gaza, economic and social conditions remain miserable, while the recently celebrated economic growth in the West Bank has been limited to a few cities and is not built on a stable political framework or an autonomous economic foundation. The Palestinian Authority's attempt to build a state under occupation has all but failed. Palestinians and other non-Jewish citizens of Israel, despite their citizenship, continue to suffer discrimination in various ways.

Israel continues to control almost all the territory of what was once the Mandate for Palestine, and has so far not been willing to part with what Palestinians regard as the minimum necessary to enable the creation of a territorially viable Palestinian state. Demographic developments are making Palestinians a majority in the whole area of pre-1948 Palestine (Eldar 2012). A situation with a minority controlling more than 80 percent of the territory and suppressing the majority of the population is not sustainable.

The so-called peace process has brought neither peace nor process. That is, not only has it failed to provide peace, but its continued existence is also owed to the necessity of maintaining the "process" at the expense of a peace whose contours and implications none of the interested parties would likely accept (LeVine 2009: 180f.). The failed Palestinian attempt in 2011 to gain recognition at the United Nations has been characterized as the final burial. The new UN vote in 2012 to grant Palestine nonmember state status was an important Palestinian psychological and political victory, but it changes little in reality.

The present paradigm of dividing the land geographically has not worked, in spite of thirty years of continual efforts, numerous plans, and endless talks—or talks about talks—involving the two parties, the United States, the European Union, and large parts of the international community (Tyler 2012). And there are solid reasons why it is not working: physically there is not much left to divide, and politically the necessary political will has not been mobilized.

Put simply, a two-state solution seems no longer in the cards. A one-state solution most likely never was. In the view of the authors of this volume, it is time for a rethink. If the land cannot be shared by geographical division, and if a one-state solution remains unacceptable, can the land be shared in some other way? Is it possible to imagine another way that can provide an opening out of the present deadlock?

It is into this situation that we introduce the concept of parallel states. Can one design a scenario with a *new type* of two-state solution: one Israeli state structure and one Palestinian state structure, in parallel, each covering the whole area, and with equal but separate political and civil rights for all? Such a scenario would mean decoupling the exclusive link between state and territory, and replacing it with a link between the state and the individual, regardless of where he or she lives. Two state structures, parallel to or "superimposed" upon each other, would thus cover the whole area of Mandatory Palestine.

The question of who should belong to which state could be addressed either by nationality or by choice or by some combination of both. Thus people in the whole area could be able to choose freely to which state they would belong, and at the same time have the right—at least in principle—to settle where they liked within the whole territory. Citizenship could then be the result of an individual's free choice or nationality, and would follow the citizen throughout the territory.

Such an arrangement would likely lead, on the one hand, to a mainly Jewish-Israeli area consisting of the bulk of present-day Israel and a number of the larger Jewish settlements in the West Bank. But this area should also be open for Palestinians wishing to live there, initially perhaps in limited numbers, until the structure won general acceptance and confidence from both sides. Israelis living in this area would be under Israeli jurisdiction, but individuals living there could also be free to choose to belong to the Palestinian state, and thus to be under Palestinian jurisdiction.

In the same way, one could imagine a Palestinian area consisting of the West Bank and Gaza, and maybe parts of the areas in Israel where Palestinians now predominate. Such an area would, however, in the same way be open for Jews-Israelis—and others—who wished to live there, perhaps with corresponding numerical limitations initially. These Jews-Israelis would be under Israeli jurisdiction and belong to the Israeli state, despite living in Palestinian-predominant areas. Dual citizenship could be an option in some cases, while differing levels of political rights could be elaborated, allowing Palestinians or Jews to participate in local or regional governance while maintaining national ties to their own state.

The application of such a structure to present geographic and demographic realities might have to be complemented with the notion of separate "heartlands": areas where present separation patterns remain and continue to be legally protected. These should be more limited areas around the major economic and security concentrations, such as Tel Aviv and Ramallah (see map 1.1).

Thus, two parallel state structures could cover the whole area, with separate heartlands but with soft and porous borders between them. Israelis and Palestinians could each claim their own state with its own special character and identity, but they would complement each other and not be mutually exclusive.

In such a structure, both states would keep their own national symbols and their own government and parliament, as well as maintaining distinct foreign policy and foreign representation. They could choose to join in a defense union, an economic union, or a customs union, or any combination of these, with one currency, one labor market, and joint external border management. Elements of this can, to some extent and in practical terms, be said to be in place today, even if one-sidedly and with strong forces pulling in different directions.

Of course, there would have to be joint, integrated, or in any case harmonized legislation in a number of areas, including areas like communications, road traffic, police, and taxation. In other areas, such as civil law and family matters, jurisdiction in many parts of the world has already followed religion rather than territory for hundreds of years, and such areas would thus not necessarily present a major problem,

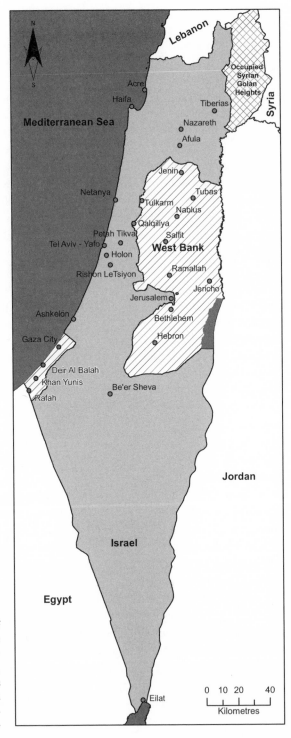

MAP 1.1. Overview of
the area of Israel and the
Palestinian territories.

Projection: UTM 36N.
Source: United Nations
Office for Coordination
of Humanitarian Affairs.
© Lina Eklund, 2013.

although admittedly parallel legal systems by definition involve complications.

The Parallel States framework would be an innovation in international politics, in international law, and in basic constitutional matters. The scenario would differ from both a federal and a binational system but would have elements of both.

Before outlining in more detail how such a scenario could be imagined, we need to take a look at some basic elements of the conflict, and also at recent developments in the understanding of sovereignty and what they mean in the present-day world.

BACK TO BASICS

The contemporary conflict between Israelis and Palestinians is generally regarded as territorial at its core, with the key issues said to include land and borders, Jerusalem, settlements, and refugees. Yet defining the conflict in these terms has not yielded meaningful progress toward a peaceful resolution. A longer and deeper perspective is inevitable. The search for an end to the conflict must go back to its beginning (Agha and Malley 2009).

Basic fears, concerns, and aspirations of the two sides have to be addressed. Exploring these is likely to highlight different perspectives and concerns from Israelis and Palestinians, but also to reveal some fundamental elements common to both.

For Israelis, security is a sine qua non, and an existential issue. The quest for security was the basis for the establishment of the state of Israel, and the Jewish state satisfies the fundamental Jewish-Israeli need for Jews to be in charge of their own destiny, to have a place on earth secure from persecution, and to protect their own identity (see, e.g., Strömbom 2010). Closely linked to the Jewish identity is the Jewish people's specific attachment to the Holy Land.

For Palestinians, the defining issue is not security as such but the loss of land—in itself a key security issue—linked to existential fears of an ultimate loss of identity. Palestinians feel a physical threat wherever they are, be it in Israel, the Occupied Territory, in camps, in neighboring states, or in the diaspora. Palestinians also have a need for dignity, equality, and justice—focused in particular on the issue of return and on a full recognition of the *right* to return.

In contrast to Israelis, many Palestinians early on did not in the same way consider statehood a primary objective, even if this appeared to be the case for several decades, particularly for the leadership of the Palestine Liberation Organization (see, e.g., Khalidi 1997: 19ff.). Palestinian nationalism and the drive for a nation-state found institutional expression in the PLO in the late 1960s. As the peace process has waned, the notion of statehood has been receding for many Palestinians. They wish to get rid of Israeli occupation, but not necessarily to divide the land. Ending the occupation and implementing justice remain central, along with an abiding attachment to the land (Karmi et al. 2011; Klein 2010).

For both sides, basic issues are thus security, identity, and access to the land. Most other issues can be subsumed under these basic categories. To have a chance to succeed, the quest for peace must begin by imagining ways to ensure mutually satisfactory solutions to the following issues:

- Is it possible to end the occupation and fulfill Palestinian needs of return in ways that can be harmonized with Israeli security needs?
- Can a Palestinian state be set up, and a Jewish state preserved, while at the same time both peoples have access to the whole land?
- Is there a way to think in terms of a new kind of two-state structure that could meet the most important demands of the two sides?

These are questions that need to be addressed in the search for ways forward, in place of the tired focus on geographical division of the territory. Instead of dividing ownership of the land horizontally into two different sovereignties, ownership could be divided vertically into different functions, and the hitherto-exclusive link between statehood and territory loosened. Thus an alternative scenario is imagined, based on the principle of shared sovereignty and political authority. But let us first take a quick look at how the concept of sovereignty has come under debate, in academic circles and elsewhere, in the past few decades.

## DIVISIBLE SOVEREIGNTY

In the world outside the Middle East, control of territory has ceased to carry the same meaning it once did, and also in the Middle East changes are taking place. Economic and political power no longer grows only out of power over the land. Access to markets, technology, information, and the rule of law are equal—and often more important—elements creating economic and political power. Power has new contents, borders are becoming porous, and states are no longer the only important actors. Many argue that sovereignty as we used to understand it is largely becoming a thing of the past.

The concept of sovereignty has eroded under the pressure of globalization. The impact of universal principles and universal structures suggests new dimensions in how states relate to one another and to their citizens. The role of borders is changing (see, e.g., Newman and Pasi 1998). People and goods can still largely be kept out—or in—but borders no longer protect against ideas, modern communications systems, or modern weapons systems. Recent developments in various parts of the Middle East serve to underscore this point.

International law and principles have been perforating national boundaries, and various transnational structures limit both the legislative and the executive space of national political bodies. External influence is increasing at all levels. Political leaders are now not only deemed responsible to their own people, but are also increasingly held accountable to international bodies for their deeds. National economic sovereignty is being undermined, and is in some cases little more than a formality, and even large countries can find their scope of action limited by international institutions. A growing body of international legislation and international administrative law is regulating ever-larger fields of national life (Kingsbury, Krish, and Stewart 2005).

The nation-state as we know it is no longer the undisputed final product of the international system. History did not end, as some have suggested, but the Westphalian era—characterized by the primacy of the nation-state—may be coming to an end, and the nation-state may in the future be regarded as a historical parenthesis stretching from the mid-seventeenth century until the twenty-first.

The erosion of sovereign political authority has affected both external and internal aspects of sovereignty. In both cases, sovereign space has been ceded to other actors than the nation-state as such: international institutions, transnational companies, major cities and organizations, and even private citizens and other nonstate actors.

As a consequence, the indivisibility of sovereignty has come to be increasingly questioned (Krasner 2005). The "classical" view of Westphalian sovereignty—that sovereignty lies exclusively in the hands of states, is inherently indivisible and inherently territorial—is now much disputed. Scholars from a number of fields claim that this classical, traditional view of undivided sovereignty is in need of being critically rethought (Agnew 2004; Sidaway 2003). It is pointed out that the norm of indivisibility has throughout history served as a veil, hiding actual power relations. In reality, sovereignty has always been divisible, and the exercise of political authority has often been derived from several sources, both external and internal. Thus it is argued that Westphalian sovereignty has constantly been violated (Krasner 1999), and that "it is the myth of Westphalia, rather than Westphalia itself, on which today's understanding of the principle of sovereignty rests" (Lake 2006). Stephen Krasner has termed this state of affairs "organized hypocrisy" (Krasner 1999).

Several scholars have proposed a distinction between de jure and de facto sovereignty (Murphy 1996) and implied that de facto sovereignty differs from the pure de jure, "original" Westphalian notion. Some argue that discussions about sovereignty have always concerned de facto sovereignty, and cannot be seen from an either-or perspective (Lake 2003). Exploring the concept of divisible sovereignty, Oliver Jütersonke and Rolf Schwartz argue that the current world order might be better described by transcending the Westphalian notion of indivisible absolute sovereignty and replacing it with one "that allows for the transferral of sovereign prerogatives across multiple agents" (Jütersonke and Schwartz 2007).

They, along with other scholars, also argue that divisibility of sovereignty is nothing new, and that the pre-Westphalian understanding of sovereignty, as expressed by Hugo Grotius (in principle indivisible but with "a division sometimes . . . made into parts designated as potential and subjective"), is more open to the notion of divisibility. In the Westphalian era the idea of divisible sovereignty was manifested in several respects, in particular during the colonial period with, for example, the Protectorate and Dominions system or the Mandate system of the League of Nations. The federal system of government found in many states is also heir to this politico-epistemological tradition.

In the present world, "new governance structures have emerged that reflect the de facto holders of sovereign powers within states" as well as power asymmetries between sovereign states, write Jütersonke and Schwartz (2007). Scholars have come to speak of a "New Middle Ages" (Rapley 2006). Several elements point to a state of affairs in which sovereign equality and indivisible sovereignty are no longer the central pillars of statehood. Not only have new governance structures and new international structures widened the spectrum of de facto power holders, but the content of power itself has also changed, acquiring new dimensions. All of this has led to an increasing fragmentation of public space, and in many cases situations in which the state no longer controls parts of its territory. In some cases this has gone as far as functional state failure, where "the state may continue to have international legal sovereignty, but the element of territorial control that defines Westphalian conceptions of sovereignty no longer applies" (Jütersonke and Schwartz 2007).

They argue further, following on the work of seminal twentieth-century explorations of the issue (cf. Henry Sumner Maine, as quoted in Keene 2002: 107), that sovereignty is best understood as a bundle of sovereign prerogatives that can be delegated and disaggregated, and they offer examples such as security control, the provision of external security, the right to legislate, the right to pass judgment and to grant pardon, and the right to tax people. Such an understanding of sovereignty differs from the traditional legal understanding based on the sovereign equality of states. For a further discussion of how sovereignty can be deconstructed and how this relates directly to the notion of parallel state structures, see chapter 3 in this volume, "Parallel Sovereignty: Dividing and Sharing Core State Functions," by Peter Wallensteen.

This view of sovereignty, as linked to the fulfillment of basic state services in the effort to guarantee and protect citizens' basic human needs, is a backdrop to the debate about the introduction of the principle of "Responsibility to Protect" in the international legal framework (ICISS 2001). The growing international acceptance of this principle constitutes a major blow to the traditional understanding of sovereign equality, what Krasner has named "conventional sovereignty" (Krasner 2005: 85), and points to a performance-based notion of sovereignty, where a state has to "earn" its sovereignty by fulfilling its obligations toward the people residing in its territory (Jütersonke and Schwartz 2007).

This being said, it must be noted that when we look at current state practice the principle of indivisibility remains strongly held. An important aspect of this reality is that the political projects behind the intellectual construction of indivisibility are not taken into account. The idea of sovereignty, and with it the presumption of indivisibility, was born with the modern state, in the midst of political conflict and transformation. Jean Bodin, Thomas Hobbes, and others at the time sought to justify the creation of central authority in the wake of internal unrest and civil war, and "to legitimize and propagate a central secular state against the remnants of feudalism and the external vestiges of the universal church." Thus "the principle of sovereignty was never meant as a description of practice nor as a foundation for a positive theory of international politics but as a normative ideal in the service of state-building" (Lake 2006).

In much the same way, in the present situation, the principle of indivisibility is asserted as part of a state-building process, on the one hand against the vestiges of colonialism, on the other against tribal or other subnational or transnational loyalties. Indivisibility was asserted in opposition to rival theories and principles, in the Middle Ages as now, and all the time in practice sovereignty remained divisible. "We ought not to mistake political programs for reality," writes Lake (2006).

One of those who have taken the lead in developing a critique of the notion of the indivisibility of sovereignty is Jens Bartelson. In chapter 2 of this study—"Can Sovereignty Be Divided?"—he discusses the paradoxical relation between the ideal of indivisibility in theory and the recurrent division of sovereignty in political practice, and suggests a reconceptualization of sovereignty in terms of the relationship between rulers and ruled. Bartelson suggests that whenever there is a mismatch between the claims to sovereignty made by a ruler and the subjects' perception of that ruler's legitimacy, sovereignty has to be divided to sustain or restore legitimacy.

## PARALLEL SOVEREIGNTY

Applying the preceding discussion and Bartelson's comments on the division of sovereignty to the basic ideas of the Parallel States Project (PSP) could begin by addressing the dilemma that occurs when "recognition fails to take place because of the absence of a common allegiance among those subjected to governmental authority," when "any claim to sovereign authority on behalf of the latter is likely to remain unrecognized and thus also unsuccessful." Bartelson mentions several different solutions: secession, federation, regional autonomy, the special case of the European Union, and division along communal lines leading to parallel structures of government.

The two latter forms of solution—the EU model of division along functional lines and parallel structures of government—are examples of shared sovereignty. History shows many cases of shared sovereignty, such as federations like the United States and Switzerland, as well as condominiums. While a federation is characterized by vertically shared sovereignty, with different levels exercising different functions, a condominium represents horizontally shared sovereignty, with two states sharing power over a certain territory, normally in borderlands between them. This model has applied to land areas such as Andorra and the Sudan, and to lakes and seas such as Lake Constance and the Caspian Sea, as well as to rivers such as the Mosel (Samuels 2008).

With sovereignty eroded and divisible, the exclusive and previously sacrosanct link between sovereignty and territory has begun to fade. In other words, sovereignty's function as political authority may be divided into, on the one hand, the authority over citizens, and on the other, authority over the territory. Until now these two have been exclusively linked. The questions then arise: Is it possible to cut this previously exclusive, if now in many cases fading, link between sovereignty and territory? And is it possible to imagine political authority over a particular territory exercised in common by two actors, while at the same time those two exercise exclusive authority over their respective citizens? In such a case, the mutual links of loyalty between state and citizen would be retained, and thus the legitimacy of the state in relation to its citizens. The territory itself, on the other hand, would become objectified and able to be given over to common administration.

How would such a construct relate to the notion of self-determination, a crucial partner-concept to sovereignty, particularly in regard to the issues of "right to rule" and state legitimacy? In the previous century, liberation movements the world over contested Westphalian sovereignty and the legitimacy of colonial states. In this way they successfully contributed to the development of the right to self-determination of peoples as an international norm. This principle dates back to the American and French revolutions, and was revived after World War I and particularly after World War II, as a guiding principle in international relations in general and in the decolonization process in particular. It is an irony of history that many of the regimes that took power from the colonials turned to clinging even harder to the Westphalian sovereignty vis-à-vis their citizens, with often disastrous consequences for their peoples.

The principle of self-determination underwent a reassertion over the past fifty-some years. In effect it calls for the people's sovereign rights. The Universal Declaration of Human Rights refers in Article 21 to the will of the people as the basis for the authority of government. In other words, state sovereignty should not derive its legitimacy from the control of a specific territory per se; the will of the people it claims to have under its control must also be respected and must be the source of the state's authority. As expressed in the International Covenants on Human Rights, the core of the international human rights law, "All peoples have the right to self-determination. By virtue of that right they freely determine their political status and freely pursue their economic, social and cultural development" (Deng 2010).

Self-determination is a principle that sets the framework for the people's political rights. In exercising their right to self-determination, a people can "freely determine" their status and thus decide which status and form of government suit them best. There is consequently no contradiction between the right of self-determination and the choice of a different form of sovereignty, such as parallel sovereignty, and of a state structure other than the classical, traditional, territorially determined state.

The notion of parallel sovereignty is, in the context of other forms of organization of political power, a novelty in degree rather than in kind. The difference from a condominium arrangement is that parallel sovereignty denotes shared power not just over a specific territory between two states, but over the whole area covered by the two states. This can be regarded as revolutionary compared to the traditional notion of condominium, wherein common or joint sovereignty normally is exercised as an additional feature on the periphery, while exclusive sovereignty still reigns at home. But parallel sovereignty, or parallel political authority, can also in principle be regarded as yet another form of shared power, even if its application implies a specific set of institutional arrangements.

To a certain extent, it can be argued that a Parallel States structure is reminiscent of the European Union's architecture, wherein the member states have voluntarily ceded layers of sovereignty to a common supranational level of government, while retaining other layers on an exclusively national level. A Parallel States structure could however be seen as an inverted EU model, wherein the two states retain separate superstructures on the top level and create a body of common elements thereunder.

The closest comparison from all the various peace proposals that have been made in the Israeli-Palestinian context is probably the Clinton parameters, and more specifically the ideas about Jerusalem. In these parameters, certain areas would be subject to Palestinian and others to Israeli sovereignty, divided along ethnic lines, while certain areas would have shared sovereignty.

In chapter 3, Peter Wallensteen deconstructs the notion of sovereignty, develops the notion of divided sovereignty, and divides sovereignty in practice first into horizontal and vertical dimensions and then further into different government functions. He demonstrates that there are different ways of distributing the exercise of these functions between different bodies-states.

What, then, could a Parallel States structure look like in practical terms?

## PARALLEL STATES—A PROVOCATION AGAINST CONVENTIONAL WISDOM

In a Parallel States structure, sovereignty or political authority over the territory could be shared between the two states in layers, with a number of state functions being exercised separately and a number of functions performed in common. State sovereignty could be primarily linked directly with the individual, and only in a secondary way with territory. Citizens of both states could be free to move and settle in the whole area, and internal physical barriers could be lifted.

Obviously it is conceptually demanding to imagine such a structure in practice, with two states existing in parallel on the same piece of land. To think in these terms is a provocation against both conventional wisdom and international law. There is no direct precedence in history, although parallel power structures and legislations were not uncommon in medieval Europe, as well as in the Ottoman Empire (Majer 1997). The closest historically proven model is the condominium. Two states covering the whole of the same piece of land is something else—the states' structure, though similar in architecture, would, in important respects, have to be of a different character from the modern state as we know it.

The basic question is how two parallel sets of political agency could exist side by side and cooperate on the same territory. Such a structure would require a clear horizontal division of powers between the two states, as well as a vertical division between different state functions—with some functions exercised separately and some held in common—combined with some form of permanent bilateral negotiation mechanism to resolve issues as they arise.

The states could retain their national symbols, have separate political bodies, be responsible to their own separate electorates, and retain a high degree of independence both in internal and in international matters. But this independence would obviously have to be curbed by mutual regard for the other in a reciprocal manner. There could be two heads of state, two governments, two Parliaments, and two administrations. Foreign policy is an area where one could imagine two separate policies and each state having its own international representation; but naturally a certain degree of coordination would have to take place in matters of common interest. There would have to be clear limitations on the authority that either state could exercise over the territory. Many state institutions could retain a "normal" character, but the scope of their power would have to be modified and take into account the power of the other, parallel, state structure.

A number of the questions that would have to be addressed are not unique for a Parallel States structure—they are relevant both in a one-state solution and—for some of them—in a two-state solution of the more traditional character. In this volume, focus has been directed particularly toward security, economic, and legal aspects, all of which present unique challenges.

## SECURITY A KEY ISSUE

Security and defense would be of paramount importance in a Parallel States structure, as well as in a more conventional two-state structure. This poses particularly vital questions, in that security is a basic need for each side in existential and concrete ways. To craft a common Israeli-Palestinian security strategy, outlining how Israelis and Palestinians could cooperate and ultimately join forces in a common security system, covering external borders as well as internal order, is a challenge that should not be underestimated.

A joint external security envelope, with a high degree of cooperation on external security and with joint or coordinated external border control, has to be envisaged. It is worth noting, though, that already today there are elements of an internal security structure that contains separate institutions and security forces, but also a high degree of coordination.

Because of the centrality of the security issue, two extensive chapters in this volume deal with it, one from each side. They each outline basic security needs, discuss the implications of a Parallel States structure for the realm of security, and outline basic issues to be addressed in a joint security strategy.

In chapter 4, "Security Strategy for the Parallel States Project: An Israeli Perspective," Nimrod Hurvitz and Dror Zeevi discuss the prevalent Israeli narrative and how it has shaped the Jewish identity and the sense of being under siege, with all of the consequent distrust implied. They outline Israeli threat perceptions, and discuss the risks and opportunities of a Parallel States structure against this background. Hurvitz and Zeevi also analyze security concerns from an Israeli perspective, and discuss how to maintain the security of Israeli citizens in a Parallel States structure—envisioning a situation in which Israeli military capabilities are somewhat reduced over time, the Palestinian party develops some defensive capabilities, and a third, international military force is introduced, both to deter and to tackle threats.

In the corresponding chapter from a Palestinian perspective, "Palestinian National Security" (chapter 5), Hussein Agha and Ahmad Samih Khalidi discuss the basics of Palestinian national security, its needs, interests, and threat perceptions, as well as doctrinal elements such as "nonoffensive defense," and outline Palestinian strategic dilemmas. Agha and Khalidi relate Palestinian national aspirations to the Parallel States framework, and discuss how it addresses as a matter of principle many fundamental issues of the conflict. But they also note that it contains significant problems and raises a number of security issues, such as how to address the imbalance in military capability and create a system of constraints. It is worth noting that all the authors underline the need for a lengthy implementation period.

## REGIONAL STRUCTURE AND "HEARTLANDS"

A Parallel States structure can be designed in different ways, but in principle the basic building block is the individual and the cement is the loyalty of the individual to the state. In its pure form, two state structures would extend in parallel over the whole territory, with only the individual at the base. But of course in reality, there are a number of substructures between the state and the individual—regions, counties, cities, villages—each with its own administration.

A Parallel States structure could thus on the one hand be said to be a top-bottom creation, where the political architecture is constructed from the top. On the other hand it could also be seen as a bottom-up structure, where the building blocks are the local communities and the division at the top a logical consequence of their different composition.

The basic principle for deciding who should belong to which state is—like the rest of a Parallel States structure—something that has to be negotiated between the two parties. The division could be based on nationality or individual choice or some other mutually agreed-upon mechanism. The option of dual nationality must also be taken into account, and would most likely play a substantial role—not least regarding Palestinians who are currently Israeli citizens.

One possible architecture involves substructures being given the right to choose which state to belong to, on a regional level. This would most likely yield a rather broad patchwork of different allegiances. Another possibility is to have local communities given the choice, which would provide a more fine-tuned patchwork. In both cases, the result would most likely follow rather closely existing population concentrations (see map 1.2).

The question then arises, Would this not be the same as a classic territorial division, but on a different basis? Well, no, because these different regions or local communities would have no state borders between them, only their populations' different allegiances. The two states' powers would extend over the whole territory, to their respective citizens in the whole area, with the economy eventually integrated, and legislation and jurisdiction either unified, harmonized, or in many cases based on criteria other than nationality. Local communities would, for example, have powers over certain matters of regional import, whereas matters such as communications, roads, traffic rules, and the like would have to be unified or at least harmonized.

If a village were to opt out of belonging to a particular state— a choice that could be made by referendum or could be based on nationality—there must remain a possibility for individuals living in that village to choose to belong to the other state. One could imagine a system not unlike that in present-day Europe, where individuals living in a city or village can carry different passports, and thus have one national identity and another local or regional identity.

Regardless of the approach chosen, two distinct "heartlands," each corresponding to population concentrations, would most likely be formed, building on present realities. One can picture a scenario with a Jewish heartland around the coastal plains, and particularly the area around greater Tel Aviv. Likewise, one can see a Palestinian heartland in areas around Ramallah and other cities in the West Bank, as well as in Gaza. Jerusalem is a special case that would require its own approach (more on this later). Such heartlands could be given special characteristics and be of different sizes and shapes. They should in principle be thought of as different from, for instance, the core areas that are discussed in the security chapter by Hurvitz and Zeevi, which exist mainly for military purposes such as barracks and training areas.

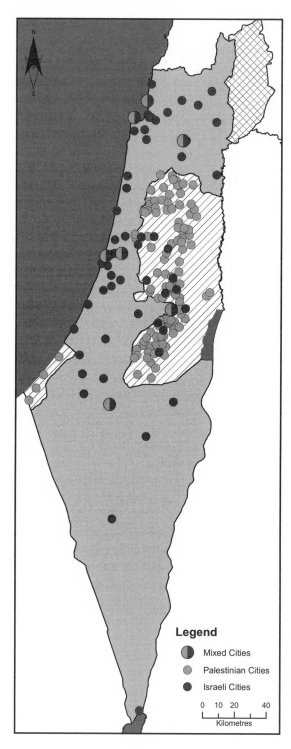

MAP 1.2. Israeli and Palestinian population density.

Projection: UTM 36N. Source: United Nations Office for Coordination of Humanitarian Affairs. © Lina Eklund, 2013.

Thus there is a continuum of different scenarios that could be envisaged, depending on how the question of administrative division was addressed. At one end there would be a total spread of two separate but parallel state structures over the whole territory, and at the other one could imagine two separate heartlands covering most of the territory, each with extraterritorial jurisdiction over its citizens in border areas and possible enclaves. The latter scenario would not be very far from some of the models discussed in certain previous negotiations and peace initiatives (Quandt 2005). To a certain extent it can be said to take its point of departure from the thinking behind the so-called Beilin–Abu Mazen Plan of 1996 but extending the notion of extraterritorial jurisdiction to cover larger areas on both sides of a border, areas that would be subject to parallel jurisdiction. Such a construct could possibly be labeled "overlapping states."

The situation of Gaza in a Parallel States scenario, as in any scenario, would require special attention. In comparison to a territorial division with two Palestinian entities, which would have to be physically connected one way or another, a Parallel States concept would by definition open up borders and make such a connection unnecessary, at least in the longer run. In a transition period, present borders and crossings might have to be retained temporarily, and could be lifted gradually.

Gaza occupies a limited but territorially contiguous area, and has a demographically homogeneous population of purely Palestinian origin. This makes Gaza a natural candidate to become a core area in a future Palestinian state, as well as in a Parallel States scenario.

Special attention to the specific problems of Gaza would be necessary, particularly in the economic arena. The Gaza economy would on the one hand have to be rapidly strengthened, and on the other especially protected in order to have a chance to grow from its present level and not become a bottomless pit of poverty in an otherwise wealth-producing economy. These issues are discussed in the chapters on economy.

To the extent that the political and religious climate of Gaza is different from other Palestinian areas and Palestinians in Israel today, special attention would also have to be devoted to these issues. The religious dimension is discussed in a special chapter.

## ECONOMIC STRUCTURE

In spite of all their differences, the Israeli economy and the Palestinian economy can be said to constitute one macroeconomy. There are both institutional and real links among the various nodes of this system. The whole creates very unequal dynamics, largely characterized by a center-periphery relationship. The integration that many imagined would occur in time has not taken place; nevertheless, elements of an economic union are present. There is an external customs envelope, a common currency, and the remains of a joint labor market, albeit with great obstacles, as there are also to the flow of goods.

One of the most important lessons of Oslo is that no sustainable economic development is possible without a stable political environment and a resolution of basic political issues. This lesson has, to a certain extent, been repeated in the past few years. Odds are that concepts such as Netanyahu's "economic peace" will suffer a similar fate (Alpher 2008).

A Parallel States structure could build upon the remaining elements of economic cooperation, but also upon the basic principle of the free flow of goods and people between the different parts of the macroeconomy. The aim would be real integration between the Israeli and Palestinian economies, building upon their complementarities while avoiding the continued Israeli structural dominance that was written into the economic component of the Oslo Accords. Indeed, avoiding the risk of cementing present inequalities would be a crucial goal and component of any Parallel States structure. Palestinian development needs would have to be addressed in a realistic and comprehensive way.

Only if Israel's economic supremacy (owing to its advanced state of development in all areas) is balanced with massive international support directed toward Palestinian development can there be long-term prospects for a viable and sustainable joint Israeli-Palestinian economy. Should this be realized, prospects for long-term economic development in a joint economy under a Parallel States structure could be more promising than under division in a traditional two-state structure.

One area where the developmental cost of taking a benign view of the realities of Israeli occupation of Palestinian territory has been particularly evident is that of water resources. The uneven distribution of scarce resources is all too apparent, and the gaps appear to be growing. Sharing authority over common resources is a central pillar of a Parallel States structure, which makes such a structure particularly suited to deal with scarce natural resources such as water. Shared sovereignty over water resources is likely to lead not only to more equitable distribution of resources, but also to more efficient ways of using them.

In his chapter "An Israel-Palestine Parallel States Economy by 2035" (chapter 6), Raja Khalidi outlines components of Palestinian national economic security and underlines the need for a transfer of sovereignty to Palestinian institutions. He discusses how a Parallel States economy can apply to, and exploit, the concept of divisible sovereignty to create a more functional and equitable economic relationship between the two states, and concludes that the road to convergence could go through either initial separation—to allow a robust Palestinian economy to be built up—or integration to correct the distorted economic union.

In a corresponding chapter from an Israeli point of view, "Economic Considerations in Implementing a Parallel States Structure" (chapter 7), Rafi Bar-El discusses the benefits and constraints of the forced openness that a Parallel States structure implies. To minimize the negative effects and the risk of economic colonization, he suggests development in two stages, with an initial period of independence and economic borders leading eventually to full openness. The two authors thus are not too far apart in their analyses.

## LEGAL INTEGRATION AND HARMONIZATION

Legal pluralism is nothing new. Two or more legal systems have existed side by side in several countries and regions throughout history. Medieval Europe is one example, with the Catholic church, princes and fiefdoms, the guild system, and other entities each exercising jurisdiction over their subjects regardless of location. The Ottoman Millet system had Muslim, Christian (both Armenian and Orthodox), and Jewish jurisdictions existing side by side, with the legal system following the individual regardless of location within the empire (Majer 1997). In the Middle East as well, civil legislation has often followed religion, and parallel jurisdiction is a fact of life, including in Israel.

In a Parallel States structure, each state would have jurisdiction over its own citizens. This would probably be rather uncontroversial in areas of Jewish or Palestinian concentration, such as in the "heartlands" that would be likely to develop. In other regions—such as border areas between the two communities, in mixed neighborhoods, as well as in Jerusalem—a certain element of extraterritorial jurisdiction could be envisaged. A large part of the jurisdiction in these areas would have to be joint or at least harmonized. Each side could keep its court system, but a system of mixed courts might have to be developed to take care of clashes of jurisdiction and other conflicts likely to arise. All of this is complicated, but hardly impossible to solve, considering historical precedents and similar situations in other parts of the world.

A Parallel States structure is not inherently designed to promote social, human rights, or gender issues. Obviously, by addressing the conflict as such the PSP aims to improve the human rights situation for those who are oppressed, be it by the other side or by their own. As to gender issues, by suggesting changes in the legal system on both sides, the PSP offers an opportunity to introduce legislation that can promote change. These issues are further discussed in the relevant chapters.

Bearing in mind that the nature of the issues in the legal field is more technical than political, and so to say reflects the political choices to be made, we have decided to treat this area from a technical legal perspective, rather than from separate national perspectives. The chapter on law is thus a compilation of written and oral contributions from various participants throughout the course of the project.

## JERUSALEM—ONE CITY

Jerusalem is a special case—in a Parallel States scenario as well as in any other scenario. Jerusalem as a political and religious symbol requires a carefully crafted system of government that takes into account the interests of the two sides, of the three religions, and of all other elements that together make up the city's unique character. A system of parallel jurisdiction seems particularly suited to satisfying the needs of both Palestinians and Jews, and perhaps Jerusalem might be seen as a microcosm that could serve as a laboratory for a Parallel States structure writ large.

Neither a renewed division of Jerusalem nor the continued domination of one side over the other can be a recipe for a sustainable long-term solution. The two communities will in all likelihood have to be given a more equal say in the running of their city, and more equal spaces to live and work there. A Parallel States scenario could provide the institutional structure for living together and organizing the limited space in the interests of both communities and of other stakeholders.

There is nothing in a Parallel States structure preventing both states from having Jerusalem as their capital. The Israeli side already has its main political institutions in Jerusalem, and many previous proposals for a two-state solution have contained provisions for Jerusalem to be the Palestinian capital.

It would seem that an initial implementation of parallel sovereignty could be applied to Jerusalem. In fact, many of the various proposed solutions to the complex issue of Jerusalem have contained elements that are in some cases close to the Parallel States framework, and some kind of joint administration is part of almost all proposed solutions, apart from those that involve one side's total domination of the other. This applies in varying degrees to proposals such as the Beilin–Abu Mazen Plan, the Geneva initiative, the Clinton parameters, and more lately the Jerusalem Old City initiative, an academic exercise initiated by the University of Windsor in Canada. The Clinton parameters, with their mix of shared sovereignty both horizontally and vertically when it comes to the Old City and East Jerusalem, offer perhaps the closest comparison. A Parallel States scenario would, however, go much further than any of these proposals in creating a structure that would guarantee both access for all and the right to live in the city, as well as a long-term basis for security and the preservation of identity for both peoples and all three religions.

## RELIGION—FROM OBSTACLE TO PEACE TO FORCE FOR RECONCILIATION?

It is clear that any discussion of parallel states must involve considerable attention to culture and religion, an issue that Mark LeVine and Liam O'Mara IV take up in their contribution to this volume. The Israeli-Palestinian conflict may have its origins in a nationalist conflict over land but it has always been significantly "culturalized," and this is nowhere more obvious than in the religious rhetoric on both sides. Only by appreciating the unique concerns of the different religious constituencies can their needs be addressed, and religious belief—Jewish, Christian, and Muslim alike—potentially become a more positive force for peace and justice.

As LeVine and O'Mara point out, both Jewish and Muslim religious nationalist claims to the territory of Palestine-Israel revolve around the need for divinely grounded sovereignty over all the land. A Parallel States scenario, by removing the linkages among the individual citizen, specific segments of the larger territory, and sovereignty, allows both nations to imagine a sovereign community over the entire territory, but in a manner that is not exclusive of the other group's claims to the same land.

A Parallel States vision allows citizens of all three faiths to live anywhere they choose in the whole area, which means precisely that Jews have permanent access to the biblical heartland of the West Bank and Jerusalem, which is today the heart of Palestine. The covenantal promise can then be kept, but without disenfranchising and even dispossessing Palestinians, while the imagination of the territory of Palestine as a *waqf* (an inalienable charitable endowment under Islamic religious law) acquires a level of political viability it did not previously enjoy.

Indeed, a Parallel States arrangement can help members of all three faiths transcend the most xenophobic and chauvinistic tendencies of their identities without challenging their core ties to the land. When sovereignty is no longer equated with exclusive possession of the land, the core, religious-derived bond between the individual and territory becomes easier to see. Competition over the land need no longer be a dominant factor in sociocultural identity. By changing the nature of citizenship, a Parallel States framework could encourage the creation of a public culture that would bring Jews and Muslims, Israelis and Palestinians, toward visions of a common good.

At the same time, as I explain in chapter 8 on the legal regime that would result from a Parallel States solution, the creation of two new state structures along the lines outlined in this book would encourage and even necessitate the creation of a new legal environment based on core international human-rights norms, principles, and laws. Such a grounding could be much more supportive of the fundamental rights of marginalized and even oppressed groups, such as women, Druze, Bedouins, and others than the present state and attendant legal systems are. At the same time, however desirable this might be from a normative liberal political position, imposing a much more "European" or "Western" set of constitutional principles or laws on Jews and Muslims who are quite hostile to such regimes would threaten the broader Parallel States enterprise. Thus, this arena would be one of constant negotiation.

## OPPORTUNITIES AND CHALLENGES

A Parallel States structure could meet both Palestinian and Israeli aspirations to live and work in the whole area that was once the Mandate for Palestine. Moreover, it could allow for an independent Palestinian state, and for the Israeli state to be both Jewish and democratic at the same time (an increasingly difficult proposition under present circumstances). Such a structure could bring an end to Israeli military occupation and open up the whole area for free movement of people, thus addressing as a matter of principle both the Palestinian right of return and the issue of settlements, two of the most intractable elements of the conflict.

Most important, the Parallel States vision could provide a way to end the conflict, and thus alleviate past and current grievances, as well as reduce the potential for future friction and violence. Incentives on both sides to resort to violence would be significantly reduced, and a new regional political situation and new strategic geopolitical reality would likely emerge, most probably of a less confrontational character.

Of course, a Parallel States structure would also entail a number of problems and challenges, not least in the security sphere. Among these are how to balance the joint and separate security forces, and how to organize internal security, immigration, and border controls. An international involvement would most likely be called for.

It is clear that a Parallel States structure requires a lot of confidence between the two sides—maybe more than other scenarios. The two peoples would have to live close together with different systems to regulate their lives and protect them. But any other scenario also implies living close together, thus still requiring a lot of mutual confidence. It is equally clear that at present there is an almost total *lack* of confidence between the sides. This may call for a period of interim measures. Some kind of long-term interim agreement, armistice or otherwise, might be required to provide the time and space for developing both confidence and more specific ideas about how to organize the future. But a vision going beyond short- and medium-term arrangements will certainly have to be developed to provide the necessary political energy to proceed.

## PARALLEL STATES AS AN ALTERNATIVE OR COMPLEMENT TO A TERRITORIALLY BASED TWO-STATE SOLUTION

The basic impetus behind the PSP is the lack of progress in the current peace process, or—maybe more accurately—the peace process that was. This does not mean, however, that the project necessarily has to be seen as challenging this process (to the extent that it still exists). Even if it is difficult to imagine, let us suppose that there might be progress toward a territorial solution, with two states next to each other. Would this make alternative thinking redundant?

The argument that a separation needs to precede any form of subsequent integration is a strong one, and cannot be dismissed lightly. Many Palestinians feel that they need to have their total independence first before starting to discuss other forms of living together with their neighbors. And it may be that separation is a necessary first step in any process that can move forward. But separation in itself does not solve all problems and leaves a number of the main issues unresolved, foremost that of refugees. There is also the matter of Israeli settlements in the

West Bank, and the uncertain future their inhabitants would face under many existing peace plans. Add to these the question of Gaza, and the links between the different parts of the Palestinian community, and the picture becomes even more bleak—not to mention when we include the situation of the Palestinians inside Israel. Thus the prospect that a separation as such, regardless of the specific proposal, will lead to the end of the conflict must be regarded as unlikely. It is difficult indeed to see that a territorial division can contain a fundamental vision for all these components that offers a better future.

And this is where the vision of parallel states comes in as one that could provide hope, even as a complement to other alternatives, since it is built upon the inevitable need to find a way for the two peoples to live together—something that many on both sides know they will have to do someday, perhaps sooner rather than later.

REFERENCES

Agha, Hussein, and Malley, Robert. 2009. "Israel & Palestine: Can They Start Over?" *New York Review of Books* 56, no. 19 (December 3).
Agnew, John. 2004. "Sovereignty Regimes: Territoriality and State Authority in Contemporary World Politics." *Annals of the Association of American Geographers* 95, no. 2: 437–61.
Alpher, Yossi. 2008. "It's Not the Economy." *bitterlemons*, November 24.
Deng, Biong Kuol. 2010. "The Evolving Concept and Institution of Sovereignty: Challenges and Opportunities." *AISA Policy Brief* 28 (June).
Eldar, Akiva. 2008. "The Jewish Majority Is History." *Haaretz*, October 16.
Halper, Jeff. 2008. *An Israeli in Palestine: Resisting Dispossession, Redeeming Israel*. London: Pluto Press.
ICISS (International Commission on Intervention and State Sovereignty). 2001. *The Responsibility to Protect: Report of the International Commission on Intervention and State Sovereignty*. Ottawa: International Development Research Centre.
Jütersonke, Oliver, and Rolf Schwartz. 2007. "Slicing up the Cake: Divisible Sovereignty in the Pre- and Post-Westphalian Order." Paper presented to the European Standing Group on International Relations, Turin Conference.
Karmi, Ghada, et al. 2011. "The One State Solution: An Alternative Vision for Israeli-Palestininan Peace." *Journal of Palestine Studies* 40, no. 2 (Winter).
Keene, Edward. 2002. *Beyond the Anarchical Society: Grotius, Colonialism and Order in World Politics*. Cambridge: Cambridge University Press.
Khalidi, Rashid. 1997. *Palestinian Identity*. New York: Columbia University Press.
Kingsbury, Benedict, Nico Krish, and Richard B. Stewart. 2005. "The Emergence of Global Administrative Law." *Law and Contemporary Problems* 68: 3–4.

Klein, Nebachem. 2010. *The Shift from Border Struggle to Ethnic Conflict.* London: C. Hurst.

Krasner, Stephen. 1999. *Sovereignty: Organized Hypocrisy.* Princeton, N.J.: Princeton University Press.

———. 2004. "Sharing Sovereignty: New Institutions for Collapsed and Failing States." *International Security* 29, no. 2 (Fall): 85–120.

———. 2005. "Sharing Sovereignty." *Journal of Democracy* 16, no. 1 (January).

Lake, David. 2003. "The New Sovereignty in International Relations." *International Studies Review* 5, no. 3 (September): 303–23.

———. 2006. "Delegating Divisible Sovereignty: Some Conceptual Issues." Paper presented at the workshop "Delegating Sovereignty: Constitutional and Political Perspectives," Duke University Law School.

LeVine, Mark. 2009. *Impossible Peace.* London: Zed Books.

Majer, Hans Georg. 1997. "The Functioning of a Multi-Ethnic and Multi-Religious State: The Ottoman Empire." *European Review* 5, no. 3 (July): 257–65.

Murphy, A.B. 1996. "The Sovereign State System as Political-Territorial Ideal: Historical and Contemporary Considerations." In *State Sovereignty as Social Construct*, ed. Thomas J. Biersteker and Cynthia Weber, 81–120. Cambridge: Cambridge University Press.

Newman, David, and Anssi Pasi. 1998. "Fences and Neighbours in the Postmodern World: Boundary Narratives in Political Geography." *Progress in Human Geography* 22, no. 2.

Pedazhur, Ami. 2012. *The Triumph of Israel's Radical Right.* Oxford: Oxford University Press, 198ff.

Quandt, William B. 2005. *Peace Process.* Washington, D.C.: Brookings Institution Press.

Rapley, John. 2006. "The New Middle Ages." *Foreign Affairs* 85, no. 3 (May–June): 95–103.

Samuels, Joel H. 2008. "Condominium Arrangements in International Practice: Reviving an Abandoned Concept of Boundary Dispute Resolution." *Michigan Journal of International Law* 29.

Sidaway, J.D. 2003. "Sovereign Excesses? Portraying Postcolonial Sovereignty-scapes." *Political Geography* 22, no. 2 (February): 157–78.

Strömbom, Lisa. 2010. "Revisiting the Past, Israeli Identity, Thick Recognition, and Conflict Transformation." *Lund Political Studies* 160.

Tyler, Patrick. 2012. *Fortress Israel: The Inside Story of the Military Elite Who Run the Country—and Why They Can't Make Peace.* New York: Farrar, Straus and Giroux.

# CHAPTER 2

# Can Sovereignty Be Divided?

JENS BARTELSON

## INDIVISIBLE SOVEREIGNTY

Ever since Eris threw the proverbial golden apple among the goddesses, it has been tempting to blame the tragic outcome of that episode on the vanity of the latter rather than on the cunning of the former. But what made the apple of discord into a bone of contention was the inscription on it reading, "To the fairest." Apples are divisible, but the attribute of being the fairest is not, and whenever some good is perceived as indivisible, the seed of a zero-sum game is sown.

This is true for sovereignty. Although there is nothing to indicate that political authority cannot be divided, sovereignty is commonly taken to mean *supreme* authority. And being supreme entails being indivisible. As Hans Morgenthau once argued, "If sovereignty means supreme authority, it stands to reason that two or more entities—persons, groups of persons, or agencies—cannot be sovereign within the same time and space" (1985: 341). According to this belief, sovereignty cannot be divided without ceasing to be sovereignty per se, and this in turn distinguishes sovereignty from other forms of power and the sovereign state from other forms of political association. To divide sovereignty between two or more authorities within a single state, therefore, would be to dissolve that state, with its constituent parts becoming new sovereign states or further dissolving into lesser parts.

Yet scholars have long disputed whether indivisibility is a necessary attribute of sovereignty, and the notion of indivisibility is one of the main obstacles to a successful redefinition that could make better sense of those instances in which sovereignty has been de facto divided between different actors within or between states (Walker 2003). Within most states, sovereignty is internally divided among different branches of government, not even the executive being vested with supreme authority. By the same token, external sovereignty is constantly constrained through contractual and other arrangements between states (Krasner 1999). In these instances where sovereignty is de facto divided, it has been objected, such divisions are overruled in times of crisis and war. According to this view, sovereignty is galvanized whenever necessary under a single will, since in "any state, democratic or otherwise, there must be a man or group of men ultimately responsible for the exercise of political authority" (Morgenthau 1985: 344).

Some critics of the doctrine of indivisibility have focused on its ethical implications, and on its apparent conflict with universal moral and legal standards. Perhaps if indivisible sovereignty had not been taken for granted as the most basic characteristic of statehood, much intellectual labor could have been more productively invested, and many modern institutional arrangements would have been easier to comprehend. But even if the notion of indivisible sovereignty seems to have lost much of its analytical purchase, abandoning the notion has been difficult. Many of those who have questioned the concept of sovereignty itself have made its indivisibility their prime target, yet their criticism has done little to change the ways in which the concept is understood and applied within political and legal theory (Bartelson 2001). Indivisible sovereignty cannot simply be wished away, as it is fundamental to our understanding of what a state is and how the international system functions. And since the concept of sovereignty is integral to modern political order, and constitutive of its master distinction between international and domestic politics, questioning that concept calls the entire system into doubt.

This indicates something important about the concept of sovereignty and its relation to political practice. The presumption that indivisibility is a logical property of the concept of sovereignty has made the notion of sovereignty resistant to redefinition. Sovereignty itself is little more than a symbolic form by which we have come to perceive and organize our political world, and as such it does not stand in any necessary relationship with that world, other than perhaps as a distant blueprint. Thus indivisible sovereignty is little but a fiction that has been instrumental in the constitution and justification of political authority, and this quite irrespective of whether the actual structures of authority have conformed to the fiction. Yet as Foucault (2003) has reminded us, beneath and in opposition to that fiction, we find a discourse according to which society is permeated by struggles between races and classes, with the effect of making politics a continuation of war by other means.

This leaves us with two intriguing questions that I would like to address in this chapter. First, how did the symbolic form of sovereignty take hold of our political imagination, to the point of becoming the standard way of justifying the exercise of political authority? I believe that an answer to this question necessitates a closer look at the concept of indivisibility itself, and how it entered the foundations of modern political thought. Second, if sovereignty has never been more than a fiction concealing rather than resolving societal conflict, under what circumstances do absolute sovereignty claims become acceptable to those on the receiving end? I shall start by describing how the concept of indivisibility was used in early modern theories of the state to account for the nature of political authority. I shall then propose a way to reconceptualize sovereignty so that the conditions of its divisibility become clearer in the light of its problematic relationship with political identity.

## ROOTS OF THE IDEA OF INDIVISIBLE SOVEREIGNTY

While there are important antecedents in medieval political thought, a recognizably modern conception of sovereignty first gained currency in early modern political thought. The promise of supreme and indivisible authority within a particular territory was then perceived as an antidote to the political disorder and moral doubt that beset much of Europe during the Reformation. The notion of sovereignty thus evolved in response to a political predicament characterized by competing claims to universal authority, and helped to settle those conflicts by compartmentalizing authority into distinct and bounded spaces.

To understand how the concept of sovereignty became constitutive of modern political order, let me start by describing the role played by the notion of indivisibility in the early modern accounts of sovereignty by Jean Bodin, Hugo Grotius, and Thomas Hobbes. This is not an altogether easy task, since it has to be inferred from how they used other concepts, rather than from any explicit definitions of or consistent references to the term *indivisibility* itself. Indivisibility helped these authors to solve two problems that had eluded medieval political theology and that had been further aggravated by the confessional crisis in early modern Europe. While the first concerned how to account for the *unity* of the state in terms independent of traditional conceptions of political community, the second concerned the *continuity* of such a unity in time and space and its relative ability to withstand the corrosive effects of historical and political change (Kantorowicz 1957). These problems were often formulated in conjunction and spurred a series of attempts to justify political authority without reference to divine law or to the community of mortals. As Quentin Skinner has argued, the eventual outcome was a concept of the state sufficiently abstract to render it independent of rulers as well as ruled (Skinner 1989 and 2002). The concept of indivisible sovereignty was a crucial resource in this regard, since it made it possible to account for both the unity and the continuity of the state without appeal to transcendent authority.

The credit for first having defined sovereignty in terms of indivisibility routinely goes to Jean Bodin and his *Six livres de la République* (1576). Although it is not my aim to dispute this claim, it is worth recalling that the concept of indivisibility had a long history and a rich symbolic significance upon which he and his successors were able to draw. As Bodin states in his *Six livres,* "sovereignty is the absolute and perpetual power of a commonwealth" (1). According to him, "he is absolutely sovereign who recognizes nothing, after God, that is greater than himself" (4). As for the requirement that sovereign power be perpetual, "we must understand the word 'perpetual' to mean 'for the life of him who has the power'" (6). Moreover, being absolute here means that "persons who are sovereign must not be subject in any way to the commands of someone else and must be able to give law to subjects" (11). The capacity to make laws is thus the most important mark of sovereignty, since "it is only sovereign princes who can make law for all subjects without exception, both collectively and individually" (52). From this "we may thus conclude that the first prerogative of a sovereign prince is to give law to all in general and each in particular . . . without the consent of any greater, equal, or below him" (56). From legal sovereignty other prerogatives follow, such as the rights to declare war and to negotiate peace, to collect taxes and to punish evildoers, to mandate coinage and measurement, and to compel subjects to change their language. Summarizing the import of these prerogatives, Bodin asserts that "the entire force of civil law and custom lies in the power of the sovereign prince" (Bodin 1992 [1576]: 58).

To Bodin, sovereignty is located either in a single person, in the people, or in a fraction of the people. To combine the principles of monarchy, democracy, and aristocracy is "impossible and contradictory, and cannot even be imagined. For if sovereignty is indivisible . . . how could it be shared by a prince, the nobles, and the people at the same time?" (92). Bodin answers this question by arguing that any attempt to divide sovereignty ultimately must issue either in popular sovereignty or in monarchy rather than in any blend of constitutional principles, as states that try to combine these principles are inherently unstable and dependent on outside forces for their survival, so "it must always come to arms until such a time as sovereignty resides in the prince, in the lesser part of the people, or in all the people" (104). From this simple logic he then devised an explanation of state failure, exemplified by the struggle between kings and nobles in Denmark and Sweden. The fact that the question of absolute authority was still unsettled in those countries was seen as the chief cause of their internal weakness and external vulnerability. Since sovereign power is the only reliable source of right among human beings, anarchy and the breakdown of social order would inevitably follow in its absence (Engster 1996).

Although Bodin expressed a clear preference for monarchy over other constitutional forms, the internal ambiguities and contradictions of the *Six livres* were used to support a wide range of ideological positions during the centuries to come (Salmon 1996). But at this point it is worth recalling that what mattered to Bodin was not exactly *where* sovereignty happened to be located in a commonwealth but rather that this locus had to be *singular* for sovereignty to perform its unifying function within the social body. Thus conceived, indivisible sovereignty is necessary to the unity and continuity of the commonwealth, and hence also to its relative ability to withstand internal and external threats to its existence. So by insisting that the prince is bound neither by any universal law nor by any authority other than that of God, Bodin took an important step toward replacing medieval conceptions of hierarchy with a modern notion of spatio-temporally demarcated authority (Fasolt 2004: 200–203).

By telling us what makes a state a state, the concept of indivisibility performs a similar integrative function in the writings of Hugo Grotius. To him, indivisibility is equally an essential characteristic of sovereignty, constitutive both of the state and of an international society of states. In *De iure belli ac pacis libri tres* (1625), he insists that political authority must be supreme, since "in civil government, because there must be some last resort, it must be fixed either in one person, or in an assembly; whose faults, because they have no superior judge, God declares" (274). The fact that such supreme authority has been conferred on the king by the people does not imply that this authority can be reclaimed by them, since its transfer is irrevocable. Yet in many cases, supreme authority is divided in practice, "either among several persons, who possess it jointly; or into several parts, whereof one is in the hands of one person, and another in the hands of another" (306). To handle such cases in law, Grotius holds, we must judge "by the will of him who conferred that right" (Grotius 2005 [1625]: 307). Grotius thus implies that even in those cases where indivisible and supreme authority is difficult to locate with any precision in a commonwealth, we are nevertheless obliged to assume that such sovereignty exists in principle. Again, the existence of indivisible sovereignty seems to be a prerequisite for the unity and continuity of the state, as well as for the existence of an international society of such states.

Finally, to Thomas Hobbes the concept of indivisibility becomes important when defining sovereignty and its relation to the commonwealth. As he states in chapter 18 of *Leviathan* (1651), "A Commonwealth is said to be Instituted, when a Multitude of men do Agree . . . that to whatever Man, or Assembly of Men, shall be given by the major part, the Right to Present the Person of them all . . . every one . . . shall Authorise all the Actions and Judgements, of that Man or Assembly of men, in the same manner, as if they were his own, to the end, to live peaceably amongst themselves, and be protected against other men" (121). The rights "which make the Essence of Soveraignty . . . are incommunicable and inseparable." Any division of these rights will produce nothing but discord, since "unlesse this division precede, division into opposite Armies can never happen" (127). Later, in chapter 24, Hobbes lists the division of sovereignty as one of the major causes of weakness in a commonwealth: "for what is it to divide the Power of a Commonwealth, but to Dissolve it? For Powers divided mutually destroy each other" (225). Hence, mixed forms of government are unsustainable, since "the truth is, that it is not one independent Common-wealth, but three independent Factions, nor one Representative Person, but three" (228). In Hobbes, the commonwealth exists independently of rulers as well as ruled, but it takes on such a legal personality only by virtue of being represented by an authority that is indivisible. To him, "it is the Unity of the Representer, not the Unity of the Represented, that maketh the Person One" (Hobbes 1991 [1651], 114). Thus, sovereignty and the state are coconstituted, the indivisibility of the former being an expression of the unity of the latter, and vice versa (see Skinner 2002, 2005).

To these writers, the indivisibility of sovereignty is crucial to the conceptual identity of the state, and hence also to its empirical unity and continuity. The notion of indivisibility helped these authors shift focus away from the medieval question of how a political community should best be governed to the question of what *form* authority ought to assume for a political community to stand internally united and for it best to be protected from external enemies. In the absence of a determinate locus of sovereign authority, the state itself will lose its unity and dissolve into factions, divided along the lines of status or faith. The notion of indivisibility thereby also provided a simple way to account for the spatio-temporal continuity of political authority, given the undeniable mortality of the physical person of the king and the historical mutability of territories and populations. In sum, the relatively swift incorporation of the concept of indivisibility into the very core of early modern political thought was crucial to the depersonalization of sovereignty and thus also to the emergence of an abstract concept of the state.

Yet simultaneously, as Foucault (2003: 48–55) has argued, such claims to sovereignty were challenged by a discourse according to which society is permeated by confrontations between different groups or nations. Paradoxically, this discourse emerged at the very time when the religious wars in Europe had come to an end and the use of force had been monopolized in the hands of sovereigns. It posited perpetual war as the defining characteristic of societies, and recounted their history in terms of unending struggles for and against domination between different primordial groups. According to Foucault (2003: 236), this way of understanding society remained operative until the end of the French Revolution, when it was eventually reversed by the invention of the modern concept of the nation and its fusion with that of the state, so that war eventually became a continuation of politics by other means rather than conversely.

But although this reversal shifted the locus of sovereignty from kings to people, it did so without questioning the indivisibility of sovereignty. As Jean-Jacques Rousseau was quick to point out, "whenever Sovereignty seems to be divided, there is an illusion: the rights of which are taken as being part of Sovereignty are really all subordinate, and always imply supreme wills of which they only sanction the execution" (1990 [1762]: 202). The fact that the unity of the state came to depend on the unity of the represented rather than on the unity of the representer thus did little to change this underlying presupposition, but instead left Rousseau and other advocates of popular sovereignty with the difficult task of accounting for the unity of the people and the indivisibility of *its* sovereignty. For a long time after the French Revolution, the paradigmatic solution to this problem was provided by the concept of the *nation*. Whether conceived in terms of the sameness of its members, or in terms of their allegiance to common political institutions, the nation could be conceptualized as an independent source of sovereignty only by virtue of being understood as an indivisible unity whose identity was unaffected by historical change (Hont 2005: 447–528; Yack 2001).

Thus defined, the concept of sovereignty came to be constitutive of both states and the international system of which they form part. Since sovereign states recognize no authority above their own, this implies that the international system is devoid of overarching authority, and thus is anarchical in character. Understanding modern societies as cohesive and inherently peaceful hence meant that war was banished to their international exterior. As Suganami (2007: 529) has argued, "if the practice of sovereignty is a sufficient condition of the possibility of arbitrary violence . . . it follows . . . that the possibility of arbitrary violence is a necessary condition of the practice of sovereignty." Thus the absence of centralized authority has been a permissive cause of war between states, yet the connection between sovereignty and violence seems to be a two-way street, since the quest for sovereignty often is prompted by the possibility of violence between individuals and groups.

## SOVEREIGNTY CONTESTED

But our world is different, or so we would like to believe. The assumptions once seen as constitutive of the modern political order have today become increasingly problematic. As indicated at the outset of this chapter, the indivisibility of sovereignty has long been challenged on the grounds that it has been constantly divided in practice. Complaints like these have long been common stock of liberal political theory. When the analytical purchase of sovereignty is questioned today, it is frequently on the grounds that political communities no longer are distinct and bounded, but rather interdependent and embedded within a global political order. States remain important actors within this order, but are no longer exclusive loci of authority and community. In order to handle the more undesirable consequences of economic globalization, some political authority has been relocated from states to global institutions of governance, while social and cultural globalization has made national identities increasingly difficult to sustain in practice. Taken together, these tendencies have made democratic legitimacy problematic, since the apparent loss of autonomy and identity seem to undermine the capacity of communities to determine their own fate (Tully 2002). Furthermore, state sovereignty has been challenged by claims to universal and boundless authority made by dominant actors in the system, leading to the substitution of demands for democratic governance for earlier demands for territorial integrity as a requirement of international recognition (Cohen 2008; Anghie 2009).

But if the conditions of statehood have changed, so have the patterns of conflict. In the old world, most wars took place between sovereign states, although some occasionally occurred within them. But when sovereign states no longer are the main belligerents, and the distinction between international and domestic conflicts has ceased to make much sense, wars have taken on a different character. Those wars are not wars *between* sovereign states, or wars *about* sovereignty within a particular state; rather, they concern precisely whether the conflict in question is international or domestic in nature. Those wars also tend to involve both domestic and international actors in complex patterns to the point of rendering them indistinguishable. When the underlying issues of sovereignty remain unsettled, what looks like an international war to one party will look like a civil war to another, and no one will be able to produce any definitive judgment as to its nature. Thus sovereignty remains a potent source of discord precisely in those places where political authority is weak and communal identity nonexistent or contested.

While sovereignty seems increasingly irrelevant in the part of the world in which it once was invented, rival sovereignty claims are the core of many intractable conflicts outside Europe. Sovereignty becomes a big deal in states that have failed, and many states are actually falling apart because of competing sovereignty claims raised in the vain hope of restoring a modicum of autonomy or creating a sense of national identity. Many states fail as a consequence of trying to adopt a largely outdated model rather than adapt to a world in which such claims are unlikely to deliver what they promise in terms of relative autonomy, prosperity, and social cohesion. What we witness today is thus a globalized version of the predicament described by Foucault, in which claims to sovereignty are challenged by a widespread conception of politics according to which conflict between different groups—ethnic, sociocultural, religious—is portrayed as inevitable and intractable. It would seem that the best way forward would be to drop claims to sovereignty in favor of arrangements in which political authority is divided, yet once sovereignty has come to constitute an apple of discord, achieving the necessary concord becomes all but impossible.

But how should competing sovereignty claims be handled when they inevitably arise? To say that sovereignty by definition is indivisible and therefore cannot be divided would be to do the parties the same dubious favor as Eris once did the guests at the wedding of Peleus. It would be to invite a zero-sum game that someone—if not everyone—eventually must lose. Yet telling the parties to look beyond the requirement of indivisibility and instead focus on sharing political authority proper is not likely to work either. Not only is the notion of indivisibility hard to shake off, but who is going to make sure that everyone receives their fair say under a new institutional arrangement, if there is not yet another sovereign power that can keep competitors in check? Once the rhetoric of indivisibility has taken hold, it easily becomes a self-fulfilling prophecy that is very hard for the parties to escape, and it lends itself to any authority seeking to justify its sovereignty claims.

## TOWARD A NEW DEFINITION

In order to understand better the relation between the ideal of indivisibility and the actual practice of sovereignty, I would like to suggest that we reconceptualize sovereignty in terms of the *relationship* between rulers and ruled, and then focus on how political authority can be justified in these terms (compare Loughlin 2003).

Let us start by noting that sovereignty is commonly defined as supreme authority *over* a territory and a population. According to the traditional view, the territorial jurisdiction of a government coincides, or ought to coincide, with a corresponding claim to authority over those people who happen to live within that territory. Yet our standard definitions of sovereignty give us very little guidance regarding the relation between sovereign authority and the territory over which it claims control, or regarding the relationship between sovereign authority and the population over which it supposedly holds sway. When territorial control is at stake, parties operate from the assumption that the extent of the contested territory is fixed and immutable. It seems beyond doubt that when the sticking point is supreme authority over a particular slice of space, the ensuing conflict is likely to become intractable. But when control over a population is at stake, the contours and complexity of its membership are conditioned by its relationship with sovereign authority. When sovereignty is divided in practice, this is normally done by taking apart and then reassembling established connections among sovereign authority, territory, and population in order to achieve a better match between claims to sovereignty on the one hand, and the peoples and places over which they are made on the other.

As we have seen already, this relationship has never been self-evident. Rather, as Foucault has reminded us, the fusion of authority and identity in the shape of the modern nation-state is a recent invention that was preceded by centuries of friction between claims to sovereignty on the one hand, and the seemingly inevitable struggles between social groups on the other. I have therefore deliberately chosen the term *population* in order to avoid smuggling presuppositions about communal identity into the argument, because I take the relation between political authority and identity to be one of mutual constitution rather than a relation between givens. The relationship between political authorities and the population subjected to its sovereignty claims should therefore be seen to be historically contingent and as open-ended as possible.

Redefining sovereignty in practical and relational terms might help us understand what is at stake when sovereignty actually is divided, and why such divisions sometimes are necessary in order to preserve or restore legitimacy to a government that otherwise would collapse, or spiral down toward international pariah status. Understood as a relationship between rulers and ruled, sovereignty is constitutive of a political community by virtue of accounting for the unity of the people in terms of the unity of the government, as well as conversely. But in order to be successful, any claim to sovereignty by a government depends on *acceptance* by the people that the government in question claims to represent, while the acceptance of that people in turn depends on their recognition of the rightfulness of that government.

This suggests that the relationship between rulers and ruled is necessarily a two-way street. Should such recognition fail to take place because of the absence of a common allegiance among those subjected to governmental authority, any claim to sovereign authority on behalf of the latter is likely to remain unrecognized and thus unsuccessful. So whenever there is a mismatch between the sovereignty claims raised by a government and their acceptance by those on the receiving end of the claims, sovereignty has to be divided if governmental efficiency and legitimacy are to be sustained. Hence, whenever a population is divided in the face of a sovereignty claim, political authority should be divided, and a failure to divide political authority accordingly must result in either domination or civil war.

In such situations, several solutions present themselves. Most of them have already been put into practice with varying success in the European and American contexts. The first is secession, through which those parts of the population that do not recognize the rightfulness of the government in question opt out and create a state of their own. One state thus collapses from a lack of legitimacy and is replaced by two new states, each enjoying more prima facie legitimacy than the first state. Such struggles for self-determination tend to be messy affairs, since they are likely to be vehemently resisted by the government whose sovereignty is called into question. Yet this is exactly how many states have ended and others begun. Sometimes, however, demands for autonomy and self-determination can be handled without splitting up the state. A federation is a classic response to this problem, through which sovereign authority is divided between different levels of government within the same territory, constitutionally safeguarding the sovereignty claims of the different parts by dividing these claims along the different levels. Regional autonomy represents a third way to handle pleas for autonomy by granting some independence to parts of a population on the grounds of their claim to possess a cultural and social identity distinct from that of the majority. Finally, the European Union represents a sui generis way of dividing sovereignty, by dovetailing the sovereignty claims of individual states within an institutional framework that allows for the recognition of supranational sovereignty claims as well.

Yet all these solutions reproduce the basic tenets of the doctrine of indivisible sovereignty by assuming that some overarching authority—however weak or symbolic—is necessary to keep these constructs from falling apart. In the case of secession, the logic of sovereignty remains essentially the same, since one state is simply being split into two or more new states. In the federative and regionalist cases, the federal level will in most cases retain important attributes of sovereign authority in order to be able to settle differences between communities or levels of government, or between these and the federal government itself. The European Union represents an interesting hybrid case in this regard, since the precise locus of authority required to settle such conflicts is itself contested, being subject to a constant tug-of-war between member states on the one hand and the European Court of Justice on the other.

It is not too difficult to imagine other ways of dividing sovereignty whose viability remains to be tested under modern conditions. One possible solution to the problem of sharing would be to divide governmental authority along communitarian lines within a particular territory, so that different identities and interests within a fragmented polity could be accommodated and renegotiated without the state in question falling apart. Vaguely reminiscent of certain forms of imperial governance, such a division would imply that political authority would have to be redistributed to different actors within different governmental domains, leading to the creation of two or more parallel structures of government coexisting within the same territory, each claiming jurisdiction over distinct parts of a fragmented population. Each governmental structure would then have a clearly specified set of functions to fulfill, but both would operate within the same legal framework, giving its citizens the same rights and obligations. The structure of political authority would thus follow the fault lines of social and political fragmentation rather than aspire to the creation of a unified political community on the basis of a common identity, or increase the risk of further fragmentation by insisting on the prerogatives of indivisible sovereignty.

In prima facie contradiction to the norm of indivisibility, two state-like governmental structures would instead run parallel within the same territory, catering to the rights and needs of their respective subpopulations. In this case, the division of sovereignty would simply correspond to the absence of a common identity or institutional allegiance on the part of the different populations, and the corresponding lack of compliance and legitimacy to which such situations normally give rise. Rather than attempt to restore effective control by imposing unity within a fragmented population, this solution would divide political authority in order to maximize both governmental legitimacy and the compliance of subject populations.

The obvious difficulty with this solution concerns how to divide governmental authority—in which areas and along what lines—and then how to settle disputes over competence between the two resulting structures of authority without thereby inviting the same recourse to indivisible sovereignty that this solution was intended to avoid. In practice, however, this would most likely entail the creation of a common legal authority mandated to resolve issues of competence through negotiation or arbitration, possibly under international supervision. Such international supervision would, of course, be susceptible to the objection that this merely pushes the problem of sovereignty further up the institutional ladder, and might amount to imperial governance in disguise.

That, however, might be preferable to a situation in which the only available alternatives are continuing domination or perpetual struggles between different groups within the same society.

REFERENCES

Anghie, A. 2009. "Rethinking Sovereignty in International Law." *Annual Review of Law and Social Science* 5: 291–310.
Bartelson, J. 2001. *The Critique of the State.* Cambridge: Cambridge University Press.
Bodin, J. 1992 (orig. 1576). *On Sovereignty: Four Chapters from The Six Books of the Commonwealth,* trans. Julian Franklin. Cambridge: Cambridge University Press.
Cohen, J. 2008. "Rethinking Human Rights, Democracy, and Sovereignty in the Age of Globalization." *Political Theory* 36, no. 4: 578–606.
Engster, D. 1996. "Jean Bodin, Scepticism and Absolute Sovereignty." *History of Political Thought* 17, no. 4: 469–99.
Fasolt, C. 2004. *The Limits of History.* Chicago: University of Chicago Press.
Foucault, M. 2003. *"Society Must Be Defended": Lectures at the Collège de France, 1975–76.* New York: Picador.
Grotius, H. 2005 (orig. 1625). *De iure belli ac pacis,* ed. Richard Tuck. Indianapolis: Liberty Fund.
Hobbes, T. 1991 (orig. 1651). *Leviathan,* ed. Richard Tuck. Cambridge: Cambridge University Press.
Hont, I. 2005. *Jealousy of Trade: International Competition and the Nation-State in Historical Perspective.* Cambridge, Mass.: Harvard University Press.
Kantorowicz, E. 1957. *The King's Two Bodies: A Study in Medieval Political Theology.* Princeton. N.J.: Princeton University Press.
Krasner, S. 1999. *Sovereignty: Organized Hypocrisy.* Princeton, N.J.: Princeton University Press.
Loughlin, M. 2003. "Ten Tenets of Sovereignty." In *Sovereignty in Transition,* ed. Neil Walker, 55–86. Oxford: Hart Publishing.
Morgenthau, H. 1985. *Politics among Nations: The Struggle for Power and Peace.* New York: Alfred A. Knopf.
Rousseau, J.-J. 1990 (orig. 1762). *The Social Contract.* In *The Social Contract and Discourses,* ed. and trans. G. D. H. Cole. London: Dent.
Salmon, J.H.M. 1996. "The Legacy of Jean Bodin: Absolutism, Populism or Constitutionalism?" *History of Political Thought* 17, no. 4: 500–522.
Skinner, Q. 1989. "The State." In *Political Innovation and Conceptual Change,* ed. Terence Ball, James Farr, and Russell T. Hanson, 90–131. Cambridge: Cambridge University Press.
———. 2002. "From the State of Princes to the Person of the State." In Quentin Skinner, *Visions of Politics,* vol. 2, 368–413. Cambridge: Cambridge University Press.
———. 2005. "Hobbes on Representation." *European Journal of Philosophy* 13, no. 2: 155–84.

Suganami, H. 2007. "Understanding Sovereignty through Kelsen/Schmitt." *Review of International Studies* 33, no. 4: 511–30.

Tully, J. 2002. "The Unfreedom of the Moderns in Comparison to Their Ideals of Constitutional Democracy." *Modern Law Review* 65: 204–28.

Walker, N. 2003. "Late Sovereignty in the European Union." In *Sovereignty in Transition,* ed. Neil Walker, 3–32. Oxford: Hart Publishing.

Yack, B. 2001. "Popular Sovereignty and Nationalism." *Political Theory* 29, no. 4: 517–36.

# CHAPTER 3

# Parallel Sovereignty

*Dividing and Sharing Core State Functions*

PETER WALLENSTEEN

## PEACE BY 2017: A NEW IDEA

The Israeli-Palestinian conflict goes back at least to the so-called Balfour Declaration issued by the British government on November 2, 1917, on the creation of a Jewish national home in Palestine. The pertinent text states that the British government will favor "the establishment in Palestine of a national home for the Jewish people, . . . it being clearly understood that nothing shall be done which may prejudice the civil and religious rights of existing non-Jewish communities in Palestine." There is a debate over the meaning of this declaration, but it suffices to say that such a national home exists today for the Jewish people and, also, that the non-Jewish communities do not enjoy the same rights.

A possible way to peace is through the establishment of two states, constituting a national home for each of the Jewish and Palestinian populations. In light of the Declaration and its legacy, it seems desirable to aim for a solution by 2017. This would replace a unilateral declaration by an outside party with a mutual settlement before the original document enters its second century. This chapter evaluates the possibilities for a parallel two-state structure in practice and as a central element in a comprehensive peace agreement. It is an attempt to think of ways to divide and share the core functions normally ascribed to only one state. The idea of resolving the Israeli-Palestinian conflict through a

Parallel States structure is new, logically attractive, and without an exact precedent. Thus, it is worth exploring.

## THE ROLE OF SOVEREIGNTY IN A PEACE SETTLEMENT

Sovereignty is increasingly debated in the context of global interdependence. Even major powers, such as the United States and China, are now—as the continuous financial crisis since 2008 illustrates—highly dependent on each other. For less powerful actors the restrictions on sovereignty are even greater. However, sovereignty has not ceased to exist. On the contrary, it is seen as highly desirable, and the quest for sovereignty spurs a great number of the world's armed conflicts. About half of all intrastate conflicts deal with issues related to the status of particular territories (autonomy, federal arrangements, conditional or full independence; Themnér and Wallensteen 2013).

For many exposed groups, having one's own sovereign unit is seen as a guarantee of security. Since 1945, very few states have ceased to exist through violent means (Krasner 2005: 69). At the same time, many attempts to build a new state have been violently suppressed, often reinforcing the belief in the utility of a sovereign state. Thus, sovereignty is a condition that implies security, and citizens and their leaders alike presume that one of the state's core functions is to provide exactly that. Global diplomatic recognition in the absence of real sovereignty is not enough to deliver such a measure of security. At the same time, global norms may be necessary for providing security equally for men and women (Olsson 2009 and 2011).

Furthermore, sovereignty is an expression of identity. It is a statement that "here we are, citizens of this state." It provides respect to citizens, and some degree of protection when citizens are moving around in the world. The granting of passports, for instance, is an act acknowledging which individuals are citizens whom a state is committed to protect. At the same time, the recognition of this passport means a commitment by other states to respect these citizens. This action has distinct legal consequences. Both of these points suggest that sovereignty is an unavoidable issue in resolving conflicts that deal with the formation of new states; that is, in what can be called "state-formation conflicts" (Wallensteen 2012).

In the context of the Palestinian conflict, sovereignty figures prominently in the search for a lasting solution. There are two sovereignty concerns in this conflict, and any solution requires two distinct self-ruling entities. Generically, they can be called State 1 and State 2, as the problem affects not only the particular case of Israel and Palestine. States 1 and 2 are carriers of sovereignty. Creating two sovereign units in the former Palestinian Mandate area is the essence of the two-state solution: two equal states living side by side. In the Palestinian context the political agreement on this is widespread, though not total.

The idea of parallel sovereignty (Mossberg 2010) is connected to traditional ways of thinking about the solution, but still makes an intellectual leap. The idea of two recognized states sharing the same territory, having separate state machineries with separate core functions but an agreed-upon degree of integration, opens new possibilities. This essay envisages what parallel sovereignty could look like in practice.

From Mossberg's conception, two distinct dimensions emerge. One is *horizontal* sovereignty: over whom and what does the sovereignty extend in terms of citizens and territory? This involves issues of citizenship, borders, and land. To which state do which persons belong, and what territory should be protected by which state? The second, *vertical,* sovereignty dimension concerns the functions under this sovereignty. There are different core functions of the state to consider. These are subject areas where, for instance, private enterprises, civil society actors, and market forces cannot provide the services citizens require. This core state domain includes security issues in a broad sense (not only physical security), rule of law, and a predictable order, as well as matters that can be termed social and human security.

Sovereignty is the answer to the question (as it is often put in the United States), Where does the buck stop? What authority is the "ultimate" and "responsible" one for de facto and de jure decisions? Traditionally this has been the state, and much of political science is devoted to understanding the interactions between citizens and the state (Hobbes 1996 [1651]; Tilly 1990). However, the complexities of global affairs and local politics have resulted in elaborate systems of sovereignty, as witnessed in the multilayered structure of the European Union. As it was created with an explicit ambition to promote peace, its example is highly pertinent to a discussion of Palestinian-Israeli issues. There also exist international governmental organizations to handle a whole array of matters, beginning with postal cooperation in the nineteenth century and the allocation of Internet domains in the twenty-first century.

Furthermore, there has been a renewed discussion of transitional authorities (Chesterman 2005) and new forms of trusteeship (Krasner

2005; Fearon and Laitin 2004). The discussion has connected to the experience of failed states during the 1990s (e.g., Chopra 2002) and the responsibility and ability of the international community to remedy this problem. These discussions reveal that the state—as traditionally understood—is no longer the only ultimate and exclusive source of power. International authority can take over some basic state functions, at least for a time. Furthermore, the deepening of cooperation and the enlargement of the European Union (Albi 2005; Ekengren et al. 2006) demonstrate the importance of regional competence, so to say, above the state. At the same time, the challenges of terrorism and nonproliferation have also led to coordination that means vesting more authority in the UN Security Council (Ahrnens 2007). Additionally, it has been discussed whether the global financial crisis results in more resources and power accruing to international financial institutions (Woods 2010).

Viewing these developments together, a case can be made that significant issues are now handled on regional and global levels, and the influence of state machinery is gradually being diluted. This provides for possible solutions to a great number of problems. In the context of the Palestinian-Israeli conflict it can be useful, but the solution will also have to include a more traditional understanding of sovereignty: a state with the rights of a state is an indispensable element in any settlement.

## THE HORIZONTAL DIMENSION OF SOVEREIGNTY

Sovereignty is normally considered to extend over a particular territory and its inhabitants. The territorial delimitation is a central issue in cases of state formation and is part of negotiations (or even wars) in that process. However, a territory without individuals cannot be sovereign; thus, we have to consider a state with its inhabitants. This notion includes residents, legal or not, as well as citizens. Corporations, foundations, and associations are also legal entities, and thus the subjects of a state. They are all actual or potential taxpayers, for instance. Most important, in this context, are of course the inhabitants. The fact that an individual is a resident or a citizen follows him or her all over the world and throughout life. Thus, all citizens are subject to law as a means of protection from crime as well as from other offenders against law. Human rights are more respected than ever, resulting in increased transparency and greater chances of identifying perpetrators. For instance, with the creation of the International Criminal Court and the special war-crimes tribunals, the chances for individuals to escape justice by settling in other countries is reduced: perpetrators of war crimes are no longer safe anywhere. At the same time, countries have to treat nationals of other states not only with respect but also with courtesy and service. If accused of crimes, they have a right to equal treatment and to be seen as innocent until proved guilty in a legitimate court procedure, a right asserted as early as in the Universal Declaration of Human Rights in 1948.

Furthermore, national law-making and jurisdiction are becoming increasingly transnational, as seen in the search for commonly agreed-upon regulations on criminality (money laundering, trafficking, terrorism, nuclear proliferation, sanctions evasion). This means that borders are not necessarily the end points for domestic jurisdiction. National law enforcement agents can identify alleged criminals all over the world and find ways to bring them to national courts. Legal and police relations have entered a new level of international cooperation, no doubt as a response to the globalization of crime. This also means that one state can legitimately demand from another that its citizens be protected by that state in a reciprocal relationship. Police can even operate across borders, if the states involved have agreed to allow this. Police contingents are integral elements of a number of international peace operations, for instance.

For the case at hand (Israel-Palestine), the concern is with the creation of a sovereign state that has its own territory and also a capacity to protect its citizens, wherever they are, without infringing the rights of the citizens of another state to exercise their freedoms (mobility, ownership of property, right to voice an opinion). The more integrated the two states are, the more coordination there must be between state machineries for such mutual protection of citizens and residents.

In the European Union this integration means that citizens can be arrested by police other than their own, and even be tried elsewhere, but they may also demand to be sent to their home country. Agreements exist to regulate this process and, over the years, considerable experience of such cooperation has been gained. These insights can be built upon for use in other situations. It should also be remembered that the idea of the European Union was regarded as utopian some decades back.

## THE VERTICAL DIMENSION OF SOVEREIGNTY

States provide services to their citizens. This is one of the reasons for citizens to pay taxes: there is a beneficial reciprocity in the form of services or public goods (order, access to roads, health services, etc.). To identify functions that would be performed by each state in a Parallel

States structure is a matter of some importance. Clearly, physical safety issues dominate when thinking of solutions and must be central to all negotiations. Israel wants to protect its citizens from attacks originating in the new state (whether by its authorities or by nonstate actors based in its territory). Likewise, the new state wants to be secure against infringements from its more powerful neighbor. The noninterference principle is central to the international system in its traditional form: states are not supposed to interfere militarily on the territory of others. At the same time, a state has the obligation to make sure that its territory is not used to create insecurity for its neighbors. Any solution has to include provisions dealing with improved security for both states at the same time, as well as for their citizens and residents. A state, in effect, will always have to consider the interests of other states. Sovereignty does not mean isolation, even in the most ideal circumstances.

There are hosts of other matters, notably constitutional structures, property rights, the rights of refugees, economic functions, transportation, health provisions, and more. All of these are significant in order to relieve some of the insecurities created by a protracted conflict, and some of them affect the sovereignty of one or both states. Solutions may be envisaged also for these issues, particularly if one is adding a regional or global dimension.

In fact, much sovereignty is vested in the constitutional independence of the state: that the state's leadership is derived from intrastate processes, not imposed from the outside, for instance. The state has to rest on internal legitimacy. In the present circumstances, democratic process, transparency, and integrity (i.e., the absence of corruption) are important elements.

Broadly speaking, we can divide the rule of the state into four core functions that have to be part of a final settlement: constitutional independence, economic power, security provisions, and social and human security. All four are seen to benefit citizens, residents, and even refugees. Before illustrating how parallel and shared sovereignty could work in the case of these two states, however, it is important to point to two additional aspects of the Palestinian-Israeli case: the process of implementation and its global relevance.

## THE PROCESS OF BUILDING SOVEREIGNTY

Thinking realistically, the present close integration between Israel and the Palestinian Authority has to be a point of departure. The creation of a Palestinian state entails taking over sovereignty from another unit, in this case an occupying power. It is at the same time a process of separation and a question of balancing power between the entities. This is likely to be a continuous process of wresting obligations from one entity and transferring them to another. It is likely that the dominant actor will agree only reluctantly to transfer larger domains of sovereignty to the new actor. That is in the logic of domination, and it is likely to be couched in terms of the occupier's need for security even in areas where this might be a fairly remote concern.

The reality of sovereignty transfer can itself require a cumbersome process, even when there is general agreement on the goals and steps as such. But a process will need to be agreed upon where state functions gradually are transferred from the dominant actor to the new entity. Indeed, this would be the case no matter what solution one envisaged—for instance, a traditional territorially divided two-state solution, the one discussed here, a unitary state for both nations, or other forms (e.g., the merger of Palestinian territories with other states such as Jordan).

The process can be illustrated by reference to the experiences of occupied territories in other conflicts. Two cases are Germany and Japan after 1945. Only gradually did the new constitutional regimes in these countries take over all core state functions. To have their own constitution was the easier part; controlling their own economy (own currency, own central bank) was more difficult, but still possible. For these countries to have an independent military was unacceptable to the victors. More than sixty-five years after the end of World War II, German and Japanese forces remain under external and internal restrictions. Decades after the end of the war, American forces still maintain extensive bases in western Germany with exclusive rights of mobility. The regime in East Germany rested entirely on the presence of outside forces (the Warsaw Pact armies). Even today, German forces operate only within an international setting (NATO, European Union). Japan is in a similar situation, with a continuing American military presence and a constitution that limits the external projection of force.

More recent cases of occupation testify to the difficulties of achieving an agreed-upon withdrawal.[1] The northern part of Cyprus has been occupied by Turkey since 1974; Western Sahara has been held equally long by Morocco. Large parts of western Azerbaijan have been under the control of Armenian forces since 1994, with various land-for-peace deals suggested over the years. In 2008, Russia took control of South Ossetia and Abkhazia, both of them regions of Georgia, and proclaimed them independent states. The international community has refused to accept these de facto divisions and boundary revisions. Nobody is envisaging any early settlements of these conflicts, although high-level efforts have been under way, for Cyprus in particular.

There are exceptions to this state of affairs. After twenty-five years of occupation, Indonesia agreed to a referendum in East Timor. When the result overwhelmingly supported independence, Indonesian sympathizers destroyed much of the capital. Shortly thereafter, in 1999, Indonesia gave up all of its claims on East Timor and pulled out its troops. This was a swift operation that was doomed to result in chaos, had it not been for UN involvement. In 2002 East Timor became an independent state and entered the United Nations. Its state structure, however, remains fragile. South Africa pulled out of Namibia in 1989 following a disastrous war, international sanctions, and threatening democratization. It was an orderly process under UN auspices, however. Namibia is today one of the most stable states in Africa. It remains to be seen how Africa's most recent state, South Sudan, will manage its challenges, as the country is conflict-prone, landlocked, and poor, though endowed with vast resources of oil. Continuing tensions with its northern neighbor, as well as internal ethnic divisions and a lack of infrastructure, make its prospects even more uncertain.

This overview tells us that the occupier is not likely to give up its gains easily, even if the immediate security threat were to subside. Ending occupation is a process, where continuing attention to security remains salient for the occupied populations as well as for the occupier. It is likely to be a protracted process for a Palestinian state to shake off all elements of Israeli domination. The expectation here is that it can be done through gradual reductions in hostility. Considering the many years of actual conflict, fears are going to remain for a long time even if an agreement could be concluded in the near future, for instance, by 2017.

For the dominant actor to take part in a process of disengagement, there have to be clear benefits. If not, the process is likely to result in delays, setbacks, obstructive actions, and interruptions, even a complete breakdown. If only the emerging new state is a winner, this will easily be seen as a failure by the dominant one. The occupiers are not likely to accept a change in status unless they also see gains. Thus, in a negotiated settlement, they are likely to demand something in return for ending the occupation. Furthermore, the termination of a future or potential security threat is not likely to be sufficient—there have to be other, tangible benefits. This is an element for which a regional approach could be important: if peace can provide access to markets previously closed, for instance, this would provide an incentive for the process to go forward.

Thus, a solution that favors integration between the new states is one that favors the chances for peace. It is not going to be possible to create a solution in which interactions between the two states are reduced to a minimum. Instead, a new order has to be constructed in which the interactions are many, frequent, and mutually beneficial—without creating new insecurities.

PEACE AND SOVEREIGNTY: THE GLOBAL SCENE

The Palestinian-Israeli conflict is a unique constellation of elements well known from other conflicts. The creation of new states through the breakup (peaceful or not) of earlier entities has been common. Since World War II the world has seen remarkable processes of decolonization of Western empires; dissolution of the Soviet, Yugoslav, and Czechoslovak unions; and an array of other secessions (Singapore from Malaysia, Bangladesh from Pakistan, Eritrea from Ethiopia, East Timor from Indonesia, etc.). Certainly, there have been failures and chaotic divorces, in which the breakup was less than peaceful: Congo's split from Belgium (now fifty years ago), Kosovo's continuing difficulties achieving recognition, and Somalia's breakup into three (unrecognized) parts in the early 1990s.

Even if these are exceptional cases, the failures to achieve nonviolent transitions have been costly and, in some cases, the new entities have failed to function effectively as states. The failure, furthermore, has not necessarily come at the moment of breakup, but often years later, after the newly sovereign states have not managed to exercise control over parts of their territory or have not been able to control violent challengers from within or without. The end of Israel's occupation cannot afford such sovereignty failures. It has to be an orderly, agreed-upon, and internally supported process with considerable international cooperation and realistic chances of sustainability. Furthermore, the process—however it plays out—will be of interest to other parts of the world, just as what has happened elsewhere can be significant for the Israeli-Palestinian situation. There is learning to be had from many directions.

One very abrupt, but still successful, transfer of sovereignty took place in 1965, when Zambia (formerly northern Rhodesia) had to face the Rhodesian crisis and implement sanctions against southern Rhodesia, following the latter's unilateral declaration of independence. Southern Rhodesia had been the center of power in the Rhodesian colonies. Very quickly, Zambia had to take over a number of state functions. There are some lessons to be learned, not least the importance of international support in the training Zambian administrators. This suggests that building separate institutions early is an important undertaking. However, at some point it is also essential to consider the construction of joint institutions. Cooperation is likely to be necessary in almost any future scenario in Middle East peacemaking, and particularly in the one suggested here.

There are other solutions that, though they may have failed, still constitute interesting examples. One such case is Cyprus, where consecutive peace processes have not succeeded in generating an agreed-upon outcome, but where each new process has built on the previous one. The political contention centers on how independent the two units of the future united republic should be: will it be a federation or a confederation? Compared to this, the Israel-Palestine conflict includes an agreement on a two-state solution, and thus has passed some hurdles still remaining for Cyprus.

Conflicts with similar issues are Western Sahara (should it be an autonomous area within Morocco or an independent state, as most African states and the African Union prefer?); Sudan (where the referendum in early 2011 resulted in the creation of a new state, South Sudan, which immediately faced state-building problems); Papua New Guinea (which faces a referendum on the status of the island of Bougainville in 2015), and Quebec (where the population narrowly voted against separation from Canada in a referendum in 1995). In fact, many seemingly unitary states have a number of shared sovereignties within them, though without challenging the center. For instance, the United States not only consists of the fifty states that are fully represented in the U.S. Congress, but also has separate autonomy arrangements, for instance, for Native Americans, Puerto Rico, the U.S. Virgin Islands, Guam, American Samoa, and the District of Columbia. In 1977 the United States agreed to give up its sovereignty over the Panama Canal, without the feared insecurities ensuing. Thus, there are arrangements to learn from, as well as conflicts in search of new ideas. Innovative solutions to the Israeli-Palestinian peace process will be eagerly observed internationally.

## A NEW TWO-STATE SOLUTION

National sovereignty serves nationally shared common interests. Therefore, parallel sovereignty has to build on shared, parallel interests.

As far as the *horizontal dimension* is concerned, the idea with the Parallel States solution is that there would be no territorial division at the state level. The two states would share a common international border, without a clearly demarcated interstate border between them. Existing controls on movement would instead be gradually removed as allowed by increasingly peaceful conditions. The citizens of both states, in other words, could move freely across the entire territory, as would capital, goods, and services. One question to be discussed is whether the same rights should be given to noncitizen residents and returning refugees as well.

Mossberg (2010: 43) writes that the united territory still "would entail decentralized, regional and/or local structures" building on two "heartlands." This idea leads in the direction of cantonlike entities connected to the two sovereign states. The subunits could have autonomous control, for example, over residential requirements for local citizens and could develop their own regulations concerning matters such as property transactions. A jointly agreed law could be applied to regulate such rights in order to ensure equal conditions across the two sovereignties. This issue is not pursued here, as the focus is on the vertical dimensions. The tables that follow build on the assumption that there are two states, State 1 and State 2, sharing the same territory, with freedom of movement within the entire territory, and that State 1 and State 2 are both responsible for border controls.

The *vertical dimensions* include the core functions that were identified previously: constitutional independence (identity issues, education, language, and treaty-making), economic power (currency, finance, taxation, transportation), security provisions (police, defense, private and public law, civil and criminal law), and social security for citizens, legal residents, and returning refugees—what here is subsumed under the label of human security concerns.

There are aspects of intrastate sovereignty and issues of interstate sovereignty, as well as matters of extrastate sovereignty (giving sovereignty to a regional or global organization or to another state). In the following tables this is described as giving sovereignty to State 1, State 2, to an extrastate entity (it could be the United States, Egypt, etc.), to a regional actor (the European Union, the Arab League, or another body in the Middle East), or to a global actor (e.g., the United Nations). This is a way to illustrate the many possibilities that could emerge when unpacking the concept of sovereignty. Of course, these different levels of service providers do have different access to enforcement capabilities. The global level may still be the weakest, but at the same time it is able to set norms and impact through everyday decisions and practices.

## PARALLEL SOVEREIGNTY AND INDEPENDENCE

In any Parallel States solution, the two states would be independent entities, in the sense that they would have their own symbols, constitutions, procedures for elections and changes of government, and so on. Table 3.1 specifies some typical formal functions that express a state's independence. It illustrates that structures dealing with constitutional and identity issues require that the two states be clearly, functionally separate. Each would have its own constitutional processes, particularly for decisions on formation of government, national symbols, official language(s), international representation, constitutional changes, forms of representation, educational structures, and international treaty-making. Thus, in the arenas addressed in this table, the two states are almost entirely separate, and extrastate, regional, and global actors do not have any significant roles.

However, the interconnection of the two states could also be demonstrated, for instance, by flying an interstate flag on official buildings (not the other state's flag but a shared symbol, which would have to be designed). That would have to be agreed between the two states, of course. Today it is not an unusual practice to fly two or more flags on official buildings.

Obviously, constitutions and their changes are intrastate affairs, but the parallel sovereignty might require a constitutional expression. Entering into such an arrangement would be different from ordinary interstate treaties and more similar to the process of accession to the European Union. For instance, to safeguard the relationship and improve its durability, the relationship should be difficult to change. Preferably this could be achieved by jointly stipulating that any constitutional amendment would require a qualified majority decision (one requiring a two-thirds majority, for instance). This would prevent sudden changes to the relationship by one or the other partner state.

Human rights provisions are central for both states, and each one would have to operate its own state institutions (ombudsmen, other

TABLE 3.1    PARALLEL SOVEREIGNTY: CONSTITUTIONAL AND IDENTITY ISSUES

| Sovereign over what? | Holders of sovereignty | | | | |
| --- | --- | --- | --- | --- | --- |
| | State 1 | State 2 | Extrastate | Region | Globe |
| Official language | S1 | S2 | no | no | English |
| Symbols (flag, calendar) | S1 | S2 | no | no | no |
| International representation | S1 | S2 | no | no | no |
| Constitution | S1 | S2 | no | no | no |
| Constitutional change, by | | | | | |
| qualified majority | S1 | S2 | no | no | no |
| Human rights | S 1 | S 2 | no | yes | yes |
| Representation | S1 | S2 | no | no | no |
| Citizenship | S1 | S2 | no | no | no |
| Education | S1 | S2 | no | European Union | no |
| International treaty-making | S1 | S2 | no | no | no |

forms). There is a need for a right to appeal, and thus, the national institutions could also be connected to the European system, by inscribing in both constitutions that the European Court of Human Rights is the final arbitrator.

A key element is the safeguarding of equal rights with respect to gender and sexual orientation. The two states would most likely have to have identical regulations in these areas to allow for smooth future relations. Thus, one might even think of having identical texts for the protection of these rights in the legal instruments applying to these issues.

A delicate issue relates to citizenship decisions. There could be particular provisions for mutual restrictions, so as not to allow a large influx of newly admitted citizens into either state. This could be supported also by the observation that the population density of the entities is already high. Thus, the states might agree on shared numerical clauses regarding immigration. This is a matter that would affect both states, as the Parallel States arrangement would allow for mobility across the entire territory. Both states might have an interest in not upsetting the demographic balance.

It is part of a state's prerogative to enter into international treaties. The envisioned comprehensive peace agreement establishing a Parallel States structure would be the first and founding treaty of the two-state solution. The two states would have to abide by all customary international treaties and declarations, thus providing internationally legitimate passports for their citizens and eliminating travel restrictions for all passport holders. Obviously, the two states would have their own foreign ministries and would both be seated at the United Nations.

The international community could be supportive in different ways. The global community provides a lingua franca—English—that both entities could use. It would be, of course, an advantage if each country encouraged the teaching of the other's language but realistically and practically, English might be the best alternative. It could even be specified as a second official language in both sovereignties.

This leads to the question of the educational system. Each entity would be likely to cement the system it has already, but an agreement could be worked out allowing for citizens from one sovereignty to enter the schools of the other. Furthermore, both national systems might benefit from harmonization with the European Union's Bologna process, to provide for comparability of university education with the one recently developed for Europe.

Most of the sovereignty elements under table 3.1 are well known, and standard formulations exist in the constitutions of other sovereign states. Such provisions may serve as inspiration for finding solutions to the thorny issues inherent in developing a constitutional framework for parallel states.

## PARALLEL SOVEREIGNTY AND ECONOMICS

In principle, both states should financially be based on their own tax revenue. At present, Israel and Palestine are both dependent on international support and assistance. The Palestinian Authority probably could not function without funding from the European Union and Arab states, though it is making strides in developing its own revenue base. Obviously, the current weakness of the Palestinian economy results in part from the unresolved conflict with Israel. A solution, no doubt, would be economically beneficial to both sides.

Table 3.2 raises a number of issues that have not been central to the peace processes so far. For instance, what currency should be used? Having one's own central bank can sometimes be seen as the ultimate expression of economic sovereignty; however, a number of existing countries are without one. The EU members that have introduced the

TABLE 3.2  PARALLEL SOVEREIGNTY AND ECONOMICS: POSSIBLE SOLUTIONS

| Sovereign over what? | Holders of sovereignty | | | | |
|---|---|---|---|---|---|
| | State 1 | State 2 | Extrastate | Region | Globe |
| Currency | S1 | S2? | $ | € | no |
| Central Bank | no | no | no | European Central Bank | International Monetary Fund |
| Taxation, persons | S1 | S2 | no | no | no |
| Taxation, VAT, border tariffs | new joint organ | new joint organ | no | no | no |
| Property rights | new joint organ | new joint organ | no | no | yes |
| Trade, free trade | S1 | S2 | no | European Union | no |

euro as their currency have a joint bank (European Central Bank). Some countries in the Balkans use the euro, though they are not members of the union. East Timor decided to use the U.S. dollar rather than create its own currency. So there is a choice for both states. Does each want to have its own currency, or should one entity use the currency of the other, or should both decide to adopt an international currency, or create a new common currency? Some logical and realistic choices are listed in table 3.2. It would have to be an independent decision on each side, but it requires coordination. They could both decide to use the U.S. dollar and to have the International Monetary Fund as a central bank, for instance.

Taxation of persons (individuals and juridical persons) has to follow residency; those registered in State 1 would be taxed there, for example. This would provide possibilities for interesting forms of competition, where State 2 might offer lower taxation conditions for corporations and thus attract capital. Other forms of taxation, such as a value-added tax (VAT) and border tariffs, would have to be shared according to an agreed-upon formula. There might in fact have to be a joint taxation authority, for revenue generated from joint sources of income. Such a new body could be created as a part of the settlement.

As the tax base would vary between S1 and S2, a shared policy on revenue redistribution would be necessary, and would have to be negotiated between the two entities in an interstate agreement and with an agreed-upon plan for review. It would be in both sides' interest to reduce income discrepancies. Largely, this would have to be achieved through sustained economic growth, but for the initial period, support to the poorer entity would be required.

A difficult and important issue is one of property rights, particularly properties that have been abandoned by refugees. This is not a unique situation. All protracted and comprehensive wars result in refugees leaving their homelands. Also, the experience of others moving into the seemingly abandoned territories is common. In this case, however, it was not only an effect of the war; there was also a deliberate intention to provide space for a new population. New settlements on lands that might not have been properly transferred from the original owner are a particularly sore point and would be a matter the two states would have to deal with early and head-on.

There is considerable attention to these questions in present-day Bosnia, and the Annan Plan went to great lengths to resolve similar problems for Cyprus. Some lessons may be drawn for the Palestinian conflict.

Actually, these three cases have a common root: the territories were all part of the Ottoman Empire. Cyprus's membership in the European Union opened new possibilities for using court procedures to settle issues of ownership and compensation. Some of these might generate ideas. It might be appropriate for the two states to create a joint property rights commission, preferably with external chairing. Such a commission would need to be well funded and could act like a tribunal, evaluating claims, finding solutions (restoration of rights, for instance), as well as estimating and handing out compensation. The Waitangi Tribunal in New Zealand for settling Maori claims might be another precedent.

Unlike the core functions discussed in the previous section, table 3.2 includes areas where international cooperation would be beneficial, and probably not controversial. The existence of strong global institutions could simplify such discussions. The property issue (ownership, restoration, compensation) might be the one that would require the most attention. Again, international expertise and experience from other situations might help to resolve the issues.

## PARALLEL SOVEREIGNTY AND INTERNAL SECURITY

A core function of a state is the reliable, fair, and competent provision of day-to-day security to its citizens. This is also where parallel states might find the need for considerably more thought than in the previous two categories. Two separate legal systems would need to exist side by side within the same territory; in that sense, they would be internal (intraterritorial, though still interstate) security matters.

Table 3.3 highlights some issues with which a proposed dual legal and police system would have to deal. Criminal law is an example. Such laws might vary between the two states. However, the basic principle would be that the citizens of one state should be tried according to the laws of that state, wherever the crime was committed within the shared territory. If both systems allowed for a possibility of appeal, for instance to European courts, this might increase the credibility and quality of the proceedings.

A complication would arise if the crime involved citizens of both countries. A "normal" interstate solution would be to follow the laws of the location of the crime. However, in this instance, both legal systems would cover the entire territory. Thus, it would be necessary to institute specifically agreed-upon rules for such crimes. It might be heard in the court closest to the crime scene, and thus according to that state's laws.

TABLE 3.3 PARALLEL SOVEREIGNTY AND INTERNAL SECURITY ISSUES: SOME POSSIBILITIES

| Sovereign over what? | Holders of sovereignty | | | | |
| --- | --- | --- | --- | --- | --- |
| | State 1 | State 2 | Extrastate | Region | Globe |
| Criminal law, S1 citizen | S1 | no | no | European Court | International Criminal Court |
| Criminal law, S2 citizen | no | S2 | no | European Court | International Criminal Court |
| Supreme Court, intrastate | S1 | S2 | no | new institutions | no |
| Supreme Court, interstate | new institution | new institution | no | European Court | no |
| State police, control over | S1 | S2 | international police keeping? | international police keeping? | international police keeping? |
| Police, jurisdiction | S1 + S2 | S1 + S2 | United States | European Union | United Nations |
| Interstate police | new joint organization | new joint organization | United States | no | no |

However, an interstate Supreme Court might have to be created as the final court of appeal in such instances. This would have to be a Supreme Court with judges drawn equally from the two states. In order to assure that the outcome is in line with international standards, such a new Supreme Court could include legal competence from outside, perhaps from the EU court system. A formula of three appointees from each state, plus three additional members, appointed either jointly by the two states (preferably) or by an international legal authority (International Court of Justice, International Criminal Court, or another) could be a solution. The president of the Supreme Court could be selected from among the three external members, again to minimize bias. Even if decisions were made only by majority vote, judges from one state could not alone dominate the court procedures. The two states would have to negotiate on this and they would, in effect, create a new form of interstate court. It would be only one of the many innovations this solution would require.

A number of issues—relating to war crimes, for instance—could be handled directly by the International Criminal Court, that is, they would be dealt with outside the two court systems of the two states. Again, this would have to rest on an agreement between the two states. It should be noted that some states now allow the prosecution of individuals and entities for war crimes, even if the crimes have been committed elsewhere (Belgium, for instance).

Table 3.3 shows that police structures would be complicated in a Parallel States construction. One might need to have several police systems, one for each state and one for interstate matters (compare the individual states' police forces and the FBI in the case of the United States). The state police services would have the right to intervene no matter what citizenship the culprits might have. It would be up to the courts to decide where prosecution would take place. This police force could be trained by outside actors, with those actors even assuming a monitoring role during an initial period. Such training, furthermore, would have to include gender awareness, as the security situation during and after conflict is different for men and women.

However, cases that involved citizens from both states would be under the new interstate police authority. This would be likely to involve highly complicated situations (organized crime, money laundering, conspiracies, threats to the state, terrorism, etc.). The interstate police force would be crucial for the maintenance of intraterritorial security. Its credibility would be important. Thus, it might benefit from including a strong extrastate component; in table 3.3, the United States is proposed for that role. Not only would this involve training of the police, but it might also include actual involvement or observation for an initial period, to make sure that the interstate police adhered to basic standards of conduct, for instance, with respect to arrest, interrogation, treatment of prisoners, transparency, and the like. In this particular case, the United States is likely to have credibility on both sides.

For the police system in general there have to be specific structures and routines safeguarding against abuse of power and protecting the human rights of anyone accused of crime. Preventive detention needs to be outlawed.

The issues of intraterritorial security would result in more complicated structures. This is not surprising, and would most likely be the case also for a more traditional two-state solution. These structures, furthermore, would mean the end of conflict. Obviously, the end of occupation is not the same as the end of integration.

PARALLEL SOVEREIGNTY AND HUMAN SECURITY

Table 3.4 points to some of the stronger benefits of parallel sovereignty, as it would provide possibilities for joint solutions to a host of human security concerns. These would include matters of health, transportation, water resources, and environmental matters, as well as possibilities for reconciliation. Even in a traditional two-state solution these matters have to be dealt with, but undivided territory would open new avenues for resolving some issues.

The Israeli health system is world-class; there is no way a Palestinian state could develop something similar in the near future. Thus, there would have to be some form of cooperative agreement, granting citizens of State 2 access to the resources operated by State 1. This could be accomplished simply by reserving space for State 2 citizens and then sending the bills to State 2. A better solution, however, would be a shared insurance system, in which anyone insured would have access to the health system. The insurance could, in turn, be paid by State 2 for its citizens. The alternative, of course, would be to develop a similar relationship with health providers elsewhere (in the Gulf, in Europe, or in the United States). However, a larger pool of patients would also help the health system of State 1 to develop and maintain its edge.

Transportation is a central issue, and all roads within the shared territory should, of course, be open to citizens of both states. There is a shared interest in mobility—for jobs, for recreation, for family

TABLE 3.4   PARALLEL SOVEREIGNTY AND HUMAN SECURITY: SOME POSSIBILITIES

| | Holders of sovereignty | | | | |
|---|---|---|---|---|---|
| Sovereign over what? | State 1 | State 2 | Extrastate | Region | Globe |
| National health system | S 1 | open to S2 | yes | yes | World Health Organization |
| Transportation | new joint authority | new joint authority | no | no | no |
| Water | new joint authority | new joint authority | no | new authority | no |
| Environment | S 1 | S 2 | no | yes | United Nations Environment Programme |
| Reconciliation | new arrangement | new arrangement | no | European Union | United Nations |

relations. New road construction would affect the economic and social opportunities for citizens of both states. The only solution would be to have a joint authority to make such decisions for the two states, including the use and maintenance of the currently existing road systems.

Water resources are significant for both communities and always affect neighboring states. There would need to be a shared authority with sovereign right to act within its mandate and with the resources to do so. A parallel here would be regional or binational bodies, such as the Rhine or Indus River commissions. Some agreements and embryonic structures already exist but need to be made more effective. International standards for the allocation of water need to be adhered to. Broader environmental issues also require close interstate cooperation, as one state's decision would affect the other.

Reconciliation is a relational subject. It takes many forms (individuals, families, clans, countries), and there are many ways of reconciling (economic compensation in money, land, access, scholarships; there are social and psychological dimensions as well). For the two states to work cooperatively, these issues would also have to be addressed at the interstate level. They could not be forced through political decisions, but would have to develop organically as cooperation increases. Thus, a framework should be created to bring up these issues over time and, in particular, both parties should be alert to prevent discrimination that could cement cleavages rather than softening or bridging them.

## SOVEREIGNTY, INTERNATIONAL SECURITY, AND PEACE

The purpose of the Parallel States solution is, of course, to end the conflict and provide security to the two states and their populations. How would the dual structure defend itself against threats from outside the territory? Within the shared territory, security is a matter of police operations, but international security is a different matter. Today one state is equipped to deal with that; the other has little reason to fear threats from outside its territory. The future Palestinian state's main security problem would originate with the partnering state. If that were removed in a credible way, as suggested in the previous sections, the traditional threat structure would change. A successful and mutually agreed-upon solution to the problems between State 1 and State 2 might result in dynamics that would also lead to peaceful settlements of other conflicts (between Israel and Syria, Lebanon, other Arab states, Iran). It is more difficult, however, to see that parallel sovereignty as such would have immediate implications for international security provisions in the same way as the other issues dealt with in this chapter.

Another field of inquiry might be the development of a joint defense doctrine. If one state were to have a major military apparatus and the other nothing of the sort, the relationship might be affected and it could be difficult to uphold the desired equality between the two entities. A joint defense doctrine would provide some insights for State 2 into State 1's planning, and could serve as a confidence-building measure for the surrounding states.

Clearly, parallel sovereignty and the Parallel States concept have to be taken as part of a comprehensive peace agreement, or at least as a crucial step in a process toward such an arrangement. Thus, the many issues of security would in part be dealt with outside the realm of parallel sovereignty, since they relate as well to regional security concerns. However, both states would need to have a say in such solutions. The practical measures envisaged here for a solution within the former Palestinian Mandate area could be a contribution to a larger process, again with the target of achieving a full resolution to the conflict by 2017.

NOTE

1. In a PhD dissertation project at the Kroc Institute of International Peace Studies, University of Notre Dame, Lenore VanderZee (2012) investigates the conditions under which occupation is terminated.

REFERENCES

Ahrnens, Anette. 2007. "A Quest for Legitimacy: Debating UN Security Council Rules on Terrorism and Non-Proliferation." PhD diss., Department of Political Science, Lund University.

Albi, Anneli. 2005. *EU Enlargement and the Constitutions of Central and Eastern Europe.* Cambridge: Cambridge University Press.

Chesterman, Simon. 2005. *You, the People: The United Nations, Transitional Administration and State-Building.* New York: International Peace Academy, Oxford University Press.

Chopra, Jarat. 2002. "Building State Failure in East Timor." *Development and Change* 33, no. 5: 979–1000.

Ekengren, Magnus, Nina Matzén, Mark Rhinard, and Monica Svantesson. 2006. "Solidarity or Sovereignty? EU Cooperation in Civil Protection." *Journal of European Integration* 28, no. 5: 457–76.

Fearon, James D., and David D. Laitin. 2004. "Neotrusteeship." *International Security* 28: 5–43.

Hobbes, Thomas. 1996 (orig. 1651). *The Leviathan*. Oxford: Oxford University Press.

Krasner, Stephen. 2005. "Building Democracy after Conflict: The Case for Shared Sovereignty." *Journal of Democracy* 16, no. 1: 69–83.

Mossberg, Mathias. 2010. "One Land, Two States? Parallel States as an Example of 'Out of the Box' Thinking on Israel/Palestine." *Journal of Palestine Studies* 39, no. 2: 39–53.

Olsson, Louise. 2009. *Gender Equality and United Nations Peace Operations in Timor Leste*. Leiden, Netherlands: Koninklijke Brill.

———. 2011. "Security Equality: The Protection of Men and Women by Peace Operations." Paper presented at the annual convention of the International Studies Association, Montreal, Canada, March 16.

Themnér, Lotta, and Peter Wallensteen. 2013. "Armed Conflicts, 1946–2012." *Journal of Peace Research* 50, no. 4.

Tilly, Charles. 1990. *Coercion, Capital and European States, AD 990–1990*. Cambridge, Mass.: Blackwell.

VanderZee, Lenore. 2012. "Understanding Occupation: Introducing a New Data Set of Military Occupations." Paper presented at the annual convention of the International Studies Association, San Diego, Calif., April 1–4.

Wallensteen, Peter. 2012. *Understanding Conflict Resolution*. 3rd ed. London: Sage.

Woods, Ngaire. 2010. "Global Governance after the Financial Crisis: A New Multilateralism or the Last Gasp of the Great Powers?" *Global Policy* 1, no. 1: 51–63.

# CHAPTER 4

# Security Strategy for the Parallel States Project

*An Israeli Perspective*

NIMROD HURVITZ AND DROR ZEEVI

## A NEW APPROACH TO AN OLD CONFLICT

In the eyes of old-fashioned, left-leaning Zionists, which we consider ourselves to be, the Parallel States Project (PSP) is the outcome of a crisis. It is an original way of dealing with a long-standing failure. Israel and the Palestinians have so far failed to develop a framework that will enable them to live alongside each other in a peaceful manner. After approximately a hundred years of bloodshed, pain, distrust, and a persistent unwillingness to reach a compromise, Israelis and Palestinians are close to the point at which the old two-state solution will not be applicable. And if the old ways are about to become obsolete, it is time to think about new ways to handle this conflict. A required part of the rethinking is to take a new and critical look at the values and assumptions of nationalism.

The PSP opens a venue of critical thought that reconceptualizes nationalism. In fact, the PSP is part of a growing international tendency to restructure the nation-state in the face of the fast-changing circumstances that gnaw at it, such as globalization, the "responsibility to protect," and global ecological issues, all of which require international cooperation and cut across borders. This tendency is particularly conspicuous in Europe, which is experimenting with decreasing the competence, jurisdiction, and sovereignty of its constituent states and placing them in the hands of a federalist body—the European Union.[1]

As often happens in history, the failure of an old system compels its members to reconsider its basic premises, adjust them to a changing reality, and as a consequence usher in a new political order. If the current demographic dynamics are coupled with Jewish settlements all over the West Bank, the division of the land between the two warring parties will become irrelevant. These developments will preclude the ordinary two-state solution, and will compel Israelis and Palestinians to seek fresh solutions based on new conceptualizations of the state. This is the strength and potential of the Parallel States structure: it cuts the Gordian knot of state and territoriality and offers new ways of thinking about what a "state" is and what "sovereignty" is. But can it allay the security fears and fulfill the expectations of Israelis? In this chapter we will present the motivations and fears of the Israeli side, and offer a framework for an effective security system.

## THE ZIONIST HISTORICAL NARRATIVE

To understand the aims and priorities of Zionism, it is important to remind ourselves how the Zionists depict the historical experience of the Jewish people in the two millennia between the destruction of ancient Judea and the foundation of the modern state of Israel. If we were to describe it in one word, it would be *powerlessness*. Although this account of Jewish history has been repeatedly challenged, it remains the key component of the Jews' self-view. Thus, the perceptive remark by David Biale, pointing out that "without some modicum of political strength and the ability to use it, the Jewish people would certainly have vanished,"[2] does little to change the deeply embedded view of history espoused by the contemporary inhabitants of Israel. Based on the historical account that was first articulated by the *maskilim* ("the enlightened"—secularizing intellectuals) in the nineteenth century and then adopted by the Zionist movement, which states emphatically that Jews in the Diaspora have been passive and impotent, the contemporary Zionist narrative sets itself up as the counterculture of the Diaspora Jew and as his political redemption. The dynamics of this dichotomy have been captured by Biale: "The powerlessness of the Diaspora was primarily the fault of the Jews themselves, for they had deliberately abdicated the vitality necessary for national life. The Zionists reached for their models in the more distant past, in the Bible and the militant revolutions of the Roman period. Zionism was to return this impotent people of the Book to nature and to the virtues of self-defense. The 'new

Hebrew man' would take the place of the weak and apolitical Jew. Jewish sovereignty in the Land of Israel would become the antidote for the ills of exile."[3]

Biale's depiction of the Zionist historical narrative goes hand in hand with Theodor Herzl's vision: "Let the sovereignty be granted us over a portion of the globe large enough to satisfy the rightful requirements of a nation; the rest we shall manage ourselves."[4] Although this interpretation of Jewish history is very harsh, in that it places the blame on the Jews themselves, depictions of Jewish weakness and vulnerability are based on facts and are highly convincing. Often marginalized as a people and as individuals, Jews were incarcerated in ghettos, paid higher taxes than their neighbors, were restricted in their choice of professions and education, and had limitations imposed on the use of cultural symbols. Once in a while these were exacerbated by deportation and exile. Despite the fact that Islamic governments were on the whole more tolerant than European ones, this discrimination was not limited to Christian Europe, and occurred also under Islamic rule.

With the rise of nationalism, Jews received a measure of autonomy in Europe (and later in non-European lands), which evolved into full citizenship. But despite the auspicious beginnings, as the world around them began to define states in national terms, Jews were often cast in the role of the "other" against whom the body of the nation was to be defined. This was accompanied by a steep rise in anti-Semitism, which was gradually transformed from a spectrum of religious animosities into a quasi-scientific racial ideology. Pogroms in late nineteenth-century Russia and hostile encounters from Paris to Warsaw convinced many Jews that the only possible solution would be a state in which they could lead a secure and independent life unfettered by other nations.

In the Zionist imagination, as in its practices of state-building, the establishment of the state of Israel was a means to negate the Diaspora and alter the fate of the Jews. Zionism emerged almost simultaneously in eastern and western Europe. Sometime before the Paris-based Viennese Theodor Herzl officially summoned the first Zionist Congress in 1897, a movement called BILU (a Hebrew acronym that stands for "let us depart to the house of Jacob") was created in Russia in the early 1880s, and a parallel quasi-messianic movement arose in Yemen, calling for the return of Israelites to their old homeland. Though not always conceptualized in similar terms, their common objectives were nominally to reclaim an ancient nation, but mainly to find refuge from the rising xenophobia of emergent nationalism.

Soon after they arrived in Palestine, the Zionist settlers found themselves in conflict with the inhabitants of their old-new homeland. At the same time persecution, mainly in Eastern Europe, increased daily. The combination of conflict inside Palestine and continued persecution abroad gave rise to the ethos of defense and self-reliance. Organizations such as Ha-Shomer (The Sentinel) and later Ha-Hagana (The Defense) sprang up, based on veterans of Eastern European armies and emulating local Bedouin and Ottoman military traditions. Later they were joined by such right-wing organizations as Ha-Irgun (The Organization, standing for "Military-National Organization") and LEHI (acronym for "Fighters for Israel's Independence").[5]

The deteriorating situation of the Jews in the Diaspora culminated with the uprooting and destruction of most of European Jewry during the Holocaust. In many cases those fleeing the war, and others trying to find refuge after the war ended, were refused entry into other countries, including the United States. Much of the Arab world was perceived as pro-Nazi during those events, and the leader of the Palestinians at the time, Mufti Amin al-Husayni, openly cooperated with wartime Germany. The barbarity of the Nazis, the cynicism of Western nations, and the cooperation of the Arabs with the archenemies of the Jews, coupled with the high numbers of soldiers who were killed in the War of Independence in 1948, have strengthened the sense of insecurity and the ethos of self-reliance. The vulnerability and impotence of the Jews in the Diaspora drove the Zionists to make an unequivocal demand for independence and power.

Long years of interaction with Arab and Palestinian neighbors have not done much to allay these fears. According to one prevailing Israeli narrative, the defining act in the relations between Israelis and Palestinians is the latter's rejection of several compromises offered by the international community, beginning with the 1936 Peel Commission and the 1947 UN Partition Plan. This view has been strengthened by more recent events, such as the failure of the Oslo Accords, Israel's accusation that the Palestinians rejected its offers at the Camp David summit of 2000, the second Intifada, and the transformation of Gaza into a military base from which attacks are launched against Israel. All these have strengthened the existing distrust toward the Palestinians. As a consequence, many Israelis believe that the Palestinian side will use any settlement as a springboard for more acts of terror or to present more political demands.

In broad terms this historical account has shaped the contemporary building blocks of Israeli Jewish identity, though varying Zionist currents view this narrative through different lenses. At one extreme of the political spectrum some Israelis consider this narrative of woe, suffering, and betrayal to be exaggerated. Adherents of this historical interpretation tend to take the opinions of other nations into serious consideration and lean toward compromises over land. At the other extreme are right-wing groups, many of which are religious nationalists that nurture the Jewish self-perception of standing apart from the Gentiles and of perennial persecution. Within this current are found influential religious leaders who depict the land of Israel as a divinely promised territory that no secular authority has the right to give up, regardless of any historical narrative. One of them, Harav Tzvi Yehuda Hacohen Kook, told his adherents that in 1947, after he heard about the UN Partition Plan, according to which the state of Israel was about to get approximately half of the old Palestinian Mandate, he sat at home bereaved and saddened because of the loss of the other half of the land of Israel. After the Six-Day War, when the possibility arose of negotiating with the Palestinians and ceding to them parts of the captured territories, he rejected such options and called them "sins."[6]

Despite these differences of opinion, the vast majority of Israelis believe that sovereignty over land is an essential means to defend Israel. In terms of the imperative of security all camps share the same historically informed view, which is central to every Jewish Israeli's upbringing. The enormity of European Jewry's tragedy in the twentieth century, along with the subsequent persecution of Jews in other parts of the world such as the Soviet Bloc and the Islamic world, as well as the ongoing conflict with the Arab world, elevated this ethos of security to mythical proportions and reaffirmed apprehensions of a nation under siege.

For Israeli Jews of all political hues, sovereignty over land—embodied in a strong state—is first and foremost a means of overcoming all these threats and catastrophes. Self-reliance and the ability to protect themselves, which are deemed the only antidotes for their fate in the Diaspora, are pillars of the Israeli ethos, and must be taken into consideration in any agreement with the Palestinians. Any settlement of the Israeli-Palestinian political process should therefore take this narrative into consideration.

In the following pages we shall argue that the best way to address these deep-seated fears in the context of the Parallel States solution is to maintain a clear asymmetry of power and install legal and other safeguards against loss of autonomy. In order for the Israelis to consider a political settlement that is based on shared space and open borders, they must know that if a crisis unfolds, they possess the military means and legal option to detach themselves from the power-sharing agreement, maintain strategic deterrence, and, if need be, have the ability to overcome any foe.

## CURRENT THREAT PERCEPTIONS

Based on this reading of reality, Israelis perceive three kinds of existential threats: attack by an external enemy or an amalgam of internal and external foes, demographic takeover from within, and denial of access to vital resources.

The current external threat is well known. The worst-case scenario is a nuclear Iran, supported by Hezbollah in Lebanon, with tacit and perhaps open Syrian backing, and a hostile Hamas government in the Gaza Strip combining forces to destroy the Jewish state. Although the Iranian axis in the region has had some setbacks recently, this scenario, according to most observers, is not likely to vanish completely in the wake of a peace accord with the Palestinian Authority. There are other forces, mainly in the Islamic world, that aspire to annihilate Israel, regardless of whether it comes to terms with its neighbors. There is a debate within Israel about the extent to which an agreement with the Palestinians will weaken these forces.

Long experience has taught Israelis that such threats can emerge from unexpected quarters. A takeover of a close Arab neighbor, or a change of government in an allied country such as Turkey or Egypt, could rapidly deteriorate into open hostility and materialize as a threat. The Arab Spring, which may usher in many positive changes to the Middle East's political culture, may also transform countries that have had peace agreements with Israel into bitter enemies. The rise in "people power" illustrates the fluidity of political systems in the region. Furthermore, regardless of the Arab Spring, terrorist and guerrilla organizations may come to possess weapons of mass destruction, and with a rapidly changing battlefield, the threats are multiplied and require a great deal of flexibility. Israel needs to be able to adjust its strategy and attain weapons systems that address such emergent perils.

But although external threats have a crucial bearing on Israel's need to maintain its power of deterrence, the greatest threat to Israel's security and independence is a takeover from within, either by force or by the sheer numbers of Palestinians in the land. Demographic extrapolations are central to this issue. In many respects population numbers and natural growth estimates have drawn large numbers of right-wing Israelis to the politically pragmatic line that espouses a two-state solution.

Surveys indicate that the number of Palestinians west of the Jordan River is currently slightly lower than that of Jews. Clearly even a very large minority is a danger to the stability of a nation-state, but although birthrates are gradually declining all around, this ratio is likely to be upset. In the near future Jews may once again become a minority and the Palestinians a majority. If significant numbers of Palestinian refugees are allowed to resettle within these boundaries in the framework of a Parallel States agreement, the balance is likely to tip even more rapidly.

This would undoubtedly be perceived by many Israelis as the major shortcoming of any solution that did not involve a clear separation of Israel-Palestine into two territorially distinct states, and would likely be the principal argument against the Parallel States structure. If the question of sovereignty was not clearly resolved, or if at any stage the parties were given unilateral power to alter the Parallel States agreement, its constitution, or its bylaws through countrywide referendum or elections, it would clearly be unacceptable to most Israelis.

Finally, Israel-Palestine is a land of scarce natural resources. Water is in short supply, and so are land and airspace. Much of Israel's water, for instance, comes from underground sources in the Mountain Aquifer beneath the West Bank. In the atmosphere of distrust that pervades Israeli discourse, any agreement with the Palestinians would need to address such issues.

## PROS AND CONS OF THE PARALLEL STATES CONCEPT

As stated above, although Israelis disagree among themselves about the borders of the state of Israel, most of them consider the two-state solution to be the preferred settlement to the conflict. In the absence of a two-state solution, the Parallel States structure offers Israel a combination of risks and opportunities.

The main risk would be viewed as allowing the Palestinians to participate in deciding Israel's future. The Parallel States structure would allow Palestinians to settle everywhere and to have a voice in decision-making about the future of the state, its external treaties, its legal and economic systems, and its form of government. This scenario would be viewed with deep suspicion by most Israelis, who assume that the ultimate aim of the Palestinians is to destroy all vestiges of Jewish independence. A major risk factor that would receive much attention is the demographic disparity. Israelis will suspect that once the numerical balance between the two peoples changes in favor of the Palestinians, they might bring up the charge of discrimination in the Parallel States structure, and this might lead to a change in the terms and conditions of the agreement and further erode Jewish sovereignty. These fears must be allayed.

On the other hand, the Parallel States structure offers some important opportunities, foremost among them, of course, being peace and an end to territorial claims by both sides. In the absence of a two-state solution this would provide the best settlement from an Israeli point of view. The crucial implication of a Parallel States framework is that all inhabitants of the region—Jews, Muslims, and Christians—would have access to every site in the Holy Land. Furthermore, it would also mean that the settlers would not be forced to dismantle their settlements. The Parallel States structure enables all the political currents of the Israeli public to attain their political goals.

## A SECURITY FRAMEWORK FOR THE PARALLEL STATES

This section offers an analysis of problems that are common to both sides and thus relevant to Palestinian concerns as well as to Israeli ones, but its main concern is the security of Israeli citizens as party to the agreement.[7]

If and when a Parallel States settlement was implemented and recognized by the international community, and some of the regional and international players previously hostile to the Jewish state acknowledged that the main problems had been resolved to their satisfaction, security concerns would diminish considerably. Yet the possibility that serious dangers would continue to afflict the region cannot be disregarded, and if we wish to make such a solution viable we need to allay fears about worst-case scenarios. Such scenarios are based on three distinct assumptions: the rise of new enemies and the entrenchment of old ones, changes in warfare technology, and the increased danger of internal strife.

We need to begin by acknowledging a basic threat that such an agreement may not eliminate. In parts of the Islamic world today there is an entrenched hostility toward the West, and toward Israel as its perceived outpost in the Middle East region. The Middle East would remain a highly unstable zone even if peace were reached between Palestine and

Israel. Rogue states such as Iran, and organizations like al-Qaeda or international jihadists, may grow in sophistication and power, becoming a serious strategic threat to the budding new entity. It should also be borne in mind that the Middle East remains potentially unstable, governed by authoritarian regimes and threatened by a panoply of radical internal groups. Such hostile groups may assume control of strategic weapons in countries such as Egypt, Syria, Jordan, or Iraq. The interim consequences of the series of coups and revolutions dubbed the Arab Spring are a case in point. In the wake of these recent upheavals, new governments and new unstable zones have emerged—the Sinai Peninsula and the Syrian border in the Golan Heights among them—in which organizations committed to the long-term destruction of the Jewish state have established bases. (At the same time, we also see a shift in some traditionally Islamist groups, which are now willing to come to terms with the existence of Israel.)[8]

This threat is compounded and augmented by changes in warfare technology.[9] In the recent past, wars were fought by armies, with civilians largely on the sidelines. Nowadays, as land armies in the Middle East are replaced to a large extent by easily accessible missile technology and unconventional warfare, several new issues emerge: civilians become much more vulnerable; wars may reach urban and rural areas; and a nonstate actor with access to such weapons could cause destruction disproportionate to its size and support base.

Another threat that needs to be taken into consideration in any Parallel States situation is the rising danger of internal strife. In the current situation there is a partial disengagement of the warring sides. While the wall in the West Bank and the fence separating Gaza from Israel lead to discrimination, these barriers effectively curtail the ability of Palestinian hostile groups to shift their armed struggle inside Israel's borders. By definition, a Parallel States agreement would do away with these barriers between the populations. Palestinians and Israelis would live side by side all over the country (or in large portions of it). This, all by itself, creates myriad opportunities for those who wish to cause mischief on both sides. While most of the population may seek peace and quiet, radical groups opposed to compromise or wishing to break up the agreement would find it easier to move freely and threaten civilian populations.

The model this chapter proposes takes into consideration such scenarios for the Parallel States framework. In general terms the model envisions a gradual, long-term reduction of Israeli military capabilities, and a parallel enhancement of Palestinian defensive capabilities, along with the presence of a third, international, military force on the ground to deter potential enemies and to tackle threats.

One inescapable conclusion is that as a direct conclusion of these assumptions, and in view of Israel's perception of its role as a shelter for the Jewish people, in all possible configurations the Israeli side would insist on maintaining some military advantage, full potential defensive capabilities, and—should all other means fail—the ability to deploy troops in its own defense. This should be a sine qua non of any proposed Parallel States agreement. Although such a condition may be perceived as an obstacle to the conclusion of an agreement, if acknowledged as a key issue for Israelis it will remove the single most crucial impediment to a Parallel States settlement.

Although our main concerns are threats and the ways to tackle them, in the conclusion to our chapter we also offer a glimpse into the possible advantages and opportunities for improvement suggested by a Parallel States solution.

## THE GRADUAL DEVELOPMENT OF A JOINT SECURITY SYSTEM

Since the Parallel States structure is a new and previously untested type of polity, it should be viewed as a developing structure that builds up experience (and—we hope—trust) along a long learning curve. The security structure proposed here should therefore develop over three phases. Time frames are approximate and could be changed to fit other concerns.

*First period*—transition, presumed to take up to five years

*Second period*—the first twenty-five years after the transition period is completed

*Third period*—steady-state, beginning from the thirty-first year

Our working assumption is that despite the signing of an agreement, an inherent lack of trust between the parties would persist during the first period and into the second one. This might not be reflected at the formal political level: both sides would have accepted the agreement and would have received international assurances. Yet on the ground, between midlevel and lower-level executives as well as among citizens on both sides, mutual distrust would linger.

The second period, estimated at twenty-five years, is calculated as the time required for building trust, establishing new modes of communication and patterns of cooperation, and moving from a structure based on separate armies and core areas to one in which joint institutions could function smoothly.

From our vantage point it is almost impossible to foresee conditions in the third period. Some scenarios would see a continued alignment of the two states or perhaps a merger into one state; others would accentuate the differences. At any rate, it is assumed that once the parallel states had been running for a generation, some mutually agreed-upon changes would need to be implemented based on accumulated experience.

## A NEW STRATEGIC EQUILIBRIUM

Israel is currently a regional power that wields substantial influence over the politics of the Middle East. It could be argued, for example, that simply by being a silent partner, it has contributed to the continued rule of the Hashemite family in Jordan, and may have been a factor in the long-term stability (or instability) of other regimes in the region. Yet as soon as a Parallel States agreement was signed and implemented on the ground, a new geopolitical reality would come into being. On the one hand, most Middle Eastern states would likely offer recognition to the new entity and establish cordial diplomatic relationships with it, effectively ending their enmity with Israel. On the other, Israel's power would be curtailed as a result of two main factors. In the first place, its sheer military force would need to be reduced in view of the fact that other military forces with divergent and intersecting interests would share the same space (see analysis below); and second, its ability to act would be restricted by the need to consider the effect of its actions on its Palestinian partner, and their political consequences in relation to the stability of the Parallel States structure.

To give one example, by preemptively responding to intelligence about a threat of aggression from a third party, Israel might potentially drag its Palestinian partner into a military dispute with a neighboring country. The Palestinians could then argue that another approach, such as alerting the neighboring country or approaching it through a common ally, could have defused the danger without recourse to military action. Similar scenarios could develop on the other side as well. In order to preclude such dangerous imbroglios, the agreement would need to ensure that both parties were restricted in their ability to engage in military action and were required to coordinate. Such necessary limitations would lead to further restriction of Israel's military might and reputation.

Thus, a Parallel States structure would be bound to establish a new regional balance of power, leading to unforeseen consequences for all states in the region. Radical states, formerly held at bay by Israeli deterrence, might become more powerful (Iran is a case in point). For another, guerrilla or terror organizations that today are vulnerable to Israeli intelligence-based actions would be able to operate undeterred, perhaps leading to other changes in surrounding states. One result might be that regimes that previously maintained cordial or even neutral relations with Israel might be toppled and replaced by more menacing ones.

Finally, we should take into consideration the fact that modern technology is changing the battlefield rapidly, and that small states or organizations relatively far away from the borders of the parallel states, equipped with such technology, might emerge as a strategic threat. The last two major conflagrations Israel has been engaged in—Lebanon in 2006 and Gaza in 2008–9—were prompted by missiles launched into civilian centers in the north and south of the country, respectively, sometimes from a considerable distance. We may assume that the struggle against unconventional warfare and ballistic missile technologies will continue in the future, not least by virtue of restrictions on the use of force against terrorists finding shelter among the civilian population. Once again, the need to take into consideration the standing of the parallel state may create new and unforeseen difficulties in fighting this menace.

Hence, a worst-case scenario for Israelis should assume an increasingly radical Middle East and, from the vantage point of the Parallel States structure, a heightened level of threat on the one hand and a restricted ability to respond militarily on the other. Many of the problems described here could be offset by efficient cooperation between the parties to the Parallel States agreement, and between them and the neighboring states.

THREAT ANALYSIS

Possible threats to Israel in a Parallel States situation should be divided into two clusters: all-out war and low-intensity war. These archetypes could also be seen as a continuum with two distinct end points—total war on one end and minor acts of resistance on the other—but there is a dividing line that allows us to treat them as quantitatively and

qualitatively distinct. Each cluster should be divided into various prob-
abilities. In order to assess as many threats as possible we assume that
the parties—Israelis and Palestinians—might under certain circumstances act as aggressors against each other even with a Parallel States
agreement.

*All-out War*

Since the Parallel States structure would be a final status agreement
accepted internationally with seals of approval by the Israelis, the Palestinians, and the international community, the threat of all-out war
would be reduced. It is assumed that the agreement would include an
international commitment for a defensive umbrella over the territory.
Furthermore, one of the most prominent characteristics of any agreement would be a breakup of current spatial divisions and a continued
integration of the two populations. In other words, Israelis and Palestinians would gradually come to be more evenly distributed throughout
the whole area between the Jordan River valley and the Mediterranean.
Since latter-day warfare in the region is based to a large degree on massive use of ballistic missiles against clusters of civilian population, we
assume that any major external attack on one of the parties, at least
until the end of the second period (twenty-five years), would be con-
strued as an attack on both sides, and in that sense the Israelis and
Palestinians would be each other's safeguard. All these factors, taken
together, would serve as strong deterrents to any belligerent state.

Yet the risk of war would not be eliminated. Even with the two parallel states up and running, external threats would persist both against
the territory as a whole and against each of the parties. Although Palestinians would begin to settle in former Israeli territory and Israelis in
Palestinian areas, for a long time to come the core areas of both groups
would remain clearly demarcated in terms of ethnicity, religion, and
citizenship. From across the borders we perceive mainly threats to the
Israeli side. There could also be external challenges that disregarded
potential damage to the Palestinian side from regimes and groups that
would see the Parallel States structure as betrayal of an Islamic or Arab
national ideal.

There is growing concern about the possible introduction of tactical
unconventional weapons, either airborne or clandestinely over land or
sea. If and when potential enemies of either state obtained precision-
guided munitions, it would be possible to target an Israeli neighbor-

hood or institution with little or no collateral damage on the Palestinian side, or vice versa.

Another possible source of all-out war that we cannot afford to disregard is the other party to the agreement: a premeditated Israeli assault on the Palestinian side or a Palestinian attack on the Israeli side. In such a case it is to be assumed that the compatriots on each side would flock to their respective heartlands, creating a clearer target for the other party's armed forces. It may also be assumed that third parties would enter the fray at a later stage. This scenario might bring about a renewed refugee situation and the entire area of the parallel states would serve as battleground for both sides.

Finally, we have to consider the possibility of a concerted attack by both internal and external forces against the other party to the agreement (for example, a joint Israeli-Jordanian attack against the Palestinian side, or a joint Palestinian-Syrian attack against the Israeli party). This type of attack is probably the toughest challenge facing each of the parties to the agreement.

## Low-Intensity Warfare

Even as the danger of all-out war gradually diminished, the danger of terror or guerrilla operations could rise steeply as a result of several factors.[10]

Groups might emerge on both sides interested in disrupting the Parallel States settlement, which would seem to some to be a betrayal of a historical birthright. Such groups could try to provoke mayhem between the parties. There could even be state-initiated or state-condoned guerrilla acts during the initial phases of negotiations, aimed at changing the parameters of the deal and improving bargaining positions. Radical organizations across the borders might also do their utmost to infiltrate the parallel states territory and use guerrilla tactics to create a semblance of internal strife in order to sabotage the agreement.

As implementation of the plan progressed, removal of restrictions on internal movement of Palestinians and Israelis within each other's communities would facilitate the infiltration of arms and munitions. If each side issued its own identity documents and controls (see the discussion below on border control), this might lead to difficulties in assessing the validity of documentation and in supervising terrorist elements. In general, border control would need to be less restricted than it currently is. Each side would, of necessity, be more lax in checking its own compatriots and their guests, leading to breaches in airport, seaport, and border-crossing security. If both sides opted for separate entry points on all borders, infiltration of weapons and combatants would become much more difficult to restrict. Finally, an influx of returning refugees and immigrants as part of the Parallel States accords could serve as an ideal cover for terrorist elements and provocateurs attempting to infiltrate the territory.

## LAYERS OF SECURITY

In order to create effective defenses against the threats described above, the parallel states should create a multilayered security network based on international and regional commitments, as well as on the presence of international forces. Ultimately, however, Israel will insist on its right to defend itself. When all else fails, it will keep relying on its own security forces as a fail-safe defense mechanism.

The country's security would be assured in the first instance by international guarantees. United Nations General Assembly and Security Council resolutions to defend the Israeli and Palestinian parties against all aggression should be integral to the agreement. The Israeli side would demand long-term guarantees against attempts by any party to overturn the agreement unilaterally and would insist that the agreement could be altered only by mutual consent.

This should be supplemented by bilateral nonaggression agreements, primarily between the two main parties but also with neighboring states. In fact, such agreements with all of Israel's neighbors should be a precondition to any Parallel States framework. On this bilateral level one cannot overemphasize the importance of confidence-building measures as part of each side's security.[11] Here the most important aspect is education. Efforts should be made by both sides, even before a Parallel States plan was implemented, to begin educating their respective publics through all channels about the other side's narrative, language, and culture, and about the possible advantages of the new agreement.

A crucial layer of defense for the parallel states would be provided by the gradual integration of populations. Here, one of the first questions to consider would be the status of Israel's current Arab population and whether its status would change as part of the agreement. Israeli Arabs could be viewed as an accelerator of the integration process if they were formally to become part of the Palestinian state, and an obstacle if they remained part of the Israeli state (and thus unwilling to share their benefits or compete for labor with their Palestinian compatriots). In any case, we view integration as a long-term process that would not be concluded in the first generation, in which case it would not be a security deterrent until the third phase of implementation.

As a further layer of security, the Israeli party should insist on protection by a trusted third party like the United States or an international force such as NATO (which stands here as shorthand for any international organization with substantial military capabilities that would be trusted by both parties). At present we perceive five options: (1) being brought under the protective umbrella of the U.S. military, with a special force of limited size stationed in the area at least until the end of the second phase; (2) being brought under the protective umbrella of NATO under the same conditions as the U.S. force above, without joining the organization; (3) joining NATO with noncombatant status, thereby maintaining a strict separation between Israel's own military capabilities and those of NATO; (4) joining NATO as a full member; or (5) deploying a UN force composed of troops from several countries acceptable to both sides.

From the Israeli perspective, the preferred option at present would be an American protective umbrella. In view of the checkered experience Israel has had with UN forces, the United Nations would be the least likely option. If NATO turned out to be the selected option, we would recommend that both parties not join the organization initially, but at a later stage their membership could be considered.

Finally, the ultimate defense of the Jewish population, if all other guarantees and security measures failed, would be the Israel Defense Forces (IDF), well trained and equipped, and in times of peace stationed in a remote military area.

## BASIC REQUIREMENTS—ARMY AND POLICE

In view of the assumptions presented above, we have to conclude that a danger of instability and an elevated level of threat to all parties could persist well into the implementation period of a Parallel States agreement. It would therefore be essential that during the first period of transition (three to five years), the IDF maintain its current structure and deployment to deter possible foes. During this period an international force would be introduced, and would begin to build its bases and study the arena. Meanwhile, a Palestinian army or police would gradually be built with the assistance of the international force.

During the second period (up to twenty-five years), in order to counter the multiple threats, there should continue to be three separate military forces in the shared territory: a Palestinian one, an Israeli one, and an international one. In addition, we propose the establishment of a unified police force. During the third period (after thirty years), we perceive the possibility of Israeli and Palestinian forces gradually integrating into one force, and of the international force phasing out.

In the meantime, the relationships among the three military forces, and between them and police forces in charge of internal security, should be carefully defined and delineated. In principle, the two parties should be allowed to use nothing but civilian police forces in times of peace, and should be required to leave the handling of all externally initiated military and terror threats to the international force. The Israeli and Palestinian military forces should engage only if a certain carefully defined threshold was crossed. Unless and until this line of defense was breached, the international force should be in full command, and the two other armed forces should restrict themselves to their barracks and training areas.

To be able to fulfill their duties undeterred, both sides should have autonomous military territories, to serve as barracks and training grounds for the separate armies. In addition, camps and training facilities should be set aside for the international security force. In view of current threats, it is suggested that the IDF would maintain two such territorial heartlands: one in the northern part of the Jordan valley and another in the Negev Desert.

## The International Force

The international force is expected to be necessary for the entire second period, and its role could be reevaluated at the end of the period. At present, from the Israeli perspective, the United States seems to be the preferred option, as it has proved itself capable of actual military operations when necessary and is trusted by both sides. Failing that, some other kind of nonaligned force such as NATO should be invited to send a suitable contingent for the purpose. One reason for selecting NATO over similar organizations would be its ability to draw on considerable additional forces from nearby in Europe and the Atlantic should the need arise.[12]

If NATO was brought in, the Israeli party to the agreement should not join NATO as a full-fledged member during the first (transitional) or second periods; rather, NATO would provide a defense umbrella for the territory and station forces there, as a manifestation of the international commitment to uphold the agreement. Eventually, if the new political structure was stable and economically viable, full membership in NATO (combatant or noncombatant) should be considered. Perhaps in an interim stage Palestinians and Israelis could be eligible to serve in the NATO international force as volunteers or as adjunct units under its command. This could be seen as the kernel of future joint Israeli-Palestinian military cooperation, which could develop into a joint army in the third phase of implementation.

The composition of the international force stationed in the country (order of battle, in military terminology) would be determined by the changing security requirements. At a minimum it should include combat aircraft, elite rapid-deployment units, surface-to-surface missiles, multilayered surface-to-air defense systems, intelligence, engineering, logistics, and other necessary functions.

At this stage it would be difficult to define the possible tasks of the international force, but as a general rule it would be the first line of defense for the territory. Any threat to the parallel states or to either of its parties would first be met by the international force. If, and only if, this force failed in its mission to protect the sides, or declined to take on the responsibility, should the other forces present get involved.

### The Palestinian Military Force

Our working assumption is that the Palestinians would not face the same types of challenges as either the Israeli party or the Parallel States structure as a whole.[13] In our estimation, the main threats posed to the Palestinian party would be of two kinds. The first might arise from the Israeli party to the agreement, following (or preceding) a breakdown of the Parallel States structure or a crisis in negotiations. A second threat might materialize as a result of terror activities initiated from the outside (al-Qaeda–type organizations resentful of the Palestinian-Israeli accord) and from the inside (Israeli or Palestinian extremists who might see the agreement as a betrayal of a divine promise).

Locally emerging terror threats would be dealt with by police and internal security forces, with possible assistance from the international force when requested. As discussed, threats arising beyond the shared territorial borders would be addressed by the international force. Palestine's military force should therefore be structured in such a way as to be able to respond mainly to the scenario of an attempted Israeli takeover. In our view, the setup should be mainly defensive and agreed upon as part of the accords.

As stated above, it seems essential that the Palestinian party, like the Israeli one, define a heartland in which its military forces would be deployed and their training would take place. In fact, we propose two heartland areas: one would be the area around Ramallah and Nablus, and another would be in the eastern side of the Negev Desert.

### The Israeli Military Force

Under the conditions described above and in view of the basic security concerns that stand at the heart of Israel's ethos of peril and survival, it is imperative that the Israeli side have a fully autonomous security force, capable of deterring and keeping at bay all reasonable external threats if need be, until such time as these threats are deemed immaterial by the Israelis.

Unlike the two other military forces mentioned above—the international force and the Palestinian force—which do not yet exist and would be tailor-made for the parallel states, the IDF would be required to undergo substantial change, a process we expect to be problematic and even traumatic for the nation since so much of its common culture is tied to the defense imperative. Although we propose that each side define its own laws of military service, we would recommend that the framework of a conscription army be maintained for the foreseeable future, perhaps with a gradually shortened service obligation (now standing at three years for men, two years for women). Also, in view of the rapidly changing modern battlefield and the pace of technological change, it is essential that Israel's security mandate be broad enough to allow for the necessary adaptations to new modes of warfare and new weapons systems. In other words, the Parallel States agreement should define Israel's military in terms of flexible defense capabilities and not simply in terms of units and weapons.

### Heartlands or Core Areas

During the transitional period, the IDF should maintain its current deployment along Israel's borders, except in the Palestinian heartland. In the second period the army would gradually redeploy into the core (heartland) area, contingent on developments on the ground and on the gradual introduction of the international force. Eventually, most of the

Israeli armed forces would be restricted to these core areas in the Negev and the Jordan valley, where training would take place and strategic weapons would be kept.

A problem may arise concerning the concentration of training facilities, arms, and equipment in two relatively small zones. We foresee a difficult discussion about the size of this region, restricting in effect the size of the joint Parallel States area. One approach would be to consider deployment of parts of the armament and personnel, such as flight squadrons, in other areas of the country, perhaps under the supervision of the international force. Another alternative would be to provide training facilities in other countries, in which case a NATO framework would also be advantageous.

## Civilian Police Forces

While the three military forces would deal mainly with external threats, civilian police forces should be established, whose task would be to maintain order among civilians, counter internal threats of terror, and curb acts of vandalism and hate crimes. In order to bypass the perennial question of composition and hierarchy, we suggest that police forces be locally organized, maintained by municipalities and local councils, and coordinated by an overarching police commission with a joint command structure, responding to problems that transcend municipal boundaries.

## Intelligence and Information Gathering

This section refers to the problems of gathering intelligence inside the joint territory in view of its sensitive implications for internal stability, and is restricted to discussing some of the problems that could arise, without recommending solutions. It is obvious that each party to the agreement, mainly in the early phases of implementation, would have to keep an eye on the other party. Mutual mistrust and fear, coupled with real threats, would demand good intelligence. By its nature, intelligence gathering is an illegal and underhanded intrusion into the other side and thus could have serious repercussions for the stability of the agreement. Here we propose to differentiate among several kinds of information gathering modes.

There should be no particular problem with information based on VISINT—visual intelligence gathering using binoculars, telescopes, and planes. This would be facilitated by the fact that the two nations share the same territory and air space. Some types of ELINT and SIGINT, electronic data gathering and collection of information from airborne signals, would be slightly more problematic because in some cases they might involve a breach of privacy. Gathering information from the phones and computers of Israelis and Palestinians, either through radio frequencies or from land lines, should therefore be permitted only after obtaining special consent from a joint court.

HUMINT, intelligence based on spies, agents, and other human sources, would on the one hand become more accessible in the absence of borders and the integration of populations. Recruitment and operation of agents would become much easier than it currently is. On the other hand, traditionally HUMINT has been the most destructive of intelligence activities in terms of the social and political costs of exposure, making it potentially more volatile than other forms of intelligence gathering and more dangerous to the stability of the parallel states. Here, too, court consent would be required.

The sides to the agreement should be made aware of these limitations and come to a clear understanding about the perils of intelligence gathering and the ways to overcome them.


CRISIS MANAGEMENT
*Containing Threats and Preventing Violence*

In contrast to the present climate of suspicion and hostility, the Parallel States structure would enhance internal security mainly by creating common purpose, common cause, and common interest in both parties to preserve it. The main challenge for all parties would therefore be deterrence, prevention of violence, and, in case of an outbreak of hostilities, primarily defense of the civilian population and preventing the total breakdown of the Parallel States framework. It is clear from previous experience that the tolerance of both sides for violence generated by individuals and organizations in the other's camp is low. They are thus prone to interpret all acts of aggression as being initiated or condoned by the other party.

Preventing violence would require, first and foremost, efficient cooperation among intelligence services in order to identify and contain threats before they materialized. This effort to gather and assess all available information should be coordinated by the commander of the international force through established rapid channels of communication. In most cases, alerting all levels—national, regional, and local—to imminent danger would go a long way toward minimizing or eliminating it.

This should be handled by a permanent crisis forum chaired by the commander of the international force. The forum should make the international force privy to the state of affairs, to accumulated intelligence, and to assessments of both parties. It should then decide on the process of continued intelligence gathering, on informing other regional players, and on continued coordination between the parties on all levels.

As a deterrent to acts of aggression from within the shared territory, any agreement should clearly define the full responsibility of each party not to promote violence on several levels, ranging from direct initiation to lesser offenses of material encouragement, ideological support, negligence, and laxity. The agreement should also define sanctions for breaches of confidence as manifested by moral support of government officials for terror or guerrilla organizations. Such sanctions could range from reducing financial assistance to one of the parties to prosecuting leaders in an international court.

### Combating Aggression

When acts of violence cannot be averted or deterred, an effort should be made to contain them and to prevent further escalation inside the shared territory. In order to put in place serious mechanisms aimed at preventing escalation, we should study the breakdown of security cooperation during the second Intifada in order to see what kinds of structures withstood the crisis and continued to function. It is our impression that some of the District Coordination Offices, staffed by people acquainted with the other side's language and culture, kept on working despite the hostilities. These should perhaps be considered an essential mechanism.

In case of an attack of unknown provenance that is not existentially threatening, the agreement should state clearly that no retaliatory action should be taken until all parties concerned had convened and ascertained that the forces behind the attack had been identified, and an appropriate response agreed upon between the two parties and the international force, by mediation or by arbitration if need be. Only if all these measures failed should the parties resort to using their own military forces as an act of self-defense.

### Border Control

In principle the parallel states would span the entire territory with few internal borders except for core areas and military heartlands on both sides. Even borders between core areas and the rest of the country need not be physically demarcated by fences or walls, but merely understood as regions in which a different set of laws applied. Yet there is a possibility that these borders would in times of crisis become more entrenched. This situation should be taken into account and allowed for if the need arose.

As for the border crossings between the shared territory and the outer world, we envision two possibilities. One would be joint border control, and the other would be a continuation of the principle of division of sovereignty, resulting in coordinated but separate border crossings.

One of the main symbols of sovereignty is control of external borders, including the power to make independent decisions about the inward and outward flow of people and goods. Thus, we assume that each party would consider control of border entry points by land, air, and sea without interference from the other side an essential part of its display of sovereignty. This issue is further complicated by the sensitive issues of the Israeli Law of Return and the Palestinian Right of Return. Schengen-type agreements (referring to the agreement that controls movement across borders in the European Union) could be reached as to numbers of immigrants (or, in other words, number of citizenships granted) by each party, the list of countries requiring visas, and other crucial details.

Yet separate border controls would have many drawbacks. They could lead to a series of difficulties and security breaches resulting in failure by both parties to fully secure their territory. Mechanisms should therefore be put in place to assure that no unwanted weaponry or other matériel could be brought into the country, as well as to prevent entry of terrorist elements. These would include, once again, intelligence coordination and sophisticated security devices on the borders.

While we view a unified system of border crossings as preferable and estimate that it could reduce threats to security, we acknowledge that it raises a host of other problems that are legal in nature, including, for instance, a fully coordinated system of diplomatic relations. Just to give one example: would Palestinians give up their right to visit Iran if there are no diplomatic relations between Israel and Iran? This is essentially a matter for legal experts. But it has a direct bearing on security issues.

A joint system of border control would require a series of measures including a trained border police force consisting of similar numbers of Israelis and Palestinians. A prior agreement on foreign relations would need to be implemented. Both parties would have to agree on entry and visa policies, and each party would be required to respect visas and other permits granted by the other side. This also has to do with the decision whether to have separate embassies and consulates abroad or joint ones.

Furthermore, decisions on immigration policies, and on the issuing of passports and other travel documents, would have to be coordinated. Joint local committees should be formed to resolve problems as they arose on the ground, and senior committees to resolve issues of principle. A mechanism of arbitration for cases in dispute should be established. This chapter will not deal with the formation of a customs union, but this issue clearly also has security aspects.

Another matter to consider is control of the shared territory's external lines of demarcation. Patrolling the fifteen hundred or so kilometers of land and sea boundaries should be entrusted to the international force, but use should be made of cameras and sensors available to both parties in order to ensure that efficient security was maintained at all times.

## CONCLUSION: STRENGTHS, WEAKNESSES, OPPORTUNITIES, AND THREATS

From the vantage point of Israel's security, the Parallel States structure's major strength lies in the fact that the Palestinian-Israeli conflict would be officially over and that many states previously at war with Israel would officially recognize the new entity. This would most likely reduce the number of potential enemies over the long run and improve security for the Israeli people. Since it provides both sides with free access to their historic homelands and ancient sites, it would also be bound to reduce internal motivations for aggression. Assuming that resolution of the refugee problem would be part of any Parallel States agreement, it should also decrease (if not altogether bring to a halt) the danger of terrorist activities originating in the Palestinian diaspora.

Another point of strength, referred to earlier, may be described as the "mutual human shield" situation: both populations would merge over time to some extent, making attacks on one party to the exclusion of the other more difficult, though not altogether impossible.

Security guarantees by the international community and an overarching military umbrella as delineated above would add an important element of strength to the proposed structure. This would hopefully be bolstered by bilateral nonaggression accords between the parallel states and all their neighbors, with clear mechanisms for mediation and arbitration.

The main weakness of the Parallel States framework as regards Israel's security is the increased danger of terror activities facilitated by the dismantling of internal boundaries. Speeded-up immigration of former refugees; the elimination of fences, walls, and barriers; and an open labor market would all be a boon to those planning guerrilla operations. Tracking the movement of hostile elements in the territory would become more difficult.

Another weakness has to do with limitations to be placed on Israel's military strength and deployment, and the fact that in essence it might be required to depend on an external force for its basic security. Restrictions on areas available for training and maneuvering could severely cripple the readiness of the army unless a creative solution, such as training abroad, were found. In sum, from the Israeli point of view, the main weaknesses of a Parallel States structure are the danger of diminished control over the activities of hostile elements and the loss of military supremacy in the region.

A Parallel States agreement presents new security opportunities for both sides. An international force might be more impartial and balanced in its handling of threats and attacks, and in the long run could offer an opportunity to decrease the danger of war and the aggressive profile of Israel vis-à-vis the Arab and Islamic world.

In the long run it also offers an opportunity to combine Israeli and Palestinian forces, allowing both sides to create a joint defense force. Other opportunities could present themselves in the areas of intelligence gathering and deterrence. A viable and effective Parallel States structure could enhance intelligence cooperation against possible threats, resulting in a more effective response.

Threats to the new entity would still abound. We perceive the main threat to be internal strife. The tripartite military force, along with regional and international guarantees and bilateral agreements, could reduce the threat of external state aggression. Yet groups of disgruntled Palestinian and Israeli citizens in the new shared territory, motivated by religion or racism, might not accept the compromise and opt to use the newly granted freedom of movement to create havoc and destabilize the situation.

NOTES

1. For a survey of federalist ideas and their implementations in Europe, see M. Burgess, *Federalism and European Union: The Building of Europe, 1950–2000* (London: Routledge, 2000).

2. David Biale, *Power and Powerlessness in Jewish History* (Tel Aviv: Schocken Books, 1986), 6.

3. Biale, *Power and Powerlessness,* 146–47.

4. Theodor Herzl, "The Jewish State" (1896), in *The Arab-Israeli Conflict: An Introduction and Documentary Reader,* ed. G.S. Mahler and A.R.W. Mahler (London: Routledge, 2010), 40.

5. For an overview of the Zionist-Palestinian conflict, see B. Morris, *Righteous Victims: A History of the Zionist-Arab Conflict, 1881–2001* (New York: Vintage, 2001).

6. For a report about his views, see a recent article in *Haaretz,* September 20, 2012, 20–21. It would be interesting to compare the religious rationale behind Harav Kook's positions and those of Hamas in its Charter and religious thinkers who support this position.

7. For a discussion of traditional Israeli security policy, see Zeev Maoz, *Defending the Holy Land: A Critical Analysis of Israel's Security & Foreign Policy* (Ann Arbor: University of Michigan, 2006). See also Efraim Inbar, "Yitzhak Rabin and Israeli National Security," *BESA Center for Strategic Studies, Security and Policy Studies* 25, at www.biu.ac.il/Besa/books/25/analysis.html. Gil Merom, "Israel's National Security and the Myth of Exceptionalism," *Political Science Quarterly* 114, no. 3 (Fall 1999): 409–34. David Rodman, "Israel's National Security Doctrine: An Introductory Overview," *Meria* 5, no. 3 (September 2001): 71–86. For a wider perspective on present and future issues, see Yehezkel Dror, "Political-Security Statecraft for Israel," *BESA Center for Strategic Studies, Security and Policy Studies* (June 2009, Hebrew); and Meir Elran, Owen Alterman, and Johannah Cornblatt, eds., *The Making of National Security Policy Security Challenges of the 21st Century: Conference Proceedings* (Tel Aviv, Institute for National Security Studies, 2011). Most of these studies assume either a continuation of the present state of affairs or a two-state solution. Their relevance to our topic is therefore limited.

8. See, e.g., Hussein Agha and Robert Malley, "The Arab Counterrevolution," *New York Review of Books* (September 29, 2011).

9. On changes in technological warfare, see Michael O'Hanlon, *Technological Change and the Future of Warfare* (Washington, D.C.: Brookings Institution, 2000).

10. On low-intensity warfare, see Daniel Marston and Carger Malkasian, eds., *Counterinsurgency in Modern Warfare* (Westminster, Md.: Osprey, 2008).

11. Gabriel Ben-Dor and David B. Dewitt, eds., *Confidence Building Measures in the Middle East* (Boulder, Colo.: Westview Press, 1994).

12. On NATO's new policies, see Brian J. Collins, *NATO: A Guide to the Issues* (London: Praeger, 2011). On the possibility of deploying NATO forces in Israel, see Hall Gardner, ed., *NATO and the European Union: New World, New Europe, New Threats* (London: Ashgate, 2004), 306.

13. Hussein Agha and Ahmad Khalidi, *A Framework for a Palestinian National Security Doctrine* (London: Chatham House, 2006).

# CHAPTER 5

# Palestinian National Security

HUSSEIN AGHA AND AHMAD SAMIH KHALIDI

For an understanding of how the Parallel States concept relates to the fundamentals of Palestinian national security, it is important to take a close look at the Palestinians' basic security needs, interests, national goals, and threat perceptions, as well as the possible elements of a national security doctrine. These sections provide the background to the discussion at the end of this chapter of how Palestinian security would be affected in a Parallel States structure.

## PALESTINIAN NATIONAL SECURITY
### Basic Palestinian Realities

In broad historical terms, the Palestinians view themselves as having been on the receiving end of the Zionist movement's and then Israel's overwhelming coercive and military power for more than a century, and as victims in a conflict that has been imposed against their will. Dominant Palestinian realities since 1948 include dispossession, displacement, dispersal, occupation, attempts at subjugation and humiliation, and a consequent fundamental insecurity. As of today, roughly one-half of the estimated eleven million Palestinian people live outside their historical homeland; the remainder live under Israeli occupation in the West Bank and East Jerusalem, under conditions of perpetual siege in Gaza, or as second-class citizens of the state of Israel.

A large Palestinian diaspora has spread across the Arab world and beyond since 1948. Normal access and interaction between those who remained on Palestinian soil and those outside are hampered by geographical distance and political reality. Within the territories occupied in 1967, two-thirds of the population lives in the West Bank and Jerusalem, and they are largely isolated from the remaining third, currently besieged in Gaza. The West Bankers are surrounded by roadblocks, Israeli settlements, Jews-only bypass roads, economic closures, and other measures that constitute Israel's "matrix of control" over the region.[1] Finally, some 1.2 million Palestinian Arabs live in a separate political sphere from their historical brethren, as citizens of their main historical antagonist—Israel.

After losing more than three-quarters of their patrimony in 1948, the Palestinians' national-territorial loss was completed by Israel's occupation of the West Bank, Gaza, and East Jerusalem in 1967. Since that time, the Palestinian people have been either under Israeli rule, in exile, or living under the parastate rule of the Palestinian Authority or Hamas. Rough estimates suggest that about ten thousand Palestinians have lost their lives and some eighty thousand have been injured in the Occupied Territory over the past four decades, with at least 750,000 acts of imprisonment or "administrative detention" (including multiple detentions) over the same period. Tens of thousands of others have lost their lives or livelihoods as the conflict has spilled into adjacent countries such as Jordan and Lebanon.

The experience of extended occupation and continuing violence has created an acute sense of national exposure and vulnerability. Those in the Occupied Territory remain subject to vastly superior force. And Israel's Arab citizens suffer from growing social and political discrimination, in addition to the tensions created by ongoing national conflict between Arabs and Jews. Palestinian communities abroad have also been subject to violent assault and mass dislocation by unsympathetic Arab regimes. Even in relatively normal circumstances, statelessness and refugee status impinge upon basic rights, such as freedom of movement and of residence, and the ability to forge a decent and predictable livelihood. Overall, a sense of persecution and fundamental insecurity are integral parts of the Palestinian national landscape.

## National Interests

There are different levels of Palestinian national interests. At the most basic level lie the *core* (or existential) interests that pertain to national survival. These are fixed and fundamentally nonnegotiable. *Vital* interests have to do with the welfare and well-being of the Palestinian people, and the boundaries between core and vital interests are often indistinct and subject to change. National interests are normally viewed in the context of statist attitudes and concerns, but in the Palestinian case, nonstate interests can carry over into a postindependence era.

Palestinian core interests include preventing the destruction of the Palestinian people; remaining on national soil; freedom from foreign rule; safeguarding national territory; providing a safe haven for Palestinians; and preserving the Palestinian way of life, mode of governance, and basic institutions. We will say a few words about each of these.

The most fundamental interest is to prevent the destruction or the annihilation of the Palestinian people and ensure their ethno-national survival. This entails acquiring adequate means of protection from existential threats or from the use of overpowering force against Palestinian communities both at home and abroad.

In light of past traumas of displacement and dispossession, deterring or preventing threats of enforced depopulation (known as "transfer" in Israel) is another core interest. This applies to the Palestinians living in the territories occupied in 1967, as well as Israel's Arab citizens. Any future state or peace agreement should consolidate the Palestinians' demographic presence on their national soil, and ensure that the experience of 1948 can never be repeated.

Ending the 1967 occupation is clearly a pre-state interest, but if the boundaries of a Palestinian state or the conditions of its establishment do not fully coincide with Palestinian national aspirations, the newly established state may pursue the struggle to end any residual Israeli occupation or perceived illegitimate presence. Ending the occupation is also a prerequisite for the realization of other basic Palestinian needs such as good governance, a sustainable level of economic development, social welfare, and a normalized existence.

Protecting and preserving any national territorial base on which the Palestinian people can build a safe and secure future is another core interest. Safeguarding national territory entails protecting national borders, sovereign airspace, and territorial waters, as well as maintaining access to vital resources such as water and other natural assets both onshore and off (food, gas, oil, etc.).

Palestinians should have the immutable right of access to their national soil, in both ordinary and extraordinary circumstances (such as an imminent threat to diaspora communities), and to partake freely in national life as prescribed by Palestinian custom and law.

Preserving the Palestinian way of life entails protection of the freely chosen mode of Palestinian representation and governance; safeguarding Palestinian political and civil institutions, customs, and traditions; and affording the conditions for them to flourish freely and without foreign intervention.

At the next level, Palestinian vital interests comprise the following: resolving the refugee problem; maintaining the collective; ensuring independent, authentic representation; and having a capital in Jerusalem and guardianship of holy places.

The refugee problem is the most persistent psychological and moral reminder of the national catastrophe of 1948, and it is a central predicament that defines Palestinian political and daily reality. Providing an acceptable settlement of this problem is a central political theme and a vital national interest. Although the exact terms of an acceptable settlement remain hard to define, any solution will require an acknowledgment of the depth of the wound of dispossession, addressing the basic moral and material needs of the refugees, and alleviating their conditions both in the diaspora and on national soil.

Ensuring that the Palestinians remain a coherent national collective, and preventing fissures and intra-Palestinian schisms that may undermine its integrity (as well as preventing others from exploiting such fissures), are vital Palestinian interests. Unity also implies a certain degree of consensus in public affairs and a rejection of internecine bloodletting, and is seen as a supreme public good. The current Fatah-Hamas split is universally reviled not only because of its negative political implications, but also because it is widely seen as a threat to Palestinian national security.

Maintaining an authentic and independent representation that articulates Palestinian demands and provides for Palestinian moral and material needs is a further vital national interest. Without such an agency, other non-Palestinian parties may act on the Palestinians' behalf in a manner that is inimical to their interests. Historically, the surrounding Arab states have interfered in this manner—for instance, Jordan, which once claimed the West Bank as sovereign territory and thus asserted the right to speak for Palestinians. In the pre-state context, the Palestine Liberation Organization (PLO), and to a lesser extent the Palestinian Authority, have also served in this role, although the post-2007 Hamas-Fatah split and the emergence of a Hamas-run Gazan entity have dented the overall legitimacy of the Palestinian Authority's representation. A

Palestinian state may need to supersede the PLO and Palestinian Authority along with other parties in this respect, depending on the circumstances and terms of its establishment.

Finally, Jerusalem's holy places are the entrenched symbols of Palestinian national, religious, and cultural identity. Maintaining Islamic and Christian holy places—particularly the Haram ash-Sharif and the Church of the Holy Sepulcher in East Jerusalem—under Palestinian guardianship is a vital national interest. These symbols feed and sustain the importance of Jerusalem itself as the heart of Palestinian national aspirations, and as such they point to Jerusalem as the necessary seat of any truly independent government. Guardianship of the holy places, and a capital in Jerusalem, also provide for an exceptional Palestinian role and presence in the Arab-Islamic and Christian worlds, and present a vital source of Palestinian prestige and influence.

*National Needs*

In view of these realities, in any final status or peace agreement between Palestinians and Israel, there are certain basic Palestinian national needs that go hand in hand with both the material and the political-psychological elements outlined above. These needs include safety and protection, national welfare and prosperity, sovereign choice, protection for Palestinians in the diaspora, and international assurances that these needs will be guaranteed.

Currently, statehood in all the territories occupied by Israel in 1967 is viewed by significant sectors of the Palestinians as a means of "normalizing" their national existence, by offering a secure and sovereign national haven. To this end, they claim, such a state must be viable and sustainable, with continuous borders and contiguous territories. But the mere existence of such a state is neither a certain nor a sufficient guarantor of security. In other words, it is a necessary means to the achievement of national security, but not an end in itself. With or without a state, the Palestinian people must be able to protect themselves against hostile forces through reliance on not only their own resources, but also measures involving third parties, if and where necessary.

Insofar as modern economic interdependence allows, the Palestinians need to be able to act in their own interests and according to their own priorities. Prosperity is an essential need, especially when set against a long history of material hardship and loss, which includes the intentional de-development of the Palestinian economy by Israel since 1967, on top of the not-so-benign neglect of the Jordanian, Egyptian, and British rulers before them. It involves economic development, but is intimately linked to basic rights such as the freedom of work, movement, residence, and others. It equally involves full access to Palestinian natural resources such as water, control over the national borders, and freedom of contact with the outside world.

The Palestinians should be able to choose their own representative bodies, political structures, laws, and modes of governance, free from outside intervention or forcible imposition. Likewise, they need to be assured of outside respect for such sovereign choices, including the results of free and fair elections and their democratic choice of government.

To extend Palestinian needs beyond national soil, based on the assumption that many Palestinians will remain outside their territorial base for the long term, it is important to find appropriate mechanisms for safeguarding the diaspora population, particularly in the Arab world. This may be partly attained through bilateral agreements with host states that provide a measure of legal and political normalization for Palestinian communities abroad. Other measures, such as international guarantees of security for Palestinian communities abroad from arbitrary violence or collective punishment by third parties, may also be necessary in order to compensate for the absence of effective self-defense mechanisms.

In light of their historical experience, and regardless of any bilateral agreements with Israel and other neighbors, the Palestinians need strong external assurances of their existence and freedom. These could include an international presence designed to monitor and verify agreements and to deter hostile acts from or against Palestinian soil. They might also comprise international guarantees that the status quo future will be maintained following any agreement. Material means of development and stabilization, including foreign economic aid, are also an important element of external reassurance.

## National Goals

Palestinian goals extend along a continuum that begins with the current pre-state era and extend into the poststate era. Certain pre-state goals can be carried over into and merged with poststate interests, and the weight and nature of any individual item may vary over time. These national goals include, first and foremost, the establishment of a Palestinian state. Since the mid-1970s, and especially following changes consequent to the emergence of the Palestinian Authority on Palestinian territory in 1994, Palestinian strategic goals have pointed toward the establishment of a viable, territorially contiguous, independent state on the West Bank and Gaza Strip with its capital in East Jerusalem. This was to be accomplished via a negotiated settlement with Israel in the case of the Palestinian Authority and PLO, and as part of a long-term *hudna* (truce) as far as Hamas is concerned.

There is a consensus that any Palestinian state should provide good representative government and be based on a constitutional separation of powers. It should respect basic freedoms and the rule of law. In short, and from a national security perspective, the Palestinian state needs to be *worthy* of preservation and defense.

But achieving statehood cannot be decoupled as a national goal from a resolution to the refugee problem, and cannot be seen to come at its expense. Finding a viable resolution to the refugee problem is a prerequisite for any sustainable settlement based on statehood. Without an acceptable solution, a Palestinian state would only create new fissures and tensions within the Palestinian polity that would likely threaten both its own stability and that of refugee host countries.

Should a Palestinian state be established, the focus and order of Palestinian national goals may shift. Much depends on the nature of the state, its jurisdiction, its territorial extent, and the commitments that it makes as part of an agreement with Israel. The more pre-state core and vital interests are satisfied as part of such a settlement, the more likely it is that poststate goals will center on maintaining and securing its underlying elements. Nonetheless, setting statehood as the sole centerpiece of national-security thinking would be both misleading and wrong. Palestinian national security is inevitably affected by the difficulty of setting definitive lines that demarcate pre-state and poststate challenges.

*Threat Perceptions*

Palestinian national security concerns comprise both *existential* threats and *current* security threats. Existential threats, by their nature, affect core interests. Current or ongoing security threats touch upon core interests, but also relate to a broader band of interests. Existential and current threat perceptions are relevant both before and after the establishment of the Palestinian state. As circumstances change, some perceptions will be modified, dissipated, or carried over from one phase to the other.

The most significant, existential threats arise from the continuation of the conflict with Israel. These include

- the use of superior Israeli force in aggressive, preventive, coercive, or punitive actions;
- the threat posed by settlements and land seizures to Palestinian territorial integrity and prospects for viable statehood;
- Israeli domination of the pace and direction of Palestinian economic life, and the prevention of normal social and economic development;
- Israeli control of Palestinian borders and movement within, into, and out of Palestinian national soil;
- Israeli control of Palestinian vital resources such as water, and assets such as offshore oil and gas; and
- the perennial threat of mass deportation and ethnic cleansing.

Threats to Palestinian core interests also arise from external factors affecting the diaspora or the Palestinian cause in general. Such threats include

- violence aimed at Palestinian communities abroad, such as the assaults in Lebanon during the civil war of 1975 and mass displacement from Kuwait after the 1991 Gulf War;
- threats arising from third-party conflicts with Israel, including the threat and possible use of weapons of mass destruction, such as a potential Iranian-Israeli confrontation, a threat presaged by the Israeli-Iraqi confrontation during the 1991 Gulf War;
- attempts by Arab and other parties to control political decision-making or to determine the shape of Palestinian representation; and
- attempts to dictate the terms of a political settlement, or to bypass Palestinian rights by concluding "separate" Arab deals with Israel on refugees, borders, or the water issue.

Within Palestine itself, there is a more immediate range of current threats that arise from ongoing Israeli military and nonmilitary actions. These include

- unilateral acts designed to create facts on the ground, such as the creation of bypass roads, or the demarcation of political and security lines via the Separation Wall in the West Bank;

- practices such as siege, closure, and disruption of normal daily life, as seen in Gaza in particular since 2006;
- assassinations, incursions, punitive raids, property damage, and home demolitions carried out by Israeli state and nonstate elements, including settlers;
- archaeological digs or infrastructure works that pose threats to the status and sanctity of holy sites, and in particular to the Haram ash-Sharif compound in Jerusalem; and
- applying arbitrary powers of arrest and detention, and the use of petty harassment at checkpoints and roadblocks.

Palestinians in the diaspora also experience a range of current threats. These include

- social, political, and legal discrimination, as in the case of Lebanon;
- insecurity and uncertainty in daily life arising out of statelessness, and the consequent inability to travel freely, secure employment, or manage problems of residence;
- interventions by Arab and other states in Palestinian domestic politics, using tactics such as providing a base for opposition media, or for political and military activities; and
- sustained regional instability and internal strife, which may endanger the safety and livelihood of diaspora communities.

A clear demarcation between long-term or existential and current or second-order threats is not always possible. Long-term occupation or reoccupation of Palestinian areas, massive Israeli settlement expansion, enforced transfer of the Palestinian population, and wholesale destruction of the Palestinian Authority, PLO, or Hamas leadership or institutions can appear as either an existential or a lesser security concern. The distinction is often a matter of intensity and degree, and the two often operate in parallel. Within the Palestinian territories, Israeli measures that produce current concerns can reinforce and exacerbate existential insecurity. Externally and in the diaspora, existential and current insecurities also interact; resolving the one does not necessarily dissolve the other. Alleviating significant current security concerns for the Palestinian population in terms of their normal daily life in the Arab diaspora may not be sufficient to mitigate their existential fears about the future safety and stability of their communities.

*Assets and Liabilities*

The Palestinians possess a number of significant assets and key liabilities in their struggle with Israel. Salient among their assets is their resilience. The Palestinian people's commitment to the national struggle has remained strong over almost one hundred years of continuous conflict. Losses have been high, but strong underlying societal bonds based on the family are a source of long-term resilience and reinforcement in the national struggle.

Finding a resolution for the Palestinian-Israeli and Arab-Israeli conflicts is seen as central to regional and world affairs, in part because of the unique status of the Holy Land for the three great monotheistic religions. It is also a function of the region's geopolitical significance, the presence of oil, the emergence of the global jihadist threat, and the rise of Islamist political power. Similarly, the existence of strong regional Arab and Islamic popular feelings on the Palestinian issue affects the behavior of neighboring states and the major international parties. All external parties, including Israel and the United States, are constrained by potential ripple effects of actions affecting the Palestinians on other Arab states, including those at peace with Israel or major Islamic players such as Turkey and Iran.

Another asset for the Palestinian people is the demographic trend. Both Palestinian and Israeli demographers have independently estimated that the Arab-Jewish demographic balance in the area of the former Palestinian Mandate as a whole is approaching parity, or will do so in the near future. Demographics have a vital impact on the politics of the struggle, both in the Occupied Territory and in Israel, which faces a growing Arab population, as well as in surrounding Arab states. The growth of the Palestinian population within Israel has helped to motivate hawkish factions to advocate the establishment of a Palestinian state that would include the transfer of a significant percentage of the Palestinian population of Israel (particularly along the border regions) and some territory to the West Bank or Jordan.

Paradoxically, some factors that might at first glance appear to be liabilities can act in the Palestinians' favor. Among these factors is the diaspora. Dispersal of the Palestinian people across a number of countries helps to sustain interactions between the Arab-Islamic hinterland and the Palestinian cause. It also serves to broaden the bases of Palestinian action, and impedes the ability of hostile forces to take effective operational or political counteraction. Also, Palestinian weakness and vulnerability have created a certain margin of international sympathy that partly compensates for the imbalance of power. This has been reinforced by a growing perception that the Palestinians have suffered a historical injustice, whereas Israel is increasingly perceived as obdurate, overbearing, and excessive in its responses.

On the other hand, the Palestinians' most significant liability has been their inability to acquire conventional self-defense capacity. At the same time, they have also been denied any significant ability to defend themselves via the negotiating process with Israel, and the demand that they demilitarize has become part of this process. Such vulnerabilities are likely to remain, unless the Palestinians find new means to defend themselves either through their own efforts or via agreement with Israel.

The Palestinians also face structural disadvantages. Although Israel remains a central concern, it is not the only source of potential threat to the Palestinians as a people or as a putative state. The Palestinians are likely to remain at a disadvantage in most of the traditional indices of power compared to all other relevant regional players. Providing national security for the Palestinians goes beyond the bilateral relationship with Israel and touches on their position and posture within the wider region.

One crucial asymmetry arises from the specifics of the Israeli-U.S. strategic relationship and the absence of any equivalent on the Palestinian side. Although American backing for Israel is not unqualified, in many cases the Palestinians face not only Israel itself, but U.S. policies that support the Jewish state as well. Palestinian and Israeli relations with Europe are more complex, but the net result is similar.

Other liabilities are physical. Within the Palestinian territories of 1967 there are significant geostrategic realities that are among the primary determinants of Palestinian national security-insecurity. The lack of physical continuity between the West Bank–Jerusalem and the Gaza Strip divides the major Palestinian population centers and allows Israel to sever or manipulate Palestinian lines of contact with relative ease. The divide is also cause for political and psychological bifurcation within the Palestinian polity, as seen both in their international orientations and in their cultural outlooks. Palestinian territory is extremely narrow and crisscrossed by a road network that can be used by conventional military forces, and the Jordan River provides no real obstacle to invasion. Finally, the Palestinians have little access to the outside world: Gaza is the only bit of Palestinian coastline, and it lacks port facilities. All the border crossings, meanwhile, continue to be dominated by more powerful neighbors.

Finally, population dispersal complicates political and operational command and control, and adds to the fragmentation and factionalization of Palestinian politics, as well as aggravating the possibility of external intervention in and manipulation of Palestinian affairs.

### Elements of a Postconflict National Security Doctrine

Any potential Palestinian national security doctrine must be grounded in the realities facing the Palestinians, today and in the future. It must seek to identify strengths and weaknesses, and deploy assets to best effect. It should set Palestinian strengths against an opponent's points of weakness or vulnerability, and avoid exposing vulnerabilities to an opponent's advantage. In the absence of a permanent agreement ending the conflict with Israel, the Palestinians must seek to maintain and defend their national goals.

Insofar as the issue of force is an integral part of national security, the Palestinian use of force should be bound by international laws, norms, and conventions. The Palestinians' right to the use of force should be no less than that of other nations or states in similar circumstances, and should be consistent with their humanitarian, moral, and legal obligations. Palestinians' use of force should not be tailored to meet offensive or aggressive political goals outside this framework.

However, no matter what shape or structure a Palestinian political entity may take, it is unlikely to acquire sufficient force to provide for a militarily sustainable defense of Palestinian citizens and territory against potential aggressors. Force or the threat of force cannot be the central element in a Palestinian national security doctrine. While it is a vital complement to defensive notions, other nonmilitary means must provide the first recourse for the Palestinians.

An important consequence is that Palestinian national security must be predicated on notions of strategic *prevention* and *deterrence* rather than any active operational modes such as a second-strike capability. In essence, the goal should be to build a multitiered regime of diplomatic, political, and psychological as well as military barriers sufficient to protect Palestinian interests, and to dissuade any potential aggressors from the pursuit of their goals via the use of force. The ultimate purpose of the Palestinian defensive regime should be to ensure that any hostile party will face as many obstacles as possible in resorting to force and will pay a high human, political, and moral price if they choose to do so.

With this in mind, a Palestinian national security doctrine could be based on five planks, detailed in what follows.

### Nonmilitary Defense

Palestinian national security should be guaranteed via binding commitments from the international community to prevent external transgression or aggression against Palestinian citizens and territory. These commitments should be folded into a comprehensive peace package, but could also be separately agreed upon as part of a stabilization program. Guarantees need not be state-centered and may precede the establishment of a Palestinian state. Guarantees could cover such things as the inviolability of agreed-upon borders—even within the context of a Parallel States solution there will be some core areas of national import—and the integrity of Gaza–West Bank passage. Declared guarantees could be accompanied by a pre-agreed system of sanctions and countermeasures should either side violate its commitments or otherwise threaten the status quo.

Palestinian national security can be further enhanced by bilateral agreements with Israel (as obviously necessary in the case of a Parallel States structure) and neighboring states. Items such as a declaration of "no first use" of force or nonaggression pacts could reinforce any detailed security arrangements on the ground and would be intended to reduce both sides' ability or willingness to resort to force.

Additionally, a Palestinian state may seek to join a multistate alliance such as NATO with noncombatant status such as that held by Iceland, although the precise mission of Palestinian armed forces in such an alliance would need to be elaborated. Under such a formula the Palestinians could accept NATO early warning stations on their territory and have shared data links with Israel as a substitute for a similarly intended Israeli presence. Palestinian membership in alliances need not preclude or conflict with Israel's or any other regional party's aspiration to do the same.

Readiness to solicit and accept international guarantees and alliances signals a certain faith in the international community's ability to play a role. But the Palestinians must take into account the possibility that any system of external guarantees can break down in times of crisis, and may constitute an insufficient deterrent. Certain powers would also find it politically difficult to intervene effectively on behalf of the Palestinians, for instance, the United States. And it is hard to conceive of other parties intervening against the will of the United States. From the Palestinian perspective, there appears to be no effective enforcement mechanism to ensure that international guarantees are translated into action.

Palestinian defense can be enhanced by a calibrated strategy of mass mobilization and civil nonviolent action, including large-scale peaceful civil disobedience, disruption of communications, sit-downs, strikes, and so on. This strategy may be used to raise the cost of occupation, and nonviolent mass action may appear increasingly effective as a means of ending the Israeli occupation, particularly as other developments in the region have demonstrated the potency of such methods.

The Palestinian side also needs to be able to exploit the asymmetry of power by encouraging media transparency in order to add inhibitions and restrict a would-be aggressor's freedom of action. Palestinian experience overall reinforces the view that media coverage generally serves the Palestinians' interests and helps to focus world attention on their concerns.

### Self-Defense, or Nonoffensive Defense

Like all other nations, Palestinians cannot be denied the right to self-defense. While they might agree to negotiate limitations on their military posture, they should not be expected to forfeit their rights altogether. One key is to ensure that Palestinians are not singled out by demands for total demilitarization or forced to rely on outside forces alone. In short, the Palestinians would need some level of protection against Israeli or other military threats—without undermining Israel's security or that of Palestine's other neighbors. Indeed, without retaining the right to self-defense and to determine its own defensive needs and priorities free from external diktats, a Palestinian state would be politically unsustainable, and would be abrogating its responsibilities toward its own citizens, thus potentially undermining the very security it seeks to provide.

One option would be to adopt a posture of nonoffensive defense. This is a strategy based on tactics and weapons that maximize defense and minimize offense, and in some cases may lack offensive capacity entirely. A Palestinian nonoffensive defense regime should incorporate no armor, artillery, or long-range protected weapons systems, among others. This can be seen as a unilateral confidence-building gesture. In view of the constraints often felt by outside actors, in most confrontations a Palestinian nonoffensive defense might seek to prolong operations and raise the enemy's costs as far as possible. In case of open conflict with another party, such a regime should be geared to exploiting the time factor so as to facilitate external intervention in the Palestinians' favor.

Intelligence becomes a vital tool to preempt and prevent hostile action, and to provide sufficient breathing space to bring the other elements of a Palestinian national security doctrine into play. Palestinian nonoffensive defense, therefore, needs to incorporate high-level tactical and strategic intelligence capabilities, including assistance from abroad. Access to high-grade intelligence from satellites, for instance, could serve to reassure the Palestinians about the intentions of regional powers, and could help prevent crises or tensions that arise from misinformation or misunderstanding. Palestinians would also need to rely on human intelligence (HUMINT) capabilities, including the ability to anticipate and monitor developments in Israel and elsewhere. HUMINT activities could, however, be a source of serious friction between the Palestinians and Israel, as both are likely to distrust the other's motives for some time to come.

Force is a last-resort defensive measure to be taken only in extremis. The Palestinians do not seek to pursue their aims by force and may require significantly less force potential than other parties to the conflict. However, if faced with an evident existential threat, Palestinians should resort to whatever means are necessary to ensure their national survival, including the use of whatever means of force are available. Self-defense must remain a cornerstone of Palestinian national security and force the ultimate fail-safe should all other means of prevention or deterrence fail.

### An International Military Presence

"External reinforcement" in the form of a permanent or long-term international military presence backed by a multilayered system of mutual commitments and international guarantees may prove a necessary measure. Such a presence would take over from Israeli forces as they withdrew from Palestinian territory. A limited international military presence in the Jordan River valley before or after a political settlement could serve Palestinian interests. It could help police the outer envelope, and could be tasked with supervising Palestinian-Israeli border crossings, ports, and airports within an agreed-upon mandate and time frame. International military personnel could also be deployed along the Gaza–West Bank corridor to guarantee its integrity. Beyond that, an international force might be essential to observe and verify compliance with any agreement. To this end, it might need to have the authority to inspect Israeli and Palestinian military installations and potential dual-use facilities.

From a strategic perspective, an international military presence would present a dual advantage. First, it would help limit Israeli options regarding the use of force. Second, it would impose a barrier to hostile attempts, from within or without, that would seek to use Palestinian territory as a springboard for attacks against Israel. Whereas no foreseeable international presence is likely to take upon itself an active peace-enforcement role in confronting Israel or other potential invaders, its very presence should help to neutralize the military importance of Palestinian territory and add to the stability and sustainability of bilateral security arrangements between the parties themselves.

### Diaspora Security

The Palestinians face a formidable challenge providing security for their people as a whole, considering the proportion not living on national soil. At the most basic level, a Palestinian state could serve diaspora security by offering an unqualified haven, much as Israel does for Jews. But a passive haven may not provide an adequate safeguard for all possible contingencies. Indeed, it is possible that the existence of a Palestine state or entity might serve to *undermine* the security of Palestinian communities abroad, by encouraging host countries to deport or evict Palestinians on the grounds that they now have a state of their own. Such circumstances could be exacerbated should there be future tensions between the Palestinian state and the host countries, or should Palestinian communities be targeted for other reasons (as with the case of the Palestinian community in Iraq after 2003, and the Palestinian refugees in Syria after 2011).

The inability of a Palestinian state to intervene directly and forcibly to protect diaspora communities requires other protective measures. One possibility would be the development of extraterritorial legal mechanisms such as those currently adopted by Israel. Such measures would imply that the Palestinian state has a moral and legal obligation to protect all Palestinian citizens against threats and actions that target them as Palestinians. While the range of options for active implementation of such a law may be limited, its mere existence could provide psychological reassurance for diaspora communities and act as a minimal deterrent against hostile or discriminatory acts that have a clear national or ethnic bias.

In addition, clear and credible international guarantees are required to ensure the security of Palestinian communities abroad, perhaps in particular from the Arab League. These guarantees could extend some extraterritorial protection to Palestinian communities by proscribing acts of large-scale ethnically or nationally based discrimination such as transfer or mass deportation. Such guarantees could also incorporate financial inducements and compensation packages from the international community for those countries that have hosted large Palestinian refugee populations in the past and are likely to continue hosting diaspora communities. It may also be necessary for the Palestinian state or entity to reach bilateral agreements regulating the legal status of residual Palestinian communities abroad as well as their responsibility toward their hosts and vice versa.

### Internal Security

Internal security bears directly on both the domestic balance of power and external relations with other parties, primarily but not exclusively Israel. As a result, internal Palestinian security comprises two dimensions: first, the consolidation and monopolization of the use of force by the Palestinian state or its precursors; and second, a proscription on the use of force by nongovernmental (or "opposition") forces directed against third parties.

From the Palestinian Authority or statist perspective, the greatest threat on both counts comes from the presence of independent armed opposition groups with separate political and ideological agendas. These groups can provoke (and have provoked) Israeli reactions that affect the ruling Palestinian Authority. But in a situation of political flux and uncertainty, opposition groups may also serve a national purpose by providing a tacit backup to the ruling authority and as a means of indirect pressure on external parties. The internal political price of "taking on the opposition" can be too high and can violate the sanctity of the Palestinian collective, unless wedded to clear-cut and tangible political and psychological gains that can be seen to justify a threat to national unity.

Palestinian pre-state behavior is likely to differ from poststate behavior with regard to internal security. As state interests consolidate, and as the price that the state has to pay for tolerating dissident opposition rises, the imperative of enforcing internal security to safeguard against external assault will strengthen. So will the tendency to suppress armed opposition groups with separate agendas. But the crucial factor remains that of the political horizon. Without a political settlement in sight that meets Palestinian minimal national goals, internal security will remain susceptible to the politics and vagaries of the Palestinian-Israeli conflict, including tolerance for militant groups that are seen to serve Palestinian national interests in the pre-state period.

Ultimately, the truism that one side's security cannot be achieved at the other's expense remains the key to disentangling the legitimate concerns of each side. How, when, and indeed whether this can be achieved is still in the realm of deep speculation. Finding a way out of the present quandary, however, is not a matter of intellectual or political self-indulgence, but of profound import to the future lives and safety of Palestinians and Israelis alike.

## PALESTINIAN SECURITY IN THE PARALLEL STATES STRUCTURE

A Parallel States solution raises a number of vital questions pertaining to Palestinian national security as described in the first part of this chapter, while also addressing many of the basic Palestinian needs and aspirations.

As opposed to solutions based on territorial-national partition, the Parallel States solution meets a fundamental Palestinian aspiration to live and work throughout the historical Mandatory Palestine, albeit with potentially significant qualifications and restrictions. Although the precise territorial and jurisdictional boundaries of both parallel states remain to be defined, the Parallel States structure implies that the entire land of Palestine will be open as a matter of principle to Palestinians, including "core" Israeli regions such as Tel Aviv or Haifa. A corollary is that the existence of parallel states would address the issue of the Palestinian right of return, and would allow members of the refugee and diaspora populations to reside in any area of Palestine-Israel that they chose, with the understanding that they would be bound by the laws of the relevant governing national authority. The Parallel States solution thus offers a possible means of resolving one of the most intractable elements of the current conflict.

The plan allows for the emergence of an independent Palestinian political state or entity with jurisdiction over the entire Palestinian people, land, and resources. Insofar as it includes all Arab Palestinians and a broader territorial base under its rule (including, potentially, current Palestinian citizens of Israel), the Parallel States model offers a much more extensive mode of self-government than the two-state model. It addresses another fundamental Palestinian national concern by bringing an end to military occupation of the lands taken in 1967, and the consequent enforced alienation of Palestinian soil as a result of the continued settlement and "Judaization" of Arab land. Similarly, and by extension, the Parallel States structure addresses vital concerns such as an Arab-Palestinian capital in Jerusalem and Palestinian guardianship over its Muslim and Christian holy places.

In short, the Parallel States solution addresses as *a matter of principle* many of the fundamental and most complex issues of the conflict. The Palestinian side would gain access to the land, secure the right of return, win equivalence in the form of state and sovereignty with Israel, and gain recognition of Jerusalem as a capital. To that extent, the plan would help alleviate past and current grievances and reduce the potential for future friction and violence. Within a framework of fully operational parallel states, the incentive of most Palestinians to resort to violence or to seek to overthrow the new system would be minimized. Nonetheless, significant outstanding problems would remain, and the Parallel States structure raises a number of new security issues that need to be addressed.

### Palestinian Self-Defense

A basic assumption is that Israel will maintain its overwhelming military superiority even if its force structure and offensive capabilities are drawn down over time. In light of residual Palestinian fears of Israel's use of force, a fundamental issue thus has to do with the Palestinian right of self-defense and the need to develop Palestinian capabilities to limit or block Israel's tendency to exploit its superior force for political purposes, both in the immediate and in the longer terms.

To that end, a fully demilitarized Palestinian state or entity is not an option, as it would allow the Israeli side to monopolize the use of force, as well as the decision about where and when to go to war. It would also provide a potential source for future Palestinian grievances that could undermine the Parallel States solution's long-term stability. Since the first duty of the Palestinian state would be to protect its citizens, it would have to find the means of, first, defending Palestinian land and population and deterring any Israeli attempt to reverse the agreement in the immediate or longer-term future; and, second, developing and maintaining a self-defensive capability that does not threaten or provoke the Israeli side into taking preemptive action—in other words, a defensive capability that is compatible with the politico-strategic stability and viability of the Parallel States structure as a whole. Some version of a Palestinian doctrine of nonoffensive defense, outlined earlier in this chapter, is compatible with this goal.

There are various potential mechanisms for managing the Palestinian need for self-defense while maintaining the overall equilibrium of the Parallel States structure. These include

- self-imposed limitations on the posture of Palestinian armed forces and the nature of their armaments;
- negotiated arms-limitation agreements with Israel, including a prohibition on the importing of certain types of offensive weapons;
- international guarantees that the Palestinian state-entity will not simply be reoccupied by Israel;
- border controls and a third-party party military presence along the common external borders; and
- mutually agreed-upon monitoring and verification procedures.

In view of the disparity in strength, Palestinian armed forces might have to be developed rapidly so as to provide a means of reassurance to the Palestinian population. The challenge would be to synchronize Palestinian force buildup with simultaneous efforts to assuage Israeli concerns and alleviate the pressures that could arise from any sharp change in the balance of power. The time frame for this buildup could be linked to the political transition from the current situation to the full Parallel States model, so as to ensure some degree of harmonization between its military and other components of government.

But none of these mechanisms, singly or collectively, may be enough to negate the historical legacy of the conflict, at least in the short to medium term. The Parallel States structure would not do away with the fundamental asymmetry of power between the Palestinian and Israeli sides. Regardless of any agreed-upon phased build-down of Israeli military force or parallel buildup on the Palestinian side, the Palestinians would remain at a fundamental disadvantage in all the indices of state and socioeconomic power compared to their Israeli counterpart.

*Asymmetries*

While the Parallel States structure might entail a positive change in both Palestinian-Israeli and Israeli-regional relations, the fundamental disparities in power between the two sides would remain a basic part of their mutual politico-military landscape until the plan fully took hold, and likely far beyond. Regardless of any attempt to create mediating mechanisms or agreed-upon constraints on the mutual use of force, the Palestinian entity would continue to live under the shadow of possible Israeli resort to force, or of Israeli power being used to intimidate, compel, or determine Palestinian decisions either domestically or in the arena of foreign policy.

This poses two main problems: how to address the material, psychological, and structural disparity between the parties to the plan, and how to create a system of constraints capable of preventing the Israeli side from using its superior force and capabilities as a lever against the Palestinians.

Assuming a transitional stage of three to five years and a longer-term period of twenty-five years for the full implementation of the Parallel States structure seems reasonable if the parties are to manage some of the psychological, political, and material consequences of this imbalance. Patience could be increased by positive interaction between the two entities and a clear demonstration of the benefits of coexistence under the new political regime. But there is a danger that interim challenges may threaten the long-term prospects of the project as whole. Such challenges could arise from any or all of the following: revanchist, dissident, or opportunist Jewish elements targeting the Palestinian state, its population, institutions, or leadership, and vice versa; dissident Palestinian action against the Palestinian state designed to entangle it in an interstate conflict with Israel; punitive Israeli military action against the Palestinian side if it is seen to be flouting agreements or harboring or protecting dissident elements; Israeli attempts to reoccupy Palestinian land, expel the population, or topple the Palestinian state in extremis; and intercommunal violence between the Palestinian and Israeli areas, or within mixed cities or regions.

Addressing this range of threats calls for a high degree of coordination and cooperation between the security forces on both sides, and the requisite political will to clamp down on opposition or renegade factions throughout the transitional process. But it also requires both sides to maintain the Parallel States regime as a higher interest than more immediate and potentially politically pressing ethnic or national concerns. The Israeli side would have to curb its "natural" instinct to exploit the imbalance in its favor and to apply force in response to Palestinian provocations, real or perceived, and would need to manage the extremist elements in its political system; while the Palestinians would have to adjust to the prerequisites of long-term and structural inequalities, and would need to rein in their more militant factions.

*Internal Dynamics*

Another set of challenges arises from the nature and structure of the Parallel States model itself. Whereas the new regime would address fundamental Israeli national interests, primarily that of creating a significant prospect for an end to conflict (at least in its historical form), it would also require the Israeli side to undertake a significant material, moral, and political shift relative to the Palestinians. The Israelis would have to dismantle many existing sovereign state structures and laws and give up exclusive control over the entire Palestinian-Israeli physical space. The Palestinians, by contrast, would be gaining a state, and increased control over land and population. This prospect not only could give rise to significant internal opposition on the Jewish side, but could also manifest itself in political violence directed at both the Israeli authorities and the Palestinians alike. A similar threat could arise from disaffected Palestinian elements that rejected the agreement or sought to elicit an Israeli response targeting the Palestinian state, its leaders, or its institutions.

The Parallel States proposal assumes that the Palestinian government would rule over the Arab population while the Israeli government would rule over the Jewish population. In simple terms, the Israeli side would police the Jewish population and be responsible for its actions, and the Palestinian side would police the Arab population and be responsible for its actions. But the reality on the ground poses a number of serious challenges to both sides. First, what is to be done where there are mixed cities or where the population is relatively desegregated? Second, how should citizens of one state be handled when they commit criminal or politically motivated acts of violence against the other? And third, how can conflicts be navigated when the national priorities of one side (in terms of exploitation of land and resources) are seen to take precedence over the other?

Questions like these highlight the complexity of interjurisdictional conflicts and the difficulty of distributing internal security responsibilities.

Who and how will each side deal with miscreants and dissidents, not only within the agreed-upon areas of their own jurisdiction, but when the actions of one side affect the security of the other? Joint policing may be one potential answer, but that also implies common threat perceptions and concurrence on the means to address them, as well as an element of recurring intervention in each other's affairs that could be both intrusive and problematic. It also requires a high degree of mutual intelligence exchange and trust, which would take time to foster, and which might be faced with constant political and psychological tensions and hurdles as the situation on the ground unfolded.

The Parallel States' internal dynamics could also lead to other forms of friction that had security consequences. Whereas the Parallel States regime might produce some clear demarcation in terms of the allocation of land and resources, continuing competition between the two states—or on the part of politically motivated elements within either side—could generate intercommunal tensions leading to violence. Large-scale (albeit legal) acquisition of land could, for instance, replicate the severe tensions of the 1930s and 1940s in Mandatory Palestine, as one side or the other sought to expand its territory or control at the other side's expense. Population movements might also be politically motivated, with Arab or Jewish "settlers" being deliberately implanted in each other's areas to alter the demographic balance, or moving by choice for nationalist or religiously inspired considerations. Even movements of people and land transactions of benign and commercially motivated purpose might be misread or misinterpreted by either side, at either the official or the popular level, or both.

Basic socioeconomic imbalances could also lead to the emergence of a Palestinian economic underclass that was fundamentally beholden to the Israeli economy and its demands (as was, in fact, the case before the first Intifada in 1987). While an Israeli-driven economy could help to accelerate the development and welfare of the parallel states as a whole, socioeconomic disparities that solidified along national or ethnic lines could reproduce political tensions and long-term instabilities within the Parallel States regime, and could provide fertile recruiting grounds for dissident or revisionist elements on the Palestinian side. After almost half a century of dependency and de-development, it will be particularly difficult for Israel fundamentally to transform its exploitative relationship with the Palestinian economy and enable both autonomy and sustainable and more equitable integration between the two economies.

Immigration and border control could also be a subject for tensions between the two states. One source of pressure could come from the

Palestinian side's desire to offer quick redress to the refugees by encouraging rapid or large-scale immigration. The Israeli side might perceive this as a deliberate attempt to "pack" Palestinian territories and create a new demographic status quo. Who gets in, and when and where they will be resettled, are politically charged issues that have a direct or indirect impact on security. Israeli concerns about possible terrorist infiltration could be matched by Palestinian concerns about Israel's continued attempts to use security as a justification for impeding free access to the land. An international monitoring body or border force could serve to alleviate some of these concerns.

Considering the historical impact of demography and land on the conflict, the Parallel States structure runs the danger of replicating previous (and current) experiences unless effective unilateral or joint mechanisms are set up to mitigate and manage the potential areas of friction and violence. The plan may therefore address some of the fundamentals of the conflict, but might also re-create them in other forms. Large-scale changes in control or ownership of land or movements of population would pose a significant security challenge to both sides, which could affect the strategic prospects of the Parallel States solution and undermine its internal integrity. Unchecked, they could generate any number of potential threats, from sustained low-level violence to large-scale population transfers in the extreme case. Without an agreed-upon system of control, the conflict could be driven back to its basics.

### Managing External Threats

Because the parallel states would occupy a single strategic space, how to identify and manage external threats would constitute a significant problem. Such threats might be directed either against the shared territory itself (i.e., a common threat) or against one of the national entities operating within the same space. The first kind of threat might be relatively easy to manage via enhanced intelligence sharing and a coordinated command and control system, including a possible prior allocation of roles between the two parties. The Palestinian state-entity might thus be prepared to rely on Israeli long-range missiles and air power (as well as the Israeli nuclear deterrent) to deal with particular *strategic* threats to the territory as a whole. Palestinian forces could also be designated for certain tactical or defensive roles in confronting a hostile common power or attempts to enter or invade the territory.

But thanks to their common strategic space and the fact that both sides would have overlapping territory, any action that targeted "Palestinian" soil would necessarily pose a threat to the Israeli entity, and vice versa. Furthermore, the exact object of an imminent attack might be impossible to identify—a hostile aircraft entering the parallel states' airspace, for example, could be aiming to bomb either an Arab city or target or a Jewish one—and the scope for error would be very small considering the constraints of time-space. In such an instance, there could be an agreed-upon code for operational reactions depending on the direction and scale of the threat, with both sides working on the basis of an agreed-upon "no risk" or "shoot-on-sight" policy.

But a more serious problem would arise from a threat that was directed against one of the two entities but not the other. Regardless of its intent, a hostile attack on a Palestinian target, for example, would involve a de facto violation of Israel's sovereignty and security envelope. (Similar logic, of course, applies in the other direction.) Such an attack could have various repercussions for the parallel states. It could entail material or human Israeli losses, particularly in mixed areas or cities. As it might be hard to distinguish between intended Israeli losses and collateral damage, this could force the Israeli side to react militarily or to engage in a confrontation with a third party with which it had no initial quarrel. An attack could also provoke hostile reactions from the Palestinian side if Israel were seen to be neutral or complicit in it. This could undermine trust and confidence between the parties and have severe consequences for their stability and viability in other domains. Finally, an Israeli response to the attack might not take Palestinian concerns into consideration; for example, a disproportionate response could escalate the conflict against Palestinian will.

The potential for spiraling conflict or uncontrolled and unintentional consequences is great, with every action on each side affecting the other. The danger of being drawn into a confrontation not of one's making could be significant. However, joint response to such an attack could implicate one side against its perceived national interest. Palestinian participation in an Israeli retaliatory action against a third party could drag the Palestinians into an unwanted or unintended conflict, and vice versa. Even if Israel or Palestine were to act alone against a hostile third party, that third party's response could target either or both sides of the Parallel States entity, thus escalating and expanding the conflict. The situation gets even more complicated when addressing the problem of preemption: Israel might find its vital interests threatened by a potential change of regime in a neighboring Arab country and might act to help the incumbent regime against internal enemies (as in the case of Jordan in 1970) or confront the new regime before it was able to take hostile action against Israel. This could lead that regime to hold the Palestine side accountable (as part of the parallel states) and to take punitive measures against the Palestinian population on its soil.

Similar considerations apply to substate actors that might target either or both sides. A terrorist attack on the Israeli side from Lebanon, for example, could force the Palestinian side to support Israel against the Lebanese state with which it otherwise had good or stable relations. An attack on the Palestinian side from Jordan could imperil Israel's peaceful relations with Jordan. The degree of either side's readiness to support the other might differ depending on the circumstances and might not always involve military action. The Palestinian party to the Parallel States structure might not be ready to act militarily against Lebanon but might be asked to offer politico-diplomatic support for such an attack, which could be severely embarrassing (in the case of a 2006-type war, for instance).

A high degree of advance planning and intelligence coordination could be instrumental in dealing with such problems. But the political-operational dilemmas they pose stem from the very nature of the Parallel States structure on the one hand, and the potential differences between the Palestinian and Israeli sides' relations with their environment on the other. Besides a range of potential threats to the parallel states as a whole, each party is likely have different threat perceptions, may actually be facing different threats, and may feel compelled to address them differently. The temptation to avoid getting entangled in each other's conflicts would most likely remain strong, particularly if involvement entailed a high price to be paid, or if the assessment of the nature of the threat differed substantially. This would create a source of internal tension within the two states that would cut across other elements of the bilateral relationship and apply pressure to both sides to give precedence to perceived national interests over "higher" joint concerns.

One potential solution would be to hand over responsibility for dealing with external threats to an agreed-upon international force, perhaps from NATO or another mutually acceptable body. A NATO force in particular would reinforce the Parallel States regime's power of deterrence, and would reduce the potential range of threats from hostile state actors in the region and beyond. NATO security guarantees could also encompass a nuclear umbrella, to be extended to both the Israeli and the Palestinian states separately (as an added measure of reassurance) or to the shared territory as a whole.

But an international force would also detract from the capability of each side to evaluate and act independently on perceived threats. This would entail a significant loss of freedom of action, which could pose a serious problem for the Israeli side in particular, especially when taking into account the other strategic assets that it might believe itself to be giving up in the process of acceding to the Parallel States structure. It might be less of a problem for the Palestinian side, which would generally see an international force as a reinforcement of its strategic posture. An international force would also not necessarily resolve the issue of differing threat perceptions and how to react to them. It might evaluate both the nature of the threat and the required response in a different light from one or both local parties. It might also be unwilling to take risks or pay the costs that either or both parties might be otherwise ready to incur. Additionally, merging the local parties' armed forces into the international force would complicate national chains of command and require an overall readiness to submit to outside priorities and modes of action.

The complications arising from potential external threats and hostile actions present a difficult challenge to the Parallel States solution. The development of joint intelligence and information-sharing would be of particular importance in dealing with this challenge, but it is also a political issue that could remain hostage to the broader range of inter-state relations. As with other elements of the new regime, the emergence of common interests (and possibly common enemies) may help in overcoming these problems over time. But their short-term impact could be considerable as the Palestinians and Israelis moved through uncharted waters in the initial transitional phases.

## The Regional Environment

One assumption is that by resolving the Palestinian-Israeli conflict in an acceptable and equitable manner, the Parallel States framework would provide a more stable regional environment for both the Palestinian and the Israeli sides. The plan would most likely be part of a comprehensive resolution of the Arab-Israeli conflict that included other major Arab parties or at least would provide the core of an overall solution to wider conflicts, although recent developments in the Arab world have significantly altered the role and scope of Arab engagement with the Palestinian issue. The Parallel States proposal would also need to elicit the endorsement of the United Nations, the United States, the Arab League, and most if not all other parties concerned with the conflict, along with requiring the approval of a majority of people on both the Israeli and the Palestinian sides.

One consequence might be that the range of conventional regional strategic threats, particularly from state actors, to either or both sides of the agreement would begin to recede, although other threats emanating from exacerbating regional fissures and substate actors might become more evident. An acceptable solution to the Palestinian refugee problem, however, would facilitate broader acceptance of the Parallel States plan among the Palestinian population at large and from those states that are currently hosting large numbers of refugees, such as Lebanon, Jordan, and Syria. A solution to the problem of Jerusalem would facilitate good relations with much of the Islamic world, as well as major Arab powers such as Saudi Arabia. Even regimes that are currently implacably hostile to Israel, such as Iran, might be ready to mitigate their hostility if they saw genuine and broad-based Palestinian acceptance of the plan.

In short, the Parallel States structure would be likely to produce a new, and generally more positive and pacific, regional environment for Palestinians and Israelis alike. But this cannot be taken for granted. For one thing, new regimes resulting from uprisings in the Arab or Muslim world might reject the Parallel States system or actively oppose it on political, ideological, or religious grounds. An extreme fundamentalist regime in Jordan, Egypt, or elsewhere might seek to undermine it, or might host militant groups that would be ready to act against one or the other of its components. A perceived loss or curtailment of Israeli power might embolden certain regimes such as Iran to fill the regional vacuum, creating regional instabilities that would have repercussions for the Parallel States entity. Substate actors such as al-Qaeda and its offshoots might seek to infiltrate the expanding Palestinian population and territorial base in order to attack either the Arab or the Jewish side, or both, as the current uncertainty in the region continued to unfold. And a generally positive regional response to the Parallel States regime could fade or be reversed if it was seen to be disadvantageous to the Palestinian side, or if Israeli-Palestinian relations appeared to be one-sided or subject to Israeli diktat and interests.

In that sense, relations between the two parties to the Parallel States plan may be one of the litmus tests for determining the direction of regional responses, and this factor represents a potential fault line that could be exploited by hostile regional actors, both on the state and on the substate level. On the other hand, if the plan is implemented according to the principles that have been outlined here and throughout this book, a Parallel States system holds the potential not merely of achieving a just and equitable peace between the two nations. In the long run, through refounded legal, political, and economic systems grounded more deeply in the highest principles of international law, human and civil rights, and economic fairness, such a system could offer not merely better security for Palestinians and Israelis, it could fundamentally transform relations between citizens and their states, and through it, with each other, in a manner that significantly improves the position of currently marginalized groups such as women, workers, Bedouins, and other ethnic and religious minorities. From this perspective, a Parallel States scenario holds the possibility to increase the security of all the inhabitants of historical Palestine, regardless of national identification or citizenship.

NOTE

1. See, for example, Jeff Halper, *An Israeli in Palestine: Resisting Dispossession, Redeeming Israel* (London: Pluto Press, 2008), chap. 6.

# CHAPTER 6

# An Israel-Palestine Parallel States Economy by 2035

RAJA KHALIDI

## WHY A PARALLEL STATES ECONOMY?

The same imperatives underlying the search for new ideas for a permanent-status Israeli-Palestinian political agreement drive the inconclusive debate about the optimal economic dimensions of a future peace settlement. A decade of negotiations about "economic permanent status" have been exhausted intellectually and rendered moot by prolonged occupation, expanded settlement, and the nonexistent prospects for a political settlement. A century of Zionist colonization and the past forty-four years of military occupation have created a perverse and structurally lopsided economic relationship between the two peoples. The two-state solution, as traditionally conceived and currently advocated, would have difficulty correcting this situation even over the long term.

Yet it does not take an expert to recognize that a partition of territory and sovereignty on the basis of geo-demographic realities today is most likely not a viable solution. In the view of many observers, a dead end has been reached amid the diminishing prospects for a conventional two-state solution, the unappealing prospects of an apartheidlike one-state outcome, and the unlikely solution of a unitary, secular, democratic state. For one thing, the idea of a sovereign, independent Palestinian state alongside Israel (on the 1967 or even more limited borders) is anathema to a hard core of Israelis who believe it would threaten their existential security. Similarly, the unitary, secular, one-state solution is unthinkable to most Israelis, as it implies an end to Jewish sovereignty and identity in Palestine.

A unitary state is similarly problematic for the Palestinian Arab people. Abandonment of their decades-old pursuit of national self-determination in the form of a Palestinian state and accommodating themselves to an apartheid system implies a much longer struggle for equality. They would also have to postpone a "national" economic development process and fall back on an economic resistance strategy. In such a scenario, the stages of Palestinian economic development could not be shaped by the traditional basket of policies and strategies for forming a developmental state. These very much depend on the possibility of exercising a certain level of "economic nationalism" that has characterized most successful development experiences. So in that sense, an equitable two-state solution retains its appeal as a basis for building a viable Palestinian economy.

Of all the different configurations of the Arab-Jewish economic relationship over the past century, none has been equitable or rights-based. And in the debates of recent decades on integration versus separation, no scheme has convinced skeptics on both sides. Hence the rationale emerges for exploring a halfway scheme for repartitioning Palestine that caters to both past injustice and future equity, one that simultaneously accommodates current intertwined demographic realities; provides for national self-determination and serves the security interests of both peoples; and creates an equitable balance in sovereignty, power, and resources.

The Parallel States economy option is unique in its emphasis on Palestinian sovereignty (including in its shared or constrained forms). All conventional discussions of economic permanent status start with an Israeli-Palestinian political focus. In all those "second-track" schemes (Economic Permanent Status, 1998; Economic Policy Programme, 2002; Geneva Initiative and Aix Group, ongoing) any option that might be of strategic interest to Palestine must first pass a variety of tests. Is it security-proof, business-friendly, fiscally conservative, neoliberal, compatible with good governance, complementary to Israeli economic interests, and so on? These initiatives were fundamentally flawed because the wrong questions were being asked while the only important question was being ignored—namely, does this or that strengthen Palestinian sovereignty and national economic security?

This is to deny neither the significance of the Israeli economy to Palestine, nor the entrenched patterns and dysfunctional dynamics of the economic relationship, which will be difficult to untangle. And certainly, under the right circumstances and with the correct common framework for dividing or sharing sovereign economic functions, the benefits that a small, weak, and open economy like Palestine could gain from proximity to—and eventual integration with—the stronger, developed Israeli economy cannot be dismissed. But we are not there yet, at least as long as Palestine cannot stand on its own two feet in any sovereign sense. The Parallel States economy, with its emphasis on medium-term equity, rebalancing, convergence, and common management of a broad swath of "public goods," offers a chance to create a truly viable and effective Palestinian economy alongside that of Israel, capable of interacting from a position of strength (compared to historical trends) without threatening Israel's security or identity.

## PARALLEL STATES ASSUMPTIONS AND FUTURE ECONOMIC RELATIONS

It is useful to review first the Parallel States Project (PSP) vision, particularly its economic dimensions, before proceeding to discuss the challenges any future partition of territory and sovereignty would have to surmount if it were to be relevant and viable. The discussion of sovereignty in the Parallel States context suggests how the functions and relations of parallel states might differ from those usually observed between neighboring states. As outlined by Mathias Mossberg in chapter 1, in a Parallel States structure the two states would combine separate authority over citizens with joint authority over territory. Their parallel exercise of sovereignty would be attached to their singular territorial unit. This structure is revolutionary compared to the traditional notion of condominium, in which common sovereignty is exercised as an additional feature on the periphery, while exclusive sovereignty still prevails at home.

By recognizing that we live in a globalized world we have come to accept that traditional nation-state boundaries may be eroded by various forces. Accordingly, sovereignty today is demonstrated in differing degrees over different objects (territory, citizens, functions) and through a variety of channels (security, economic, political, institutional, cultural). Hence, the possible permutations of an Israeli-Palestinian permanent-status solution appear more nuanced than the static one- or two-state dichotomy suggests. The Parallel States concept allows a variety of parameters for partitioning (or sharing) territory, populations, and resources in place of conventional partition (i.e., simply drawing a line across the map to define all borders between the two states). It hence creates more options for a balanced and just division between the two peoples, and indeed, for differing borders in function-specific areas.

Of the assumed parameters discussed within the PSP, several are of special importance to a future Parallel States economy. To begin with, the creation of two legal systems permits different forms of economic legislation, standards, and measures appropriate to each economy's level of development, without being incompatible with the conduct of normal intrastate economic relations, and without implying an exact correspondence between legal systems and territory in all situations. Having a single international border allows either of the parties control over commercial and passenger movement across borders on behalf of both, or joint presence and control. Free mobility of people and goods within the joint territory, while not necessarily implying a common trade and fiscal system, does suggest that the security-first mentality would give way to the logic of markets, development, and cooperation. The creation of one economic area does not need to mean that each party must have the same economic system so much as it implies an all-embracing framework for relations that allows the Parallel States economy to breathe, and that puts the parties' economic relations on a different level from those shared with other partners.

Just as much as it is a political necessity, reconciliation is relevant in correcting the structural imbalance that the more advanced Israeli-Jewish economy has enjoyed at little cost. And the possibility of separate economic policies in some areas and joint policies in others fits well with the idea that Palestinian Arab special development needs (in the West Bank and Gaza, as well as inside Israel) should be addressed through differentiated, regional treatment. However, in other arenas (safeguarding water and natural resources, protecting the environment, ensuring public health, etc.) there is simply no room for divergent national policies, and joint action would be imperative to survival.

To the preceding list, other principles should be added that have a bearing on the Parallel States concept as a whole and on its possible usefulness to policy-makers in the future. First off, statehood does not take precedence over sovereignty. This means that a solution to the historical conflict must recognize the root causes and that statehood is not itself the answer, but only a manifestation of the greater need of both sides for self-determination and sovereignty. Nor should statehood be a *substitute* for sovereignty: the idea of a Palestinian state with provisional borders would create precisely this problem, whereby a state would exist in name, but in a legal limbo without the sovereign powers to defend its interests. Sovereignty is a means to guarantee respect for national interests. But instead of wielding it as a battering ram to advance national interests, Palestinians and Israelis alike should see it as a defensive concept that upholds the borders and agreed-upon sharing of functions that the Parallel States economy needs if it is to deliver results to both sides.

For the Parallel States economy to satisfy each side's needs for national self-expression and security, the areas of exclusive sovereignty need to be as broad as possible. Hence, national (state) sovereignty takes precedence over shared or extraterritorial sovereign powers, but does not exclude them. Linked as it would be to global and extraregional powers and guarantors for security purposes and international legitimacy, however, the Parallel States economic scheme would admit the influence of external actors in each side's economic affairs. This means that establishing Palestinian sovereignty would necessarily imply a contraction of Israeli sovereignty as currently exercised, but without affecting its statehood. While this may mistakenly be portrayed as a threat to, or diminution of, Israel's right to exist or to its Jewish identity, within recognized boundaries the Israeli state would remain sovereign—although those boundaries would be less generous and gray than they are today.

The preceding caveats regarding the concept of Parallel States sovereignty are relevant to any discussion of Palestinian economic development prospects, and not only because the Israeli-Jewish economic experience since before 1948 has emphasized a primary role for the state in building the economy, by subsidizing strategic industries and protecting vulnerable sectors. This, in fact, provides important lessons to policymakers seeking to enable a viable Palestinian development path, and is equally important in the economic context because the "mission of economic development" for Israel has been completed, as symbolized by its recent entry into the club of "developed" economies, the OECD.

There is, therefore, a specific relevance to the challenge of building a functioning economic framework for the parallel states in emphasizing Palestinian sovereignty (hitherto nonexistent). Is it possible to envisage conceptually how, over the span of a generation, the different areas of sovereignty in the Parallel States context could come to coexist or interact in such a way that the disposition of sovereign economic powers would be optimal and attractive for both sides, and thereby provide a viable basis for a permanent system?

Metaphorically, it can be said that the functioning of the Parallel States economy should resemble the intermeshing of the wheels of an engine or a clock. Some wheels are bigger and more powerful, with more traction than others (e.g., Israeli sovereign economic power, or the operation of global financial markets). Others wheels occupy smaller spaces, but nevertheless remain indispensable to the machine (e.g., Palestinian sovereign economic power, or that part of national policy space ceded to international trade obligations as exercised in the WTO context). A well-conceived interaction of sovereignties should enable perpetual movement of the Parallel States economic system within defined parameters, whereby the whole only turned if all the wheels were well founded and smoothly spinning, their cogs well connected and geared to one another. In the area of economic relations this accurately describes the manner in which closely related, yet distinct, economies interact in a globalized world. A configuration of interacting parallel sovereignties implies the simultaneous existence of two national sovereign powers and exclusive zones (exercised by the states of Israel and Palestine within their hinterland and core territories); several functional or territorial areas of shared sovereignty, encompassing both states' territory (regional public goods) as well as contiguous zones on the periphery (utilities, transport networks, industrial zones, ports, airports, sensitive security zones); and functional extraterritorial forms of sovereignty that effectively act as brakes on the sovereignty of national economies (world trade rules, international trade infrastructure, financial markets, intellectual property rights, movement of persons, etc.).

## ISRAELI-PALESTINIAN ECONOMIC IMBALANCES

The overriding requirement for a successful adjustment of the current Israeli and Palestinian economies to a future Parallel States system is that it be able over time to redress the severe imbalance in the structural relations between the two economies. Certainly other considerations must be kept in focus, especially that the safeguarding of reasonable national economic interests and security, and different national self-determination paths and stages, call for differentiated economic policies and treatment. But if the Parallel States economy does not recognize that the only basis for historic reconciliation is an equally historic reversal of Palestinian Arab economic misfortunes, then it runs the risk of locking in current distortions and inequalities without providing a basis for equitable growth and development.

An examination of current economic imbalances is vital to identifying the future options and policies to be considered when designing an economic system compatible with the Parallel States concept. This in turn calls for an understanding of the steady attrition of Palestinian Arab economic power since before 1948, leading to the now almost absolute predominance of the Israeli-Jewish economy throughout the territory of Palestine-Israel. In doing so, it is necessary to include on the balance sheet all the remnants of the Arab economy of historical Palestine, both in the West Bank and Gaza Strip (occupied in 1967) and in the remaining Arab region of the Galilee Triangle–Negev, which became part of Israel in 1948.

No study of Palestinian Arab society and economy since 1948 can avoid explicit recognition of the wider context of the historical clash between a settler colonial project and a native population rooted deeply in the land and culture of Palestine. This conflict has not only shaped the strategic actions of Israel and framed the resistance of Palestinians, but equally is translated directly or indirectly into every law, institution, process, and instrument governing relations between Arabs and Jews in the state of Israel, as well as in the relation between the occupying power and the Palestinian people in the West Bank and Gaza. This recognition has equally led to a range of critiques, many of which understand the prospects for Arab development in the Jewish state to be predetermined by the continued Zionist nature of the state of Israel, and hence illusory by definition.

If we can avoid delving into Mandate-period economic history in Palestine, the most appropriate reference point for understanding the economic challenge faced today is the 1947 UN General Assembly Resolution 181 for territorial partition, especially its Annex for Economic Union between the two states. UNGA 181 provides an appropriate historical context for tracing subsequent developments, as well as a recognized de jure framework, however dated, for relations between an Arab and a Jewish state in partitioned Palestine. While overtaken by the military logic of Israeli expansion in 1948 and in 1967, UNGA 181 is the only internationally endorsed translation of the partition concept to resolve the struggle over the land of Palestine.

Ironically, the economic union called for in UNGA 181 is the only part of that resolution that was actually realized, as the Palestinian Arab economy within the 1949 armistice lines became part of the Israeli economy, especially after the remainder of Palestine fell under Israeli occupation in 1967. Today, economic activity throughout the area of the Palestinian

Mandate is governed by the unified economic regime (macroeconomic, monetary, trade, and fiscal) stipulated in UNGA 181. The economic union as proposed in 1947 was meant to smooth the transition from the so-called "dual economy" of the Palestinian Mandate to one unified economic system for two states. But it was premised on a naive assumption about the outcomes of union between an advanced, capitalist, urban, Jewish economy and a postfeudal (or perhaps precapitalist), agrarian, Arab economy: namely, that economic convergence would follow. As is shown below, this has not been the record of the "union" as it has evolved.

Under both the traditional and parallel two-state solutions, there are two broad strategic options for sharing economic space. These entail either abandoning the "union" in its evolved shape in favor of separation and reunion under new conditions in the future, or correcting the distorted union through an economic repartitioning that produces significantly different economic outcomes from those experienced over the past century.

In some ways, economic separation implies a process just as complex as territorial partition. The 1949 armistice lines (the so-called 1967 borders) remain the internationally accepted borders, and the basis for an eventual two-state solution. This "consensus" persists despite the growing irrelevance of those lines to the actual distribution of the Arab and Jewish populations, land, and resources throughout the territory. But assuming more flexible options for parallel states' economic borders, exactly what lines should separate the economic spaces to be occupied by two states after sixty years not only of proximity, but of a distorted union?

This task is especially daunting when the ownership of the primary economic resource—namely, land and its attendant natural resources—has been partitioned along lines mainly dictated by the logic of Jewish colonization and conquest. One author has vividly termed the process of Zionist settlement in the land of Palestine "exclavation" (Falah 2003). He describes the pre-1948 Jewish economy as emanating from its urban centers along the coast and establishing outpost "exclaves" in the midst of dense Arab rural areas, which eventually created the geoeconomic pattern for claiming sovereignty. The transfer of ownership in the Galilee since 1948 amply demonstrates this process. The windfall of land expropriated by the state from "absent" refugees saw vast tracts of exclusively Arab areas reduced to a series of barely connected "enclaves."

Since 1967 the same process has been pursued in the occupied West Bank and Jerusalem. Steady Jewish settlement has turned the remainder of Palestine into a series of "enclaves" surviving amid an ever-expanding archipelago of Jewish "exclaves" with scant regard to ownership, habitation, or access to resources. The impoverished Gaza Strip boasts the distinct feature of having become one big "ex/enclave." It is totally surrounded (enclaved) but with a sizable, demographically homogeneous and contiguous area of purely Palestinian ownership and proto-sovereignty (exclaved). So how, and exactly where, can Arab sovereignty in Palestine then be defined or reclaimed, when the demarcation of human settlement shifts every decade or so? The answer to this dilemma has as much relevance to the economic dimension as to any other in the Parallel States structure.

## Theories of Economic Integration and Israeli-Palestinian Realities

The analysis of economic "path dependence" (UNCTAD 2006) suggests that even after years of independence, some countries continue to suffer from growth-inhibiting structures that were formed during their colonial era. Once structures have been formed, the argument goes, they tend to lock in a certain evolutionary path for the country, especially under colonial conditions, such as the relation between Israel and the occupied West Bank and Gaza Strip. Under "normal" circumstances, the dynamics of integration are expected to display a pattern of economic divergence followed by convergence. In the early stages of integration, the gap widens. In later stages, a switch occurs in the dynamics and investment in the small economy becomes more attractive. As a result the poor economy starts to grow faster than the richer one, narrowing the gap.

Had economic relations between the Israeli and Palestinian economies been confined to the dynamics of normal, uncontrolled market forces, the gap between per-capita incomes theoretically should have widened in the first years of the occupation and then become smaller—an assumption described as the market failure school of the economics of occupation (Samour 2011). This supposition is widespread among Palestinian and international observers and admits the existence and possible normal functioning of "markets" in a colonial situation, which only fail to deliver development for reasons related to occupation restrictions (neatly termed by economists "transaction costs"; see, e.g., Kanafani 2011).

TABLE 6.1  PATTERN OF CONVERGENCE-DIVERGENCE IN
REAL GDP PER CAPITA (1995 DOLLARS)

| Year | Israel | West Bank and Gaza | Income Gap |
|------|--------|--------------------|------------|
| 1968–69 | 8,137 | 904 | 9.0 |
| 1975–76 | 10,964 | 1,543 | 7.1 |
| 1980–81 | 12,019 | 1,599 | 7.5 |
| 1985–86 | 12,743 | 1,708 | 7.5 |
| 1990–91 | 14,170 | 1,407 | 10.1 |
| 1995–96 | 16,458 | 1,361 | 12.1 |
| 1999–2000 | 17,310 | 1,528 | 11.3 |
| 2001–2 | 16,908 | 1,244 | 13.6 |
| 2003–4 | 16,755 | 1,169 | 14.3 |
| 2005–6 | 17,875 | 1,047 | 17.1 |

SOURCE: UNCTAD 2006.

What happened in fact was the opposite, as shown in table 6.1. The actual pattern was one of a slow convergence during the first two decades of occupation followed by divergence. Under abnormal conditions such as these, divergence simply bred more divergence, as the imperatives of Jewish colonization and Israeli occupation effectively expropriated the expected gains from "integration." After forty years of occupation, the per-capita income gap between the Israel and Palestinian economies had doubled, from ninefold to over seventeenfold. Convergence under occupation is, or should have become by now, an illusion.

By widening the focus to include all Arab "economic regions" within Israel-Palestine, table 6.2 presents two available aggregate indicators of the Arab and Jewish economies' relative size, to compare over sixty years; namely, gross national income (GNI) and welfare (per-capita GNI). Inside Israel as a whole since 1948, the path has been one of Jewish-Arab economic divergence, just as it has been since 1967 between Israel and the occupied West Bank and Gaza Strip. Taking all regions into account, a telling picture emerges of Jewish-Arab economic divergence over the past two-thirds of a century.

In 1944, the Jewish 32 percent of the population produced 49 percent of GNI. But by 2007, the Jewish 52 percent of the total population produced 89 percent of GNI. In 1944, the two economies were roughly the same size, but today the Jewish economy dwarfs the Arab economy by eight to one. Meanwhile, the pre-1948 economic welfare imbalance has been further aggravated, with the gap between per-capita incomes

TABLE 6.2  PATTERN OF CONVERGENCE-DIVERGENCE IN POPULATION, GROSS NATIONAL INCOME, AND PER-CAPITA GNI

| | Palestinian Mandate | | | Israel | | | Occupied Territory 2007 | Israel plus Occupied Territory | | |
|---|---|---|---|---|---|---|---|---|---|---|
| | Arab 1944 | Jewish 1944 | Ratio J/A | Arab 2006–7 | Jewish 2006–7 | Ratio J/A | | Arab 2007 | Jewish 2007 | Ratio J/A |
| Population (thousands) | 1,185 | 554 | 0.47 | 1,231 | 5,435 | 4.41 | 3,385 | 5,066 | 5,435 | 1.07 |
| Total GNI (thousands) | £63,000 | £60,000 | 0.95 | $14,000 | $157,000 | 11.2 | $5,600 | $19,600 | $157,000 | 8.01 |
| Welfare (per-capita GNI) | £53.1 | £108.4 | 2.04 | $9,300 | $28,900 | 3.11 | $1,465 | $3,900 | $28,900 | 7.4 |

SOURCES: Estimates based on (for 1944) British Mandate data cited in Metzer 1998; (for Israel in 2006–7) Sadan 2006; and (for Occupied Territory 2007) UNCTAD 2006.

more than trebling from two to more than seven. This gap most vividly reflects the opportunity gain of a century of colonization, expropriation, and demographic transformation.

## The Arab "Regional" Economy within Israel

Ever since the PLO formally embraced the two-state formula in 1988, it has maintained a formal recognition of UN General Assembly Resolution 181, alongside UNGA Resolution 194 on the rights of refugees. But the UNGA 181 borders have been excluded since the Madrid peace negotiations, in favor of UN Security Council resolution 242, which implies the 1949–1967 Armistice lines as the hard borders of any two-state configuration. Dropping UNGA 181 from the reference framework for negotiations also has been a silent testimony to the exclusion from the agenda of the "permanent status" of the Arab minority in Israel. It is "understood" by all that this is an internal Israeli matter, not subject to negotiation or discussion.

Although such considerations are apparently of equal relevance to resolving permanent-status issues such as the fate of refugees or of Jerusalem, we are still far from the option of a different repartition of Palestine that, for example, opens the door to Arab areas in Israel merging voluntarily with an eventual Palestinian state. Nevertheless, the question remains how an Arab regional economy in Israel can be part of the future economic system within the current configuration of Israeli sovereignty or any future hard borders between the two states.

In all areas of economic activity, the path of Arab economic "development" in Israel is at odds with that of the national, Jewish economy as seen in key socioeconomic indicators. This history lesson in the processes and systems of Jewish colonization is amply demonstrated by comparisons of the period prior to 1948, inside Israel since then, and in the West Bank since 1967. It is useful to envision future economic Jewish-Arab relations without the encumbrance of hard borders of territorial partition, though with clearly defined soft borders. If for no other reason, exclusion of the Arab economy in Israel from the developmental dividends of reconciliation would risk sowing the seeds of future insurrection that would straddle all sides of the hard borders.

My own analysis of the Arab economy in Israel has shown the extent to which its economic development path indicates a distinct, regional pattern divergent from that of the national, Jewish economy (Khalidi 1988 and 2008). Another, innovative treatment emphasizes the manner in which state policy toward the Arab economy has featured a mercantilist imperative that systematically favors and protects the Jewish economy from Arab encroachment (Shehadeh 2006). A forthcoming analysis of the most recent state-sponsored policies to "integrate" the Arab economy in Israel reveals a continuation of six decades of colonial resource-extraction processes, most recently in a neoliberal free-market guise (Khalidi and Shehadeh, forthcoming).

Regardless of the analytical framework applied, it is only necessary to highlight here the extent of divergence between the Arab and Jewish economies in Israel despite decades of proclaimed integration and equality. Inclusion of this regional economy in the Parallel States economy need not imply eventual state of Palestine sovereignty over it. However, this does not obviate the need to benefit from appropriate and feasible programs that would rehabilitate and integrate it within the broader Parallel States context. While any future forced physical transfer of Palestinian population is unacceptable, the possibility of a new assignment for sovereignty under the Parallel States configuration implies soft options as well, which could allow citizens or communities in one state's territory to opt for attachment to the other's different, if compatible, sovereign economic space.

## Toward a Break with Past Policies and Failed Ideologies

An overriding and more immediate challenge, however, is the need to salvage the economy of the Occupied Territory and to render it collectively sovereign and viable. Regardless of the fate of the Arab economy in Israel, it is in the 1967-occupied territories, on that 22 percent of Palestine supposedly reserved for Palestinian self-determination, that the heartland of the Palestinian Arab economy may be built. So not only must an eventual state of Palestine accelerate per-capita GDP growth and catch up, but it also has to somehow leapfrog into the twenty-first century in building an economy suited to these times. In doing so it must also break ties of dependency that have welded the Occupied Territory and its economies to the imperatives of Israeli colonization (Khalidi and Taghdisi-Rad 2009).

The developmental experience of the Occupied Territory since 1967 has largely reproduced that of the Palestinian region in Israel since 1948. Settlement exclaves have produced Palestinian enclaves with most jurisdiction, zoning, land-use planning, and regional planning powers subject to occupation authorities. The gradual attrition of territorial, economic, and institutional integrity between the West Bank and Gaza Strip, and between the West Bank and Jerusalem, mirror the cantonization of pre-1948 Palestine. Finally, the Occupied Territory features structural transformations similar to the Arab region in Israel, leading to an enfeebled productive capacity, weak human resource development, bankrupt local government, restricted international trade access, and chronically deficient trade with the Israeli economy. But the lessons from this pattern have yet to be recognized.

Predominant narratives in current economic policy focus on improving Palestinian quality of life (and essential public services and security) until such time as the occupation can be ended. Such approaches are of no relevance to the Parallel States framework because they effectively exclude or postpone the most crucial elements of Palestinian sovereignty. Equally problematic is that they fundamentally misconceive the needs of the Palestinian economy and the prerequisites for building an economy for a viable, sovereign state.

The most notable examples are the beliefs, largely supported by the donor community and international financial institutions, that the joint economic and trade regime (defined by the Israel-Palestine Protocol on Economic Relations, signed in Paris in 1994) can be fixed with some goodwill, that improving movement and access conditions will deliver tangible economic benefits, and ultimately that integration is feasible, desirable, and inevitable. The recurrent and failed Israeli concept of granting economic peace instead of land for peace is little more than an updated version of the material inducements to individual prosperity in place of communal development that have characterized Israeli occupation strategies since Moshe Dayan's "Open Bridges" of the 1970s and Menahem Melson's "Village Leagues" of the 1980s.

A more recent project espoused by Palestinian Prime Minister Fayyad proposes laying the foundations for the state of Palestine through statelike institution-building prior to sovereignty and through economic liberalization without structural transformation. While this project was predicated on the naive assumption that a Palestinian state would be established in 2011, it lacks developmental depth, and what the Palestinian Authority's statehood plan represents, at best, is a strategy to expand policy space for the further implementation of the neoliberal framework in policy areas over which it has currently no control. In one sense, the current historic moment echoes the transfer in an earlier era (1994) of limited economic authority (within the Israeli occupation envelope) to the newly created Palestinian Authority (Khalidi and Samour 2011).

Other, less prevalent though persistent, analyses advocated by some United Nations institutions, NGOs, and a handful of scholars have long attempted to explain precisely why "development under occupation" is a chimera. This viewpoint has focused on how a qualitatively different Palestinian development paradigm needed to emerge that recognized the realities of occupation and the extent to which the fate of the Palestinian economy has become mortgaged to Israel and its economy. This minority viewpoint deserves renewed consideration in the Parallel States context.

Both prior to and parallel to the explosion of economic policy interest in and expertise on Palestine since the 1990s, the conventional wisdom was rarely confronted by any original analyses, Palestinian or otherwise. Certainly there were some important exceptions, such as the work of the late professor Yusif Sayigh in the first, ultimately shelved, Palestinian Development Program of 1993. Such contributions not only predate the deluge of documentation and analysis carried out since, but in some respects have survived as enduring testimonies to the most crucial features and implications of the deep structural economic impact of prolonged Israeli occupation. As early as 1988 Yusif Sayigh pointed out that there can be no development under occupation (Sayigh 1986), and yet the failings of the policy environment and the misguided attempts at integration were obvious even then to anybody who cared to notice. Another such early warning that rings true today came from Mohammed Shadid: "For those Palestinians thirsty for any kind of development, no matter the political price, the immediate future seems manageable. Those Palestinians whose goal is political self-determination, in order to end the cycle of exploitation at the hands of those who control the direction of economic development, can expect an intensification of the kind of political suppression which the term 'quality of life' came to mean in 1986" (Shadid 1988: 135).

Hence a future vision for Palestinian economic development must derive from a genuine national sovereignty agenda, guided by the best policy practices of developing countries and the lessons of prolonged occupation. Such a vision must not be an academic exercise for a rosy postliberation future, but instead must contribute to a strategy for Palestinian liberation. While the Parallel States economic vision might represent an ideal—though still distant—future, the real litmus test is whether it can also relate to today's economic challenges in the less optimal and more confrontational realities of prolonged struggle over land, resources, and sovereignty.

## NATIONAL ECONOMIC INTERESTS AND STRATEGIES TO REDRESS IMBALANCES

I have emphasized the failure of Palestinian policy to adopt economic strategies geared toward ending occupation, alongside the Israeli policy success in prolonging occupation through economic peace, since the Parallel States proposal will have to address both if it is to achieve its ambitious goals. Too few experts, pundits, and policy-makers have recognized that Palestine (like all such things!) is a case like no other and should not be subject to generic, template-driven, one-size-fits-all policy formulas. And in the wake of the 2008 global economic crisis, this rings truer than ever. While conventional wisdom might have been unable to envisage that the liberal market system could fail so dramatically, with the collapse of Israeli-Palestinian cooperation since the second Intifada this should have become obvious at least to Palestinian policy-makers. Sustaining the short-lived growth gains from the post-Oslo "peace dividend" and economic cooperation has proved elusive, if not futile, with real per-capita incomes today 30 percent below 2000 levels.

The developmental cost of having remained faithful over the years to failed economic doctrines and a rose-tinted view of the realities of Israeli occupation rises with every passing day. The Parallel States structure must be able to transform what is today, for want of a better term, a bipolar Jewish-Arab economy into a mutually beneficial framework for growth and sustained development. This bipolarity is manifested in various dimensions, all of which will need to be tackled by any future arrangements: uneven performance, from crisis/depression, to recovery/exuberance, back to normality; a lopsided structure governed by the same underlying economic rules, regulations, and policy but with one Jewish dominant pole and several Arab satellite poles; and skewed resource distribution in land, water, and other natural resources, as well as financial capital (industry, investment, technology) and human-social capital.

To the extent that the Parallel States structure can apply, and indeed exploit, the more nuanced concept of divisible sovereignty to create a more functional and equitable economic relationship between the two states, it can offer more than the conventional economic cooperation or integration schemes proposed. It also suggests alternatives to the descent into a colonial or apartheid unitary state system, which is what Israel and the Occupied Territory risk becoming if current trends continue.

But avoiding these pitfalls calls for more than just careful or innovative design. More vital is that the Parallel States structure secure clear sovereign gains for Palestine, whose economy requires major support and restructuring if long-term imbalances and divergence are to be reversed. This in turn implies that the Parallel States economy must not be conceived of as some distant goal after a political settlement appears on the horizon. Instead, efforts could be focused today that are consistent with the core assumptions of the Parallel States structure regarding sovereignty, statehood, and reversing adverse path dependency. This means that the Parallel States framework should embody principles and economic goals that are necessary for the success of any negotiated two-state configuration. But these should also be relevant to a longer-term struggle for equal rights and freedom as prospects for a two-state solution recede. There is no need to invent a special new wheel for the Parallel States economy: the components of Palestinian national economic security are unchanging under any scenario, and the strategies that must be pursued to secure real Palestinian development are equally evident and imperative in any case.

## The Vital Components of Palestinian National Economic Security

Within the broader framework of the Parallel States proposal, it is necessary that Palestinian economic security be safeguarded just as all other dimensions of national security would be. This is not simply a matter of ensuring individual or communal economic security through sustained growth and development. It is also necessary that the geo-demographic, legal, and institutional features of a viable national economy be defined.

It is furthermore important that such components of a "doctrine" of national economic security be pursued by Palestinian policy-makers under any economic scenario. Such a set of goals should be consistent with the broader agenda of national liberation and serve as clear benchmarks of the extent to which Palestinian state-building efforts are geared toward securing national sovereignty rather than simply erecting its façades. The most important parameters of a strategy that advances Palestinian national economic security interests, today and tomorrow, are enumerated here.

- *Safeguarding the territorial integrity of the West Bank and Gaza Strip.* Even in a Parallel States scenario, these would remain the core regions of the Palestinian state, and their regional integration and security are prerequisites for long-term economic stability.

- *Reinforcing any Palestinian policy initiative and institutional development that removes Israeli occupation systems of control and authority.* Any new economic policy, institution, or system that takes control out of the hands of Israeli policy-makers and empowers Palestinians carries a premium over prolonged Israeli management of Palestinian economic interests and affairs.

- *"Forming" the institutions for a viable state rather than pursuing open-ended "reforming" of institutions of interim self-government.* The bulk of institutional development and reform undertaken by the Palestinian Authority to date has entailed trying to improve the functioning of self-government institutions designed and approved in cooperation with the Israeli occupying power in the early 1990s in the context of the Paris Protocol. These institutions ultimately constrained Palestinian industrialization, agricultural development, and productive investment as much by design as by application (see Khalidi and Taghdisi-Rad 2009). A break with this legacy is required if proto-state institutions are to command the heights of a national economy rather than fulfill a subcontracting role for Israeli colonial policy.

- *Delimiting and safeguarding the separate status of the Palestinian customs territory.* Regardless of the form of any permanent-status economic arrangement, Palestine's sovereignty must also find expression in a distinct and coherent trade regime suited to its national economic interests. An indispensable feature of any national economy is that it be a "separate customs territory," enjoying control over a significant part of its commercial relations.

- *Policies and international support measures addressing the special needs of a newly independent, war-torn state.* No state emerging from colonialism and conflict has been successful in navigating the early stages of its national economic development without significant recognition of its special needs by trading partners and donors. Equipping Palestine with multilateral means to enhance its economic policy space and development prospects implies treatment that allows it no less leeway in bolstering and protecting its national economic interests than other countries had as they industrialized and developed.

- *Policies, strategies, and measures for sustained growth and development having the flexibility to withstand adverse shocks and adapt to recessionary external conditions or renewed conflict.*

A corollary of the preceding point is that development strategies, macroeconomic policy, and both public and private investment act to compensate for the new state's relatively small size, weakened resource base, and shattered human capital. Doing so will expedite Palestinian economic catch-up as well as provide instruments that increase policy space to deal with external shocks.

- *Securing effective control and jurisdiction over vital natural resources within a balanced framework of multilateral cooperation.* One of the greatest lost economic opportunities of the period since Oslo has been the exclusion from Palestinian jurisdiction of most Palestinian land, water resources, and mineral riches. If Palestine does not enjoy full sovereignty over natural resources, its economic security will forever be at risk.

- *Implementing inclusive and innovative policies for naturalization, restitution, resettlement, and reinsertion of returning refugees.* To the extent that statehood and sovereignty are true manifestations of a historic recognition of the Palestinian people's legitimate national rights, they should enable the realization of the rights of refugees, especially those who opt to return to live in Palestine as citizens of the state of Palestine.

### Goals and Instruments for Palestinian Arab Regional Development

As has been emphasized throughout, for the Parallel States economy to be functional, it must be geared to Palestinian development needs, as that part of the economic equation has been disfavored, if not negated, over the past sixty years. Israel has its own development priorities and economic policy preferences, and these should not be replicated by the Palestinian economic policy regime, as they serve Israel's sovereign colonial interests. For the still-developing Palestinian Arab people, on both sides of the 1967 borders, a very different set of policy priorities is appropriate. These should reflect the special needs of the Palestinian Arab regions whose development prospects have been subject to others' colonial development considerations for the past century.

Economic policy goals consistent with a doctrine of national economic security have eluded Palestinian policy-makers until now, owing both to weak policy-making capacities as well as to the occupation regime, which leaves only limited policy-management space for Palestinian decision-making. Sovereignty should enable Palestinian national development policies focused on correcting structural distortions, powering developmental takeoff, and setting the two states' economies on a path of convergence. It is essential that progressive and people-oriented development goals be well founded in the economic policy of the state of Palestine, while also being pertinent for efforts to reverse the sustained decline of the Arab regional economy in Israel.

Some of the essential economic development goals attuned to the specific needs of a vulnerable, war-torn economy like Palestine would include sustainable poverty reduction and decent work; sectoral diversification; consolidation of the agricultural productive base; harnessing economic linkages to reduce dependence on Israel; climate-friendly industrialization; public investment for infrastructure; services and utilities; private investment to promote strategic growth and export sectors; regional development planning; effective, efficient, and transparent economic governance institutions; autonomous macroeconomic and monetary policy and institutions; and environmentally sustainable management of natural resources.

Having defined the core economic security interests and highlighted the foremost goals of economic development for a sovereign state of Palestine within a Parallel States system in the coming period, we can briefly examine the final elements in the panoply of strategic guidelines for the economy. These are the institutional and policy instruments to be deployed during, and in some cases before, the operational statehood phase. The emphasis on sovereignty is intended to highlight the need for a strong Palestinian state from the outset if a Parallel States economy is to serve its purpose and play its role in achieving historical reconciliation. This sort of institution-building will enable the emergence of those governance structures and functions that Palestine needs if it is to lead effectively the reconstruction and development effort and enjoy equitable economic relations.

There are some key functions of states in a globalized economy to which Palestine could aspire in its state-building efforts, which reinforce national economic security and sustained development, and also constitute clear milestones on the path to a sovereign future. These functions in turn imply a number of institutions and policies that should be high on the agenda of Palestinian and concerned international policy-makers seeking to prepare for a real state-formation process. These include the capacity to enforce and maintain security, without which the state cannot fulfill its economic role of maintaining law, order, and property rights along with control over geography and natural resources, and without which the economy cannot properly function and remains handicapped. Good Palestinian governance implies strong and modern state institutions and transparent and inclusive legislation to meet the challenge of managing the complex Parallel States economic relationship. In order to safeguard the maximum possible space for pro-growth development, coherent macroeconomic, investment, and trade policies are essential, while the state's capacity to mobilize social capital networks and human resources, including returnees, will be crucial. Resort to the institutions of international law and the global multilateral economic governance system will provide a safety valve to ensure that Palestinian sovereignty is not breached by its more powerful neighbors and economic partners.

## REBALANCING THE TWO ECONOMIES

As I continue to emphasize, an economic future for the Parallel States system entails, above all, launching the much-overdue process of forming a Palestine sovereign state. The state of Israel has held a monopoly on sovereignty throughout Palestine for more than six decades, and this is ultimately a dead end. Israel has also enjoyed a successful, if not model, state-building record. In the process, the imperative of expanding the sovereignty of the Jewish state throughout Palestine has meant that Palestinian Arab development has increasingly diverged and lagged behind that of Israel. Today, the Arab economy in Israel represents the most advanced form of this disintegration, the Gaza economy the most extreme example of deprivation, and the consumption boom in the West Bank is typical of the anachronistic bubbles that have always burst over past generations.

In exploring the functional forms of Parallel States sovereignty and how they might be divided or shared, while each of the two states would maintain its own distinct economy, the framework for sharing sovereignty over territory and citizens would by necessity create a third distinct economic space, which we call the Parallel States economy. Its design should be determined by a set of agreed-upon common goals, a sort of declaration of economic principles that would guide the process of managing common or adjacent economic resources and harmonizing national economic policies and cross-border relations. While the Palestine state-formation economic development agenda reviewed in the foregoing is of limited interest to Israeli or other policy-makers, how this economy will interact with Israel is of course highly pertinent. As has been stressed, an equally pressing issue is how the needs and potential of the Arab economy in Israel can best be factored into that equation. Hence, a new set of parameters to correct generations of adverse Jewish-Arab economic relations must be recognized, endorsed, and pursued by all parties, one that encompasses all regions of the two states.

A central, guiding, and overriding purpose of the Parallel States economy would be to narrow income differentials and development gaps, with the aim of achieving Jewish-Arab convergence within a generation. Economic integration would also be a common interest, but for convergence, Arab enclaves must be transformed into interconnected growth poles operating within the overall Parallel States economy. Since a repartitioning of Palestine is at the heart of the Parallel States concept, it is only through equitable sharing today (which compensates for Palestinian disadvantages) that welfare and equity may be achieved tomorrow for both peoples. Furthermore, until a point is reached where Palestinian Arab economic growth is endogenously powered, a significant transfer of financial resources from Israel and the international community will be needed to compensate for decades of lost Arab development.

To accompany political self-determination, each state must pursue its own distinct development path, suited to its identity and needs, and its own policies to promote its economic security. This means that each state's sovereignty would be maintained in its core territory, while the Parallel States economy allowed for intensive cooperation in areas (and territories) of common concern or shared resources, while a gradual process of convergence would narrow policy and institutional differences as the two states' development interests met and meshed. Even though each state would seek to secure the welfare of its own citizens and the security of its territory, the Parallel States economy must take account of Palestine's development handicaps when apportioning each state's obligations, through common but differentiated responsibilities.

Over the longer term, shared authority and compatible laws and administrations could be developed in areas of transborder public concern, especially natural resource and land use, ecological conservation, energy, and public health. In economic domains (trade in goods and services, finance, banking, industrial standards, agriculture), each state's legislation and regulations should become compatible with international standards and conventions, and thereby achieve harmony with each other. Overall, both within each state and in bilateral relations, regional development planning and public investment should favor peripheral or marginalized areas that have been bypassed by development (the Negev, Galilee, southern West Bank, Jordan River valley, southern Gaza).

## THE DEPOLARIZED PARALLEL STATES ECONOMY: SEPARATION OR UNION?

This investigation of the prospects for a Parallel States economy began by asking exactly what lines should separate the economic spaces to be occupied by two states after sixty years of proximity and a lopsided "union." The two broad options for sharing economic space imply either abandoning the current "customs union" in favor of separation or correcting the distorted union and pursuing it in an enhanced form. Both options suggest "soft" economic borders that would not necessarily always correspond to hard physical borders, and imply that in the Parallel States economy, sovereignty over different economic domains would have three dimensions. For either economic separation or union, the deployment of economic policy instruments and institutions would entail more or less emphasis on these manifestations of sovereignty: two national sovereign powers in exclusive zones; functional-territorial areas of shared sovereignty between two national sovereigns encompassing both states' territory or in contiguous zones; and functional extraterritorial (global) sovereignty that constrains the sovereignty of (all) national economies.

It should be recalled that powerful Palestinian economic policy-making and commercial interests today prefer a continuation of the current customs union (tweaked into a better deal for the Palestinian side) to the idea of cutting loose from Israeli economic hegemony. However, the preceding discussion has demonstrated how such an approach has not and will not change adverse historical trends. In addition, mistrust and structural economic bias make it difficult to see how a gradual, incremental reform of such a distorted structural relationship would ever be more than cosmetic. So as part of a viable Parallel States partition, Palestine and Israel should most likely each go their separate ways in terms of industrial and trade policy, monetary and macroeconomic management, and other sovereign economic areas.

A separate Palestinian trade and monetary regime implies strong and efficient border and customs controls between Palestinian and Israeli economic spaces, corresponding largely (but not wholly) to territorial borders. Separation also entails a distinct Palestinian tariff structure, a suitable progressive income and indirect taxation system, and a credible macroeconomic and monetary management capacity. Under this option, there would be a greater need for effective national sovereign institutions on each side of the physical border in most economic domains. For all the immediate costs the Palestinian economy might incur from the shock of delinking from the Israeli trade and monetary regime, such a shift would allow the economy to revalue and reposition itself while also establishing new trade alliances with Western and East Asian trade partners as well as with its current preferential trade partners such as the European Union. And it would not rule out renegotiating preferential or deeper trade and economic relations with Israel after an initial period.

Under such a Parallel States economic framework, shared sovereign functions would be restricted to those common-good areas listed previously (water, natural resources, energy, environment, possibly ports and airports) but exercised over the whole territory of both states. Such advanced (postnational) forms of sovereignty could be explored even more intensively in any peripheral (joint sovereignty) zones that are rich in resources, poor in human settlement, and easily managed in common.

In the same manner that Israel is today subject to the rules and regulations of the multilateral trading system and is integrated into global capital and financial markets, so would the sovereignty of the two states be restricted in these domains. However, depending on the Palestinian monetary system adopted, macroeconomic policy options would be limited to those consistent with the practices of the home country of the currency (if any) to which Palestine might be linked. If, on the other hand, Palestine opted to embark on the path to a fully independent currency, it would need to pursue proactive macroeconomic management to maintain monetary autonomy and policy effectiveness—a risky, yet not insurmountable, challenge.

Some economists might argue that the shock to the Palestinian economic system of separation from Israel would be too significant to countenance and that instead, indefinite subordination to the more stable, advanced Israeli economy is safer and the only realistic option on the table. This rests more on hypothetical constructs derived from neoclassical trade theory, not to mention "economic peacemaking" theory, than on any real-world experience. While there are not many modern examples of the economic impact of secession from economic or trade unions, at least one interesting experience may be instructive; namely, the breakup of the Soviet Union and its enforced forty-five-year-long economic integration (COMECON) of a swath of now-independent states.

Indeed, here is a case of military occupation of numerous eastern European and central Asian countries, coexisting within borders determined by the military logic of the last months of World War II (Judt 2005), with an all-powerful center (Russia) and a host of nominally sovereign, satellite economies effectively controlled and managed from the center. However much this "economic union" served the interests of the dominant economy and regime, it was flawed conceptually, disastrous economically, and ultimately unsustainable politically. And yet, from its ruins emerged the flourishing smaller and weaker Baltic and eastern European national economies, which have since become increasingly integrated into their regions, the European system, and the global economy. In just twenty years, several depressed and subject economies of the former Soviet "Union" have presented successful examples of rapid growth and newly independent, daresay sovereign, development. Who can say that a breakup of the Israeli "union" in its current configuration would not permit equally satisfactory results for Palestine?

On the other hand, a strong argument lingers (e.g., Kleiman 2007) that integration is more desirable for the Palestinian economy, if not inevitable. Following from this, of the three supposed trade regime options, the customs union remains superior for economic welfare and gains from trade considerations. The problem with such a neo-Zionist political economy is not simply that it is empirically not evident, but more important that it misdiagnoses the structural relationship between the two economies. Nevertheless, if we take our cue from the same group of economists and concede that integration is economically more beneficial than separation, it is only logical and desirable that this be a *full and balanced economic union,* attuned to the equitable vision of the Parallel States system.

Hence, economic union would imply joint Palestinian-Israeli management of the trade regime (with exemption areas carved out to protect the weaker Palestinian partner and support its industrialization); macroeconomic and monetary policy (with Palestinian membership on the board of the Central Bank and autonomous financial sector supervision functions); a common taxation and revenue-sharing framework (with adequate incentives and exemptions for the poorer Arab Palestinian regions of the Union); and preferential treatment in all economic domains for the depressed Palestinian Arab regions of the union, including within Israel, to ensure catching up.

Both economic theory and empirical evidence imply that this option might actually constitute the optimal path to achieving the purpose and vision of the Parallel States economy presented above—a sort of post-humous vindication of UNGA Resolution 181. International trade theory contends that the "normal" path of integration is the move from Most Favored Nation status to customs union to free trade to full economic union, including monetary union. Thus, it is not surprising that orthodox economists remain wedded to the idea that a breakup of the so-called customs union in favor of Most Favored Nation status is a regressive step.

However, it is clear that a successful regional trade and economic integration along the traditional path not only is theoretically possible, but has been pursued vigorously throughout the world, in developed and developing regions alike. Today, integration efforts in developing regions are more or less advanced, from the functional (and balanced) South Africa Customs Union to the stillborn Arab Free Trade Area to the more functionally effective Latin American and Asian free trade areas, and more recently to regional payment systems in Asia and Africa, and even common currencies such as the euro.

The most successful regional integration effort (at least so far) is that witnessed in Europe, with its evolution in a postconflict setting from the Iron and Coal Community and the European Common Market to the European Union and the Maastricht Treaty of monetary union. While exemplary, this gradually broadening integration effort is perhaps not most illustrative of the sort of path that Israeli-Palestinian economic union might take. However, yet another post–Cold War experience seems instructive in considering the union option, namely, the reunification of Germany in the wake of the disintegration of the Soviet Union. Of course, there are essential political differences between the two situations, especially that the Parallel States framework entails creating two parallel systems out of one, rather than reunifying a collapsing state and economy with the rest of the nation or territory cut apart from it by war.

What is relevant is the manner in which the Federal Republic of Germany's public finances assumed the debts and liabilities, obligations, assets, and monetary value of the failed German Democratic Republic economy, and integrated those regions within twenty years into a unified (one-state, national) economy, still regionally differentiated yet not divergent from the overall trend of the national economy (Flassbeck and Horn 1996). Once monetary union was decided and indeed inevitable, an intensive program was launched overnight of valuing and converting the assets and liabilities of the much poorer GDR economy, from GDR deutsche marks into FRG deutsche marks (at varying rates of parity from 2:1 to 1:1). This was followed by years of systematic, intensive, public and private investment, both within depressed regions and in their links to the rest of the economy and to trade partners to the east. Property restitution and equitable compensation were successfully managed, not to mention population and labor-force integration, while ultimately the wealth of the German union was boosted by the rehabilitation of public assets in the east. A massive resource transfer from the west ultimately made this possible, financed by (former FRG) taxpayers and through resort to international capital markets, such that twenty years later the German economy has reemerged as the powerhouse of Europe and its single currency.

## A VISION OF THE PARALLEL STATES ECONOMY BY 2035

Regardless of which path is taken, either separation or union can constitute a feasible basis for a Parallel States economy that both delimits and shares sovereignties. In any case, what should emerge from the vigorous pursuit of a Parallel States formula is not only a rapid turnaround in near-turn economic fortunes for Palestine, and a smooth transition (be it delinking or fiscal union) for Israel. But at a more advanced stage of Parallel States entrenchment, toward the year 2035, a vision for a new economy becomes evident, and not so far-fetched, achieving for both peoples

- *narrowed income disparities,* by constructing an integrated Arab economy from Galilee to Gaza, relinked to the advanced Jewish economy;
- *human capital renewal,* by removing differential access to educational and skills opportunities as well as tapping the Palestinian diaspora;
- *labor market flexibility,* by integration with differentiation—poverty reduction, social safety nets;
- *redistribution of the productive base:* restoring private property, safeguarding land and agriculture in core zones;
- *restoration of the natural resources balance,* water and mineral resources, including sustainability—a common resource;
- *sustainable and green energy,* through interregional solutions (Turkey, Syria, Egypt) and investment in renewable energies;

- *affordable human settlement,* involving immigrant-returnee absorption as mutually agreed, planned, and managed;
- *regional planning and zoning* for overlapping spheres and authorities, housing and municipal services ("declaving"); and
- *coherent economic policy-making,* with compatible macroeconomic, monetary, fiscal, and trade regimes.

## REFERENCES

Falah, G. W. 2003. "Dynamics and Patterns of the Shrinking of Arab Lands in Palestine." *Political Geography* 22: 179–209.

Flassbeck, Heiner, and Gustav Horn, eds. 1996. *German Unification—an Example for Korea?* Aldershot, UK: Dartmouth.

Judt, Tony. 2005. *Postwar: A History of Europe since 1945.* New York: Penguin.

Kanafani, Nu'man. 2011. "As If There Is No Occupation: The Limits of Palestinian Authority Strategy." Middle East Research and Information Project (MERIP), *Middle East Report* (September 22). Available online at www.merip.org/mero/mero092211; accessed October 18, 2013.

Khalidi, R. 1988. *The Arab Economy in Israel: Dynamics of a Region's Development.* London: Croom Helm.

———. 2008. "Sixty Years after the Partition of Palestine: What Future for the Arab Minority of Israel?" *Journal of Palestine Studies* 73: 24–36.

Khalidi, R., and S. Samour. 2011. "Neoliberalism as Liberation: The Statehood Program and the Remaking of the Palestinian National Movement." *Journal of Palestine Studies* 11, no. 2 (Winter): 6–25.

Khalidi, R., and M. Shehadeh. 2013. "Israel's 'Arab Economy': New Policies, Old Dynamics." Forthcoming in a volume edited by N. Rouhana.

Khalidi, Raja, and Sahar Taghdisi-Rad. 2009. "The Economic Dimensions of Prolonged Occupation: Continuity and Change in Israeli Policy towards the Palestinian Economy." Special Report. Geneva: United Nations Conference onf Trade and Development (UNCTAD).

Kleiman, Ephraim. 2007. Personal correspondence with the author.

Metzer, Jacob. 1998. *The Divided Economy of Mandatory Palestine.* New York: Cambridge University Press.

Sadan, Ezra. 2006. *The Arab Sector's Share in the Economy: Some Parameters of Arab Society within the Israeli Economy.* Tel Aviv: The Abraham Fund Initiatives.

Samour, S. 2011. Personal correspondence with the author.

Sayigh, Yusef. 1986. "The Palestinian Economy under Occupation: Dependency and Pauperization." *Journal of Palestine Studies* 15, no. 4 (Summer): 46–67.

Shadid, Mohammed. 1988. "Israeli Policy towards Economic Development in the West Bank and Gaza." In *The Palestinian Economy: Studies in Development under Prolonged Occupation,* ed. G. Abed. London: Routledge.

Shehadeh, M. 2006. *Impeding Development: Israel's Economic Policies towards the Arab National Minority* (in Arabic). Haifa: Mada El-Carmel Centre.

UNCTAD (United Nations Conference on Trade and Development). 2006. *The Palestinian War-Torn Economy: Aid, Development and State Formation.* Geneva: United Nations. Available at http://unctad.org/en/docs/gdsapp20061_en.pdf.

CHAPTER 7

# Economic Considerations in Implementing a Parallel States Structure

RAPHAEL BAR-EL

## ECONOMIC STRUCTURE AND GOALS

The Israel-Palestinian conflict continues to be immune to resolution; the concept of "two states for two peoples" that was at the heart of the Oslo negotiating process has proved inapplicable to conditions on the ground. The economic component of the peace process, which constituted the majority of the text of the Declaration of Principles famously signed on the White House lawn in September 1993 and which was the core component of the "New Middle East" vision behind Oslo, has equally failed to produce meaningful benefits, particularly to the Palestinian population.

Yet even as scholars and policy-makers search for new kinds of solutions to this long, intractable conflict, it remains true that establishing a viable postconflict economic environment will be crucial for peace to take hold. This fact applies equally to the kind of Parallel States solution discussed in this volume and to more traditional territorial solutions.

This chapter seeks to clarify the economic implications of a Parallel States arrangement. In analyzing the economic component of a Parallel States solution we assume that the fundamental principles of the plan are, broadly, as laid out in chapter 1:

· The area between the Jordan River and the Mediterranean Sea, covered today by the state of Israel and by the Palestinian Authority, would be governed by two governments, one Israeli and one Palestinian.

- With some exceptions, every individual in this area would define himself as Israeli or as Palestinian. The Israelis would be under the political jurisdiction of the Israeli government and the Palestinians would be under the jurisdiction of the Palestinian government. Individuals may choose to adopt both identities, but in this case rules for jurisdiction should be defined (probably the jurisdiction in the locality of residence would apply).

- Localities (municipalities, villages, etc.) would be defined as Palestinian or as Israeli, according to the democratic decision of their citizens.

- The area would be open internally, with no borders. This implies free movement of all citizens of both "states" throughout the entire territory.

The basic economic structure of the two economies today is one in which the Palestinian economy is almost fully dominated by the Israeli economy in every aspect. There is a huge gap between the size of the two economies: while the Palestinian gross domestic product is less than $7 billion U.S. (according to the Palestinian Central Bureau of Statistics for 2009), that of Israel reaches about $200 billion U.S. Customs regulations are decided by Israel and imposed on the Palestinian Authority. The customs union is a necessary measure in order to prevent the smuggling of imported goods between Israel and the Palestinian Authority, but it imposes a serious constraint on the ability of the Palestinians to devise their own foreign economic policy. And although the import taxes are similar, the movement of goods between Israel and the Palestinian Authority is mostly controlled by Israel, for security reasons as well as for economic reasons. For Palestinians, mobility of labor force, capital, and entrepreneurship is also limited. Labor force from the Palestinian Authority cannot freely commute for jobs within Israel. Permits are required and depend mostly on economic considerations in Israel and on the security situation at any particular time. Israeli as well as foreign capital can be transferred for economic activity in the Palestinian Authority only under Israeli control. The establishment of new major economic projects is also regulated.

Because of all these factors, as well as because of historical patterns and trends of the Palestinian economy, we confront today a huge divergence between the Israeli population and the Palestinian population in terms of income levels, human capital, technology levels, infrastructures, access to finance, access to markets, and access to international networks. These gaps impose heavy constraints on the potential for both economic cooperation and economic adaptation between Israel and the Palestinian Authority.

Any structure of an agreement between Israelis and Palestinians, whether a two-state solution or a Parallel States agreement, will require appropriate economic adaptations. There are three broad targets that should guide the elaboration of any economic structure. The first is establishing a robust basis for long-term economic growth in the region, even if this implies slower growth in the short term. The second is improving the welfare of both populations, Palestinians and Israelis. This goal includes diminution of inequalities in the distribution of income between individuals (as reflected by the Gini coefficient, or other similar indicators); improvement of economic safety (as measured by poverty rates or other measures of poverty profundity); and diminution of inequalities between regions—peripheral and central regions, Palestinian and Israeli regions. The third aim is to preserve the independence of both governments, Palestinian and Israeli, to make their own decisions about their economic strategies.

At this stage, it should already be clear that the achievement of all the enumerated objectives together is practically impossible, at least in the short run. For one thing, economic theory shows that the achievement of rapid economic growth may be associated with an increase in inequality in the distribution of income. This may be explained by the argument that economic growth involves a concentration of efforts in specific economic sectors or population groups, such as in the "Big Push" theory by Rosenstein-Rodan (1943). The diminution in inequality is expected to be achieved at a later stage, mostly as a result of a "trickle-down" effect. This theory, of course, is not generally supported by empirical findings, as found in many studies around the world, such as in Pakistan (Goheer 1999), India (Gupta 2000), and Taiwan (Hsieh and Hsing 2002).

More relevant to our subject is the fact that the principles of the Parallel States structure impose heavy constraints on the ability of each government to design an economic strategy that would meet its goals. These constraints are embedded in the structure by definition. The free movement of goods within the area implies the adoption of a joint (or at least mutually adapted) customs policy, along with a joint value-added tax policy. And the mobility of production factors, capital and labor force, at a relatively low cost of communication (as compared to the mobility cost of foreign workers) may impose serious constraints on the direct taxation policies of both sides, if undesired imbalances are to be avoided. Such constraints may lead to highly significant dilemmas in the elaboration of economic policies that would be required for the achievement of the main objectives by both the Palestinian and the Israeli governments: a policy based on an openness assumption may result in negative side effects (growing inequality, heavy dependence), while a policy based on an autonomy assumption would contradict the basic principles of the Parallel States structure.

We may therefore formulate the main problem to be analyzed in this paper in the following terms: The Parallel States framework implies almost by definition the prevalence of an economic openness between the Israeli and Palestinian economies. Such enforced openness leaves room for cooperation that may contribute to the advance of both economies. On the other hand, the constraints of enforced openness may impose significant limitations on the ability of each side to devise its own independent economic strategy that would lead to the achievement of its goals, following its own priorities. Consequently, the objective should be the elaboration of a joint economic policy through which Palestinians and Israelis would try to achieve the maximum benefits of economic cooperation, and decrease to a minimum the negative implications of the constraints imposed by openness. We can see already now that there is not necessarily a win-win solution, and in economic terms heavy conflicts of interest may arise. Because the Parallel States plan intends primarily to solve a political problem, agreements between Israelis and Palestinians may deliberately take into consideration the need to sacrifice some economic interests for the benefit of political goals.

## POTENTIAL BENEFITS FROM ECONOMIC OPENNESS

The implementation of a Parallel States structure is expected to bring benefits to all sides, at least from two perspectives: the influence of peace conditions on macroeconomic growth and the influence of economic cooperation between Israel and Palestine.

The direct influence of peace on the potential for economic growth in each individual country seems quite trivial, at least theoretically (Yamarik et al. 2010, Bar-El and Peled 2000). This influence is primarily explained by three factors. A state of peace implies lower national defense expenditures, enabling the allocation of more resources to economic activity. A state of peace also results in a better business environment. In practical terms, this can be expressed in terms of a lower "risk premium," lower price of capital, higher expected profitability of investments, and, finally, higher investments (both local and foreign) in the economy. And the better business environment may also have a positive influence on trade conditions. The opening of new world markets both for imports and for exports has a positive influence on the terms of trade: higher accessibility means lower prices for imported goods and higher prices for exports. Improved terms of trade are expected to increase profitability, exports, and economic growth.

The influence of peace on economic growth in the Middle East is not statistically proved, but we can identify a significant process of growth in times of advance toward peace. In Israel, economic growth during the years 1990 to 1996, which were characterized by a significant peace atmosphere, reached an impressive annual average of about 6 percent. During this period, Israel signed the Oslo Accords, achieved a peace treaty with Jordan, and conducted negotiations with Syria. This period was also characterized by massive immigration from the former Soviet Union, as well as expanded diplomatic ties resulting from the peace process. Israel initiated or reinstated diplomatic ties at this time with approximately forty-five countries, including many Asian and Eastern European nations that had previously adhered to the Arab boycott.

A slower advance in the peace process and an economic recession characterized the years from 1996 to 1999. In an inverse test of the influence of economic conditions on terrorism, Sayre (2009) finds that deteriorating local labor-market conditions during the second (al-Aqsa) Intifada accounted for nearly half of the increase in suicide bombings during that time. Berrebi (2007) also shows that both higher education and standard of living are positively associated with participation in Hamas or in Palestinian Islamic jihad and with becoming a suicide bomber.

The other potential benefit of the Parallel States framework is that it can significantly facilitate economic cooperation between Israelis and Palestinians, as a result of the physical openness embedded in its structure. The elimination of barriers between countries is expected to open new market opportunities for products, labor, and capital, therefore increasing the economic productivity of each of the parties involved. The benefits of cooperation may be a consequence of different factors under different conditions. Most of the factors can be roughly divided into two groups: those related to economies of scale, and those related to complementarities, as defined by Bar-El and Schwartz (2003).

Cooperation between Israelis and Palestinians can take place in a variety of economic activities and in a variety of places: a Palestinian or an Israeli or a joint economic activity, located at any place in the Parallel States area. In any case, such cooperation is expected to create benefits as a consequence of the ability to act on a wider scale. Cooperation in production, such as the establishment of bigger manufacturing plants, may allow for higher levels of efficiency. Cooperation in trade may allow for broader-based consumer markets. Cooperation in labor force (through improved mobility and access) may allow for a more efficient allocation of workers by providing a wider range of supply options (workers have a higher level of access to a greater variety of employment options). The higher efficiency in the allocation of workers may also result from the creation of more widely based demand markets (employers have a higher level of access to a wider variety of skills). And large-scale projects may be more efficient if they serve more than one state: this is the case with regard to joint airports, the joint treatment of ecological problems in adjacent regions, and joint tourism packages offering a wider variety of tourist attractions. Such projects can also more easily attract foreign investments.

Facilitating economic cooperation between Palestinians and Israelis may also accrue benefits from the potential for complementarity. Today, the prevailing separation of markets of goods and services, along with the separation of markets of production factors, inhibits the achievement of higher levels of economic efficiency by both parties. One such complementarity is that one state may be able to provide larger amounts of skilled or unskilled labor force, while the other may be able to provide a greater amount of capital, or a higher level of technology or marketing ability. Another area of complementarity involves natural resources. For example, a more efficient distribution of water may be achieved through cooperation, which aims to allocate water in the different regions of each country from the nearest sources, independently of the water's country of origin, and based on overall agreed-upon distribution (as suggested by Fisher 2000). Similarly, cooperation in industrial production may take the form of distributing the production segments (backward and forward linkages) between the two parallel states, with each state specializing in the segments in which it is most efficient. And cooperation in tourism, besides the advantages that result from scale economies, may also offer complementarity benefits, such as the possibility of visiting highly attractive places in one state, and using lower-cost accommodation facilities in another state.

Another area of potential benefit lies in what are called externalities. Externalities are defined as gains or losses to a community (i.e., macroeconomic gains or losses) that result from an economic activity but are not included in the considerations (in terms of microeconomic gains or losses) of the private business involved. For example, pollution from a manufacturing plant is considered a negative externality, or an investment in technology by a certain firm that contributes to the development of other economic activities is considered a positive externality. In both cases, the achievement of an optimal situation requires the involvement of public policy.

Bar-El and Malul (2008) considered two types of externalities—those defined as macroeconomic and those defined as sociopolitical. Macroeconomic externalities include the well-known types of economic benefits generated by a business activity or by a public project (see Malul et al. 2010). Economic activities or projects that are enabled or at least facilitated by the existence of an open economy may create incentives for additional economic activities and therefore have both an income multiplier effect and an employment multiplier effect, for Palestinians and Israelis alike. Isard (2004) argues that history provides some encouragement for the belief that investment in joint projects can be successful, either as part of a more comprehensive framework or as a stand-alone effort that can grow into a much larger cooperative process. Dacey (2008) strengthens this argument by showing that the expected small gains resulting from a small-steps approach can be positively leveraged.

Sociopolitical externalities are defined as benefits that are not necessarily measurable in purely economic terms; these include regional stability, the easing of social tensions, and the diminution of international conflicts (see Bouillon 2004; Crescenzi 2003; Forman et al. 2000; Isard 2004; Weede 2004). Saleh (2004) found a significant positive correlation between the Palestinian unemployment rate and the number of suicides, shootings, and total violent attacks.

In summary, the establishment of a high level of economic cooperation as implied by the Parallel States framework would therefore provide benefits of economies of scale and of complementarities as mentioned above, as well as noneconomic benefits, to both parties. A totally open regional economic situation enlarges markets, enables a more efficient allocation of production factors, and facilitates the specialization of each party in its field of specific comparative advantage. Noneconomic benefits include the creation of an atmosphere of common interests and a milieu of intensive cultural and social interaction.

## POTENTIAL CONSTRAINTS AND DETRIMENTS OF
## ECONOMIC OPENNESS

Beside the potential benefits mentioned above, the economic openness embedded in the Parallel States structure implies an almost full exposure of the Palestinian and the Israeli economies to each other. Considering the prevailing conditions, this exposure could lead to extremely serious dangers, in economic terms as well as in social and political terms. Two main issues should be considered in the analysis of the Parallel States framework's impact on the Palestinian and Israeli economies.

The first steps in the development of the Palestinian economy would likely require policy measures toward the stabilization of foreign trade, the initiation of manufacturing activities, the control of inflation, as well as many other macroeconomic elements, while organizational structures were established and basic infrastructures were built. The current de facto customs union between Israel and the Palestinian Authority, with no separate foreign trade policies, has led to a very heavy dependence on the part of the Palestinians on the Israeli economy. The following data by the Palestinian Central Bureau of Statistics for 2009 (yearbook of 2010, p. 419) illustrate this situation: imports totaled $3.594 billion U.S., of which $2.645 billion consisted of imports from Israel (74 percent) and $92 million consisted of imports from Arab countries (3 percent). Total exports were valued at $506 million U.S., of which $441 million went to Israel (87 percent) and $50 million went to Arab countries (10 percent).

The lack of borders between Israel and Palestine could force a continuing acceptance of the prevailing Israeli policy of exposure to external markets, and the acceptance of international agreements historically made by Israel. The imbalance in the level of economic activity is further accentuated by the existence of significant disparities in the economic structure of the countries (see Eken et al. 1997; Samara 2000).

Since we may assume that we cannot expect a regression on Israel's part from its historical policy, the Palestinian government would have almost no leeway in the elaboration of a foreign trade policy that would promote its interests. The inability of the Palestinians to protect their products as a result of the existence of an open free market also exposes the Palestinian economy to unfair competition with Israeli products. The Israeli economy is not only stronger, it is also very close to the Palestinian markets, and therefore can easily defeat most competing products. A separate foreign trade policy based on customs borders between

Palestine and Israel could facilitate the establishment of protective measures that would decrease the deficit in the balance of payments and decrease the dependence on Israeli markets for imports and exports.

The same constraints could apply to monetary policy and to many elements of fiscal policy such as income tax rates, value added taxes, and so on. In sum, the result is that the Palestinian government would have an extremely limited ability to make decisions in many elements of its economic strategy. This can be already considered a loss of some degree of economic sovereignty. And the next concern to be discussed would add an element of dependence to the loss of economic sovereignty.

The lack of borders between the Israeli economy and the Palestinian economy in a Parallel States structure would lead to the formation of an integrated joint economy, or at least to two economies with extremely strong interdependence relations. Such unprotected mutual exposure may involve heavy risks to both sides.

Heavy gaps now exist between the level of Israel's economic development and that of the Palestinian Authority. Statistics provided by the World Development Report show a gross domestic product (GDP) per capita in Israel about ten to fifteen times higher than in any other country in the region (gaps are still very high when we consider GDP in purchasing power parity [PPP] terms). The research by Arnon, Luski, Spivak, and Weinblatt (1997) indicates a similar historical picture for the Palestinian Authority. And Israel has a clear advantage in all elements that are related to the potential for economic growth: physical infrastructure, human capital, access to financial sources, technological abilities, access to markets around the world, and linkages with global networks.

This imbalance between the two economies may result in an unexpected kind of relationship between them. The relatively strong Israeli economy would naturally rely on the excess Palestinian unskilled labor force, for two reasons. First, the level of unemployment in the Palestinian labor force is extremely high: 32 percent according to the latest data, published in 2012 by the Palestinian Central Bureau of Statistics, for the year 2008. This should be added to an extremely low level of participation in the labor force—45 percent, against an average regular rate of 60 percent in Israel and other countries. Second, the daily wages of Palestinians are about 76 Israeli new shekels (NIS) in the private sector and 84 NIS in the public sector, but 140 NIS for Palestinians working in Israel or in the Israeli settlements.

In the short term, such a relationship is in the interest of both parties: Palestinians would increase their gross national product (GNP) through income deriving from Israeli activities, and to a lesser extent increase their GDP through the effect of increased local demand induced by the income from Israel. Israel, for its part, would increase its GDP and profitability through easier access to unskilled workers at relatively lower levels of income. Assuming a situation of peace, Israelis have a clear preference for Palestinian workers above other foreign workers: Palestinians are mostly commuters, do not require local infrastructures, and do not create the variety of social problems created by foreign workers. Such attractive immediate mutual interest can be expected to reinforce this pattern of economic relationship, and even establish it as a deep-rooted permanent pattern in the long run.

But such a pattern implies heavy risks. The attractiveness of an immediately increased GNP for the Palestinians may lead to a much slower increase in the GDP, and probably to a slower increase in GNP in the longer run. The availability of convenient job opportunities in Israel and their implied wage rates has a detrimental effect on the Palestinian economy by creating a version of the Dutch Disease (Bar-El and Sagi 2005). In particular, it prevents the efficient utilization of human capital as educated Palestinians find unskilled jobs in Israel that pay better than skilled jobs in the domestic economy. Thus, while the medicine of free access to the Israeli labor market offers an effective quick relief for the pains of unemployment, it may have a negative long-term dynamic effect. The local Palestinian economic policy would not focus on the creation of a long-term basis for growth, through the development of infrastructure, human capital, and local economic activities with a relative competitive advantage. In the long run, the Israeli economy would also suffer from a pattern of cooperation mostly based on the employment of Palestinian unskilled workers. Today, the development of the high-tech-oriented Israeli economic structure is determined by the availability of human capital, appropriate infrastructures, and access to finance. The increased availability of low-cost unskilled workers could lead the Israeli economy in the future to paths of lower technology and more traditional activities.

The extreme openness of the economy would also be expected to lead to a sharp loss of economic sovereignty, for the Palestinians and to some extent also for the Israelis. The strong dependence of the Palestinian economy on employment in Israel leaves little room for the elaboration of a Palestinian economic policy or strategy. Furthermore, such dependence might cause extreme fluctuations in the Palestinian economy that the Palestinian government had no power to control: any recession in the Israeli economy or any marginal changes in Israeli economic policy would directly lead to drastic reductions in Palestinian employment. The loss of economic sovereignty would be less for Israelis, but still quite significant: heavy dependence of Israeli economic activities on a Palestinian labor force would limit to some extent the options of economic policy.

In short, the substantial divergence between the Palestinian and the Israeli economies might naturally lead, in conditions of open markets and free flow of production factors as implied by the Parallel States structure, to a situation of economic colonization, in which the Israelis used the high availability of unskilled Palestinian labor force for the purpose of growing Israeli GDP, while the Palestinian economy might enjoy short-term benefits but eventually slide into a state of near-stagnation. A high level of economic integration resulting from the Parallel States structure might be subject to all the drawbacks and obstacles that have been enumerated here. The highly significant differences in the level of economic development, in economic productive structures, and in the economic, political, and social regimes of Israel and Palestine create considerable imbalances and inconsistencies. Psychological attitudes and the specific fear of Israeli economic domination impose constraints that would likely inhibit any such economic integration.

Lawrence et al. (1995) have reached the conclusion that regional economic integration is an acceptable target only over the long term, and that it should not be implemented at present, even absent political constraints.

## A DILEMMA AND SOME POTENTIAL ANSWERS

The implementation of a Parallel States solution requires answers to an extremely serious dilemma. By definition, the Parallel States system enforces on both Palestinians and Israelis a few basic economic conditions: open borders (or nonexistent borders) and free movement of goods, labor, and capital. Under normal conditions, such parameters are defined by each country, as a function of specific goals to be achieved and of specific economic strategies to be designed. In this case, the parties involved would have their own goals, but they would be denied the privilege of decision-making about the level of mobility of goods and production factors.

Such an open economy, assuming a state of peace, certainly facilitates the achievement of many potential benefits, as already discussed, as a consequence of the related economies of scale, complementarities, and externalities (economic and social). However, the actual ability to realize such benefits is heavily constrained by the many limiting factors. Basically, these factors are linked to the huge differences between Israelis and Palestinians, in economic terms but also in social terms. Furthermore, the gaps between the two societies, in the forced conditions of an open economy, might cause damage at higher levels than the expected benefits, therefore disabling any agreement on a Parallel States solution.

The question to be answered now, therefore, is to what extent it is possible to design economic policy measures that would minimize the negative effects of the Parallel States economy while maximizing the positive effects, reaching a positive balance for both parties. Formulated here are a few guidelines that would serve as a basis for the development of the economy of both Palestinians and Israelis, understanding that economic, social, and security considerations are strongly interdependent.

- *Security and goodwill.* Both parties must agree that no system of economic openness as implied by the Parallel States framework can survive a situation of violent conflict. Both parties must agree about their goodwill to live in peace with each other and to improve their mutual well-being.

- *Externalities.* Economic development of Palestine is in the interest of both the Palestinians and the Israelis. Therefore, some economic measures that would help the Palestinian economy and not the Israeli economy could be justified on the grounds of the economic or social externalities resulting from such measures.

- *Independence.* Both parties must be free to define their economic objectives independently, along with the strategies necessary to achieve them. Still, mutual coordination would be required in order to prevent or decrease negative consequences to the other party, which could lead to retaliatory measures.

- *No use of monopolistic power.* Economic cooperation must be done in good faith, with no intention of economic dominance by one party over the other.

## Considering a Two-Stage Economic Agreement

As already explained, a major problem with the establishment of the Parallel States economy is the fact that the Israeli economy and the

Palestinian economy differ strongly, which carries the risk of leading to an asymmetric situation in which Israel dominates the Palestinian economy. Such a situation would be bad for the Israeli economy and much worse for the Palestinian economy in the long run.

It therefore seems wise to propose a two-stage solution: in the first period after a peace agreement, the Palestinian economy should concentrate on building its basic physical, organizational, and economic infrastructures. A peace agreement is expected to lead to a high level of involvement on the part of the international community in the efforts to reconstruct the Palestinian economy, and most of the economic activity would probably focus on such efforts.

During this period, or at least a part of it, the independence of the two economies should be maintained, through separate fiscal and trade policies. This means that economic borders should prevail, as much as possible, enabling each party to exercise economic sovereignty (with different taxes, regulations, etc.). At the end of this stage, a solid, well-based Palestinian economic structure should allow the economy to become more open in relation to Israel, through a process of balanced economic cooperation or integration, with much lower risks of economic dominance. It is hard to define the length of this period, since it is highly dependent on the pace of progress in the Palestinian economy and on the evolution of relations with Israel. A period of five to ten years should be considered.

This does not mean in any way that the Israeli economy and the Palestinian economy should be completely unlinked. On the contrary: appropriate patterns of cooperation could stimulate the advance of the Palestinian economy toward its maturity. Cooperation should be mainly oriented toward the stimulation of an endogenous economic growth in Palestine, increasing GDP rapidly and decreasing the gap with GNP, by means of investments in infrastructure, education, organizational structures, and the like. Cooperating parties would naturally be Israel and Palestine, but could certainly also include other countries such as other Arab countries, the European Union, the United States, and more.

## Labor Force Mobility

As explained above, the Parallel States framework implies a free labor market (free movement of labor). Accepting the conclusion that a natural free market could lead both economies to a market failure (in terms of business interests leading to an equilibrium that is not optimal for either the Palestinian or the Israeli economy in the long run), intervention measures should be considered aimed at achieving an optimal equilibrium between the benefits of labor mobility and the diminution of distortions in the structure of the two economies. The approach by Bar-El and Sagi (2005) states that the policy should aim at an optimal combination of two targets: fighting Palestinian unemployment and increasing local demand in the Palestinian economy, with a minimum of instability and social tension, while laying the groundwork for long-term sustainable growth with full employment. Consequently, the flow of labor should be regulated to some extent rather than left to be determined by a completely free-market mechanism. Naturally, regulation would be more easily implemented when the two economies were separate or independent, but could still be applied after the abolition of borders.

Such a market intervention can be achieved by regulating either quantities or prices (or a combination of the two). An attempt to employ direct quantitative regulation (quotas) could encounter various difficulties, and might not be sensitive enough to changing conditions. Preferable would be regulation through prices (wages, in this case), which can be implemented through several measures.

First, Palestinians would be allowed to work in Israeli businesses only after receiving a permit from the Palestinian government. A Palestinian tax would be imposed on such working permits. The tax would reduce the demand among Palestinian workers for Israeli employment, and at the same time would enable the distribution of benefits from work in Israel to the Palestinian economy as a whole and not just to selected workers. The resulting diminution in the gap between wage levels received by Palestinians in Israel and in Palestine would also be effective in preventing the "queuing" effect: Palestinians who prefer unemployment as they wait for employment opportunities in Israel, which leads to underutilization of the Palestinian labor force.

Second, Israel should rigorously apply its own labor laws to Palestinian workers, such as social security (assuring social benefits, unemployment payments, etc.) and retirement funds, so as to avoid employment distortions stemming from unequal taxation. On the one hand, this would improve the social conditions of Palestinian workers, and on the other, the higher employer costs would reduce Israeli demand for them.

Third, assuming a situation of peace and stability, Israelis should consider a gradual diminution in the number of foreign workers, through the diminution of quotas. The replacement of foreign workers by Palestinians would not bring any significant gains to the business community responding to microeconomic considerations, but it would entail benefits to both the Israeli and the Palestinian macroeconomies, as a consequence of heavy positive macroeconomic and macrosocial externalities, as explained above.

Over the long term, growth may be secured to a large extent by accumulation of human capital and skilled labor. Preparatory measures should be taken by investing in the Palestinian education system. In particular, some of the foreign assistance should be allocated to enhancing and improving Palestinian institutions of higher education, mainly by training faculty for technical and business education. The resulting improvements in the Palestinian labor force and in the Palestinian economy would in the long run make all the intervention measures mentioned above obsolete.

### Changing the Pattern of Economic Links: Cooperation in High Technology

Since the main problems related to the opening of physical barriers are explained by the huge gap between the two economies, a solution (at least partial) may be to consider another pattern of economic interaction, one more based on advanced skill levels. Currently, cooperation is based mostly on the huge supply of unskilled Arab labor being employed by the Israelis. Although this may be an efficient response to the serious problem of unemployment among the Palestinians, it does not address the need for dynamic growth in the Palestinian economy. It also does not respond to the needs of the growing population of skilled Palestinian workers and academics, who are capable of leading innovative ventures that have high multiplier effects and could be an efficient engine for economic development in the future.

A pattern of cooperation in more advanced activities would respond to some of the risks of openness and at the same time provide the opportunity to enjoy more of the benefits of such openness. The risk of economic domination is lower when both parties are cooperating on the same grounds, with a more symmetrical pattern. The risk that Israelis focus less on their leading growth engine and more on traditional activities is reduced. And the contribution of both economies to economic growth is greater.

Israeli-Palestinian collaboration in advanced technologies, innovation, and high-tech activities could serve as a catalyst for facilitating an

Israeli-Palestinian network of innovation from which both sides could benefit, particularly the Palestinians who lack experience and infrastructure in these fields. This collaboration should include strategic partnerships, research and development partnerships, joint ventures, investor relations, relationships with consultants, and relationships with colleagues (see Kaufman and Schwartz 2008).

The technological systems of Israel and Palestine are at completely different stages of development. While Israel's innovation system is highly developed (see Avnimelech and Teubal 2005), the Palestinian Authority's innovation system is in a very preliminary phase (Schwartz et al. 2008). This introduces a new challenge: the development of a network between two innovation systems that are at different stages of development. Collaboration between Israelis and Palestinians could assist the Palestinians in gaining access to Israeli innovation networks, both national and global.

The question now is to what extent such a pattern of cooperation can be implemented in the conditions of a Parallel States structure, considering the constraints enumerated above, such as the differences in economic structures, the risk of economic domination, differences in social values and attitudes, and more. All these constraints point to a need for separate economic activity. The response, as suggested by Malul et al. (2010), is the development of patterns of cooperation in high tech that do not necessarily imply an intensive joint operation: cooperation can take place while each side works in its own territory, contributing income and growth bases to its own people. In their study of Israelis and Palestinians, Malul et al. (2010) identify a few such patterns. Two main groups are virtual models and work arrangements.

Virtual models involve (1) setting up a joint database on the Internet for various activities in the high-tech field, such as availability of workers, training, financing bodies, and so on; (2) holding joint conferences with high-tech personnel from the other side with the purpose of exchanging information and in order to learn about new possibilities; (3) holding virtual meetings and conferences via the Internet; and (4) holding virtual joint employee training workshops via the Internet.

Cooperative work arrangements might include (1) developing a joint product in which each side is responsible for a different aspect of the work, and creating a joint umbrella framework; (2) establishing business relationships between companies from both sides; (3) cooperation between academic institutions from both sides in areas of research, publishing, and more; (4) investment by Israelis in Palestinian companies;

(5) investment by Palestinians in Israeli companies; (6) having Israelis market the product of a Palestinian company; (7) having Palestinians market the product of an Israeli company; (8) consultancy or participation in management of Palestinian companies by Israelis; and (9) consultancy or participation in the management of Israeli companies by Palestinians.

After such partial patterns of cooperation are established and constraints are released over the longer term, full cooperation can be developed in activities such as (1) developing a joint product in a joint company; (2) establishing a joint body for raising funds for companies from both sides and for joint projects; (3) establishing a joint body for companies from both sides to assist in marketing to the international market; (4) joint employee training; (5) jointly establishing companies; (6) three-way cooperation among Israelis, Palestinians, and foreign partners in businesses.

## Focused Regional Cooperation Projects: More Than Free-Market Promotion

The Parallel States structure imposes free-market conditions. As explained, the immaturity of the Palestinian economy when combined with other economic and social constraints may lead to negative results, both for Palestinians and for Israelis. The intervention of both governments should therefore be focused on measures that create balanced and healthy conditions for economic cooperation, instead of leaving the whole arena to the free market. One answer may be the careful designing of cooperative projects that take into consideration the distorting factors mentioned above and provide appropriate solutions.

As analyzed by Bar-El and Schwartz (2003), joint regional projects show great potential for resolving certain pressing problems, pooling the diverse strengths of Israelis and Palestinians, and laying the groundwork for increased trade, cooperation, and interaction in the fields of agriculture, industry, energy, water, tourism, and transport. L. Haddad (1999) proposes for example a regional institutional framework for implementing integrated regional water management. Projects could be conducted on a bilateral, multilateral, or regional basis, or using the "triangle approach" in which an extraregional partner is involved. This method could be useful both for complementing the strengths of regional participants and for reducing concerns over unequal partnerships.

In agriculture, significant potential exists for cooperative research on seed varieties, agricultural technology and techniques, and dryland agriculture, as well as the diffusion of existing technologies and know-how related to efficient water use in agriculture. Fisher et al. (1994) indicate for example the existence of a complementarity between Israel and the Palestinian Authority in the development of agricultural projects.

In industry, subcontracting has been widely practiced between Israeli and Palestinian firms as a joint production technique, particularly in the electronics and textile-apparel industries. There is significant interest on both sides in continued industrial cooperation, and, especially among Palestinian firms, in raising the level of cooperation through joint ventures, which are perceived as more equitable arrangements than subcontracting. A survey by Hazboun et al. (1995) indicates a fairly high level of support among both Israeli and Palestinian firms for industrial cooperation (more than 85 percent), although the percentage varies depending on the industry and type of cooperation.

The potential benefits of cooperation in the textile industry are increasing as this industry reduces its reliance on cheap labor. The textile industry is undergoing a process of intensive change as a result of evolving technologies and marketing patterns, as well as the globalization of the production process. The competitive advantage of this industry is therefore based not solely on low labor costs, but also on access to new markets and new technologies, as well as on exposure to new fashions and changing demand patterns (Meyanathan and Jaseem 1994). The complexity of those new demands may provide a base for regional cooperation.

More broadly, joint industrial parks would offer a partial solution to the disparity between labor supply and demand and the need for industrial development. There appears to be significant support for such parks in the region.

Regarding water, the most beneficial form of cooperation in the short term would come from creating the capacity to manage shared water resources (Fisher 2000). Accurate and complete data are essential for planning a long-range water strategy, and for achieving the lowest-cost solution to the region's impending water shortages. Jordan, which has relations with all the countries in the region, could organize a multinational water forum that would coordinate the establishment of a regional hydrological network as well as training programs, and would increase the capacity for cooperative planning and management of the supply of and demand for water resources. These programs are urgently needed to lay the groundwork for informed planning and decision-making. While large-scale trade in water does not seem likely in the near future, cooperation would permit more efficient use and management of existing resources, as well as the efficient provision of an additional water supply, whether through water reclamation, increased exploitation of currently underutilized sources, desalination, or imports from outside the region.

Finally, joint tourism projects can benefit from improved infrastructure and free movement. The tourism potential in the Middle East has not yet been maximized. A key site, the Dead Sea, shows potential for multinational projects, namely, the "Lowest Park on Earth," which would benefit from joint planning with Jordan. Another key site that is yet far from being fully utilized is the Old City of Jerusalem (Isard and Hara 2002).

## CONCLUSIONS

Economic welfare is certainly one of the main goals of any society. The conflict in the Middle East, and specifically the Israeli-Palestinian conflict, is one of the most important impediments to the achievement of this goal. The Israeli economy has grown quite rapidly since the establishment of the state, but there is no doubt that the permanent conflict has significantly constrained this growth and limited Israel's ability to realize its full potential. The specific factors that played a role in deterring growth are numerous and include the high budget allocations to security, losses caused by wars and terrorism, the decreased attractiveness of tourism, and disconnection from regional markets.

The damage caused by the conflict to the Palestinian people is even higher. Existing in a state of occupation and strongly dependent on measures taken by the Israelis, the Palestinian economy's ability to develop is extremely restricted. Here, too, many factors can explain the extremely low level of income and development: the inability of the Palestinians to devise their own economic policy; restrictions imposed by Israel on mobility of labor, capital, and goods; the Palestinians' limited ability to develop their own infrastructures; and of course the costs directly incurred by the conflict itself. A peace agreement would naturally remove many of these constraints and enable both parties to achieve a better economic welfare.

In conditions of peace, the structure of economic relations between Israelis and Palestinians should naturally change, since the prevailing one is unacceptable. The question is which kind of economic scheme would be best for the achievement of a better welfare for both Israelis and Palestinians. A two-state solution as envisaged in the past few years would provide an effective answer: each state would devise its own economic strategy in view of its priorities, and both states would devise together the structure of their economic relations, bearing in mind their interests, in economic terms as well as in social and political terms.

The Parallel States solution imposes major challenges in the elaboration of an economic structure, because of the implied constraints directly related to it, explicitly the elimination of any physical borders between Palestinians and Israelis. Forced openness would impose heavy constraints on the ability of the governments to manage some of the most basic elements of economic policy: fiscal policy, terms of trade, exposure to external competition. Because of the huge gaps between the two economies, openness could lead to a situation in which the Israeli economy dominated the Palestinian economy. The consequences would be highly negative, not only for the Palestinians, but also for the Israelis.

Any newly established country engages in a process of building and developing its economy and needs to consider carefully all policy instruments required for its first steps. One approach might be an agreement by which the Parallel States structure would be fully implemented after a preparation period of five to ten years, during which time the Palestinian government would not be constrained in its efforts to establish itself on solid ground, using appropriate fiscal and protective measures, while concentrating most efforts on the reconstruction of a devastated economy. In no way does this mean that the Palestinians would not maintain economic relations with Israel and other countries in specific areas. After reaching some degree of maturity, the Palestinian economy would be strong enough to confront a relationship with the relatively strong Israeli economy.

The openness of the economies to each other under the Parallel States framework, besides the heavy constraints it imposes, certainly offers opportunities for economic cooperation, with benefits to all parties. As explained above, the benefits of cooperation are generated by the increasing economies of scale and by the complementarities between the two economies. Furthermore, such cooperation generates positive economic externalities as well as sociopolitical externalities. Since externalities are not perceived by the free market, the two governments should promote cooperation that takes into consideration the links between economic and sociopolitical factors.

A cautious consideration of the very delicate question of labor force mobility is needed, in order to contribute to the solution of problems of unemployment and low income on the one hand, while preventing the negative effects of economic dominance and distorted economic structures on the other. A system of regulation of labor force mobility that would respond to this dilemma could well be the optimal solution to this problem.

In addition, cooperation should not necessarily focus on the employment of unskilled workers. Although this sounds a bit premature, cooperation in high-technology activities has the potential to bring benefits to all sides, while avoiding constraining factors. Mutual benefits from cooperation in high technology can be achieved not only by joint projects, but also by virtual collaboration, outsourcing, knowledge exchange, and other approaches. Such patterns enable the promotion of advanced activities in each locality, contributing to GDP as well as GNP. Finally, since the free market could be a distorting factor in the implementation of the Parallel States structure at specific economic and social gaps, the focus should be on regional projects, initiated or stimulated by the public sector, in the fields of manufacturing, tourism, infrastructure, and others.

Handling economic policy under the conditions imposed by the Parallel States structure would not be an easy task. Still, the openness of both economies to each other carries a significant potential of cooperation that could bring benefits to all parties involved. An unregulated free market may lead to negative results. The existence of heavy economic and noneconomic externalities requires a cautious involvement of the respective governments in order to enjoy the promise of the benefits of openness, while carefully avoiding the constraints inherent to such a system.

REFERENCES

Arnon, A., I. Luski, A. Spivak, and J. Weinblatt. 1997. *The Palestinian Economy*. Leiden, Netherlands: Brill.

Avnimelech, G., and M. Teubal. 2005. *Evolutionary Innovation and High Tech Policy: What Can We Learn from Israel's Targeting of Venture Capital?* Haifa: Science, Technology, and Economy Program, Neaman Institute, Technion, Israel.

Bar-El, R., and M. Malul. 2008. "The Role of External Partners in Regional Cooperation Projects in the Middle East." *The Economics of Peace and Security Journal* 3, no. 1: 39–44.

Bar-El, R., and A. Peled. 2000. "Peace, National Growth and Regional Cooperation." In *Regional Cooperation in a Global Context*, ed. R. Bar-El, G. Benhayoun, and E. Menipaz, 33–62. Paris: L'Harmattan.

Bar-El, R., and E. Sagi. 2005. "Israeli-Palestinian Labor Market Alternatives: Short Term and Long Term Aspects." In *Regional Cooperation Perspectives,* ed. Gilbert Benhayoun, Raphael Bar-El, and Emmanuelle Moustier, 21–34. Paris: L'Harmattan.

Bar-El, R., and D. Schwartz. 2003. "The Potential Effect of Peace on Regional Economic Cooperation in the Middle East." *Peace Economics, Peace Science and Public Policy* 9, no. 1: 1–32.

Berrebi, C. 2007. "Evidence about the Link between Education, Poverty and Terrorism among Palestinians." *Peace Economics, Peace Science and Public Policy* 13, no. 1: article 2.

Bouillon, M. 2004. "The Failure of Big Business: On the Socio-Economic Reality of the Middle East Peace Process." *Mediterranean Politics* 9, no. 1: 1–28.

Crescenzi, M. 2003. "Interdependence and Conflict: When Does Symmetry Matter?" *Conflict Management and Peace Science* 20, no. 1: 73–92.

Dacey, R. 2008. "Leveraging the Small Steps Approach to Development." Round table: Exploring the Potential for Israeli-Palestinian Economic Cooperation: Theory and Practice, November 2007, Jerusalem.

Eken, S., T. Helbling, and A. Mazarei. 1997. "Fiscal Policy and Growth in the Middle East and North Africa Region." International Monetary Fund Working Paper, WP/97/101.

Fisher, F. F. 2000. "Towards Cooperation in Water: the Middle East Water Project." In *Regional Cooperation in a Global Context,* ed. Raphael Bar-El, Gilbert Benhayoun, and Ehud Menipaz, 159–86. Paris: L'Harmattan.

Fisher, S., L. Hausman, A. Karasik, and T. Schelling, eds. 1994. *Securing Peace in the Middle East: Project on Economic Transition.* Cambridge, Mass.: MIT Press.

Forman, S., S. Patrick, and D. Salomons. 2000. *Recovering from Conflict: Strategy for an International Response.* New York: Center on International Cooperation, New York University.

Goheer, N. A. 1999. "Poverty in Pakistan: Increasing Incidence, Chronic Gender Preponderance, and the Plausibility of Grameen-Type Intermediation." *Pakistan Development Review* 38, no. 4: 873–93.

Gupta, S. P. 2000. "Trickle Down Theory Revisited: The Role of Employment and Poverty." *Indian Journal of Labour Economics* 43, no. 1: 25–34.

Haddad, L. 1999. "Policy Implications of Endogenous Growth Theory for the Oil-Dependent Countries in the MENA Region." *Middle East Business and Economic Review* 11, no. 1: 15–27.

Hazboun, S., S. Bahiri, and N. Hashai. 1995. "Comparative Analysis of the Perception of Israeli and Palestinian Manufacturers on the Economic Implications of the Interim Settlement." In DATA Studies and Consultation, *Sustaining Middle East Peace Through Regional Cooperation: Manufacturing in the Palestinian Territories,* vol. 5 (working paper).

Hsieh, W., and Y. Hsing. 2002. "Economic Growth and Social Indicators: The Case of Taiwan." *International Journal of Social Economics* 29, nos. 7–8: 518–25.

Isard, W. 2004. "A Jordan/West Bank Development Proposal: Peace Economics." *Peace Economics, Peace Science and Public Policy* 10, no. 2: 36–55.

Isard, W., and T. Hara. 2002. "The Old City of Jerusalem as a Tourist International Magnet: An Initial Proposal for a First Step Cooperation in the Middle East." *Peace Economics, Peace Science and Public Policy* 8, no. 4: 46–59.

Kaufman, D., and D. Schwartz. 2008. "Networking: The 'Missing Link' in Public R&D Support Schemes." *European Planning Studies* 16, no. 3: 429–40.

Lawrence, R. Z., et al. 1995. *Towards Free Trade in the Middle East: The Triad and Beyond.* Cambridge, Mass.: ISEPME, Harvard University.

Malul, M., R. Bar-El, and D. Schwartz. 2010. "Patterns of Cooperation in High-Tech—Constraints, Feasibility, and Benefits: Results of a Study among Palestinians and Israelis." *Conflict Management and Peace Science* 27, no. 1: 67–84.

Meyanathan, S. D., and A. Jaseem. 1994. "Managing Restructuring in the Textile and Garment Subsector: An Overview." In *Managing Restructuring in the Textile and Garment Subsector: Examples from Asia,* ed. S. D. Meyanathan. Washington, D.C.: World Bank.

Rosenstein-Rodan, P. N. 1943. "Problems of Industrialization of Eastern and South-Eastern Europe." *Economic Journal* 53, nos. 210–11: 202–11.

Saleh, B. 2004. "Economic Analysis of the Palestinian Second Intifada." PhD diss., Kansas State University.

Samara, A. 2000. "Globalization, the Palestinian Economy, and the "Peace Process.'" *Social Justice* 27, no. 4: 117–32.

Sayre, E. A. 2009. "Labor Market Conditions, Political Events, and Palestinian Suicide Bombings." *Peace Economics, Peace Science and Public Policy* 15, no. 1: article 1.

Schwartz, D., R. Bar-El, and M. Malul. 2008. "The Concept of Virtual Incubator for Peace Science, Research and Policy Makers. Peace Economics." *Peace Science and Public Policy* 14, no. 2: article 3, 1–19.

Weede, E. 2004. "The Diffusion of Prosperity and Peace by Globalization." *Independent Review* 9, no. 2: 165–86.

Yamarik, S. J., N. D. Johnson, and R. A. Compton. 2010. "War! What Is It Good For? A Deep Determinants Analysis of the Cost of Interstate Conflict." *Peace Economics, Peace Science and Public Policy* 16, no. 1: article 8.

# CHAPTER 8

# Parallel Sovereignty in Practice

*Judicial Dimensions of a Parallel States Structure*

MATHIAS MOSSBERG, BASED ON WRITTEN AND ORAL
CONTRIBUTIONS MADE DURING THE COURSE OF THE
PROJECT BY HIBA HUSSEINI, IRIS CANOR, NIMROD HURVITZ,
ANDREW CRAIG, ABSAL NUSEIBEH, AND SHARIF SILMI

## INTRODUCTION

Is it possible to construct a legal system and a judiciary in which the principle of parallel sovereignty is a founding pillar? Can two sovereignties coexist side by side—not merely in theory, but in physical space—sharing executive, legislative, and judicial power over the same territory or parts thereof? Considering the novelty of implementing a Parallel States structure, any definitive answer will have to wait for such a structure to be put into practice. However, by attempting to discuss the legal-judicial dimension of the structure as an attempt to bring the discussion down to specifics, we might begin to identify the practical challenges that the parallel states would present.

This discussion of a parallel legal system's feasibility focuses on the practical and technical aspects of sharing sovereignty over a territory, rather than on the idea's political, security, and economic dimensions. Where appropriate, we will highlight areas of conflict, controversy, and opportunity specifically implied by the Israeli-Palestinian context, and the political and historical implications that would accompany a Parallel States solution. Simply put, while not ignoring the realities on the ground in Palestine and Israel, this discussion will refrain from dwelling on them in favor of a more objective discussion of the legal-judicial issues involved in merging two parties into one Parallel States entity.

Even within the technical and legal aspects of a Parallel States framework, there are specific concerns from the respective sides. In the legal and judicial field, cultural, religious, and governmental differences will mean that issues of fundamental importance to one party may not necessarily be important to the other. The following discussion aims to formulate the basic questions that must be addressed by both sides, and presents them from a technical legal-judicial point of view. The objective is to shed light on the general feasibility of a Parallel States solution and to examine its validity at the legal-judicial level. The issues discussed here also have a more general bearing on other conflict situations than do issues such as security, which are more context-specific.

Considering that the Parallel States structure must, unavoidably, be woven into the fabric of the conflict, we will be required to address crucial issues including settlements, land ownership, and territory, as well as the attainment of justice for all those involved. These issues will also be presented from a technical legal-judicial perspective, with a view to identifying the practical questions to be addressed in implementing a Parallel States structure.

While this more technical approach will be taken throughout the chapter, it is important to examine, initially, why the Parallel States structure makes sense in the context of the political conflict that persists between Israel and the Palestinians. It may be viewed as an attempt to deterritorialize the core of the Israeli-Palestinian conflict. By this we don't mean that territory no longer matters; clearly it is at the core of the conflict and of any possible solution to it. Rather, a deterritorialization means that the basic concerns of the two sides are met without territory as the defining element of the solution or of the relationship between the individual citizen and each of the states.[1] When we look at the history of the conflict, it is worth noting that the importance of the territorial element has changed over time, a primary example being the serious consideration of land swaps by the two sides.[2] Such developments suggest that a nonterritorial approach may be better suited and even better able to meet the primary needs of the parties.

In looking back at the Zionist project, it becomes plain that its major design was to settle the entire land of historic Palestine. The project was largely motivated by the belief that establishing a Jewish state on that land was of existential importance for the Jewish people.[3] The original need, however, was to safeguard the identity of the Jewish people by creating a space where its survival could be guaranteed.[4] These facts suggest that the territorial element is of relative rather than absolute importance as a component of a solution. A structure that ensures the survival of the Jewish nation even without an exclusively Jewish territory in Palestine would appear to go a long way toward meeting Israel's core needs.

For Palestinians, the Jewish quest for a territorial solution likewise became an existential challenge. Palestinians were forced to leave their land and instead focus on threats against both their physical and their political existence, in 1948, 1967, and onward. It was not until the 1980s, when Palestinians recognized Israel's existence and its *right* to exist, that they shifted their strategy to acquiring a specific and limited territory.[5] Once they did so, the idea of a two-state solution became the plausible and widely accepted approach to correcting the historical wrong committed against the Palestinian people while ensuring Israel's continued security and viability as a Jewish state. Thus, finding a territorial solution, and dividing the land and sharing the territory, regained importance.

Until 2000, it seemed as though this territorialization would prevail in the minds of Palestinian negotiators; that is, the solution to the conflict would involve dividing the territory into two sovereign states. The precise geography of the two states was never close to being resolved, but the broadly accepted outline for resolving the problem of settlements was solidified with the inclusion of the Clinton Parameters into the Palestinian negotiating position, in which the Palestinian leadership adopted the principle of mutually agreed-upon, one-for-one land swaps of West Bank territory for land inside the 1967 borders of Israel, if those swaps were part of a viable final status agreement.[6]

The Parallel States proposal is an attempt to reach the same goal of agreed-upon final status, but through removing the barriers of an imposed internal geography of separation between Israelis and Palestinians in favor of one that promotes political independence while also encouraging integration in the political and cultural spheres. In this regard, a deterritorialized solution is not a new concept. In the pre-state period, alternative territorial options were widely discussed but never seriously contemplated, while alternative ways of fulfilling the national dream were never widely discussed but were seriously contemplated by Jewish thinkers such as Judah Magnes and Martin Buber.[7] In the 1920s, Martin Buber and others founded the Brit Shalom movement. The movement's objective was to promote mutual respect between Arabs and Jews, and it argued that Palestine should be a binational state where both peoples would have the same rights, privileges, and obligations.[8]

This was, according to them, enough to satisfy Jewish aims. However, the more militant majority in the Zionist movement prevailed.

It is crucial to understand that as the chances for a two-state territorial solution have faded, the conflict has again become deterritorialized, but in a manner that regains an existential character. For the Palestinians, the threat of national extinction has once again manifested itself, while for large parts of Israeli public opinion, a failure at territorial division has increasingly come to mean the end of the Jewish state. In light of current circumstances, a Parallel States structure is a logical step in the continued search for a solution that is not dominated by the territorial element. It represents an evolution of the binational idea and in some ways also a step toward the concept of aterritoriality suggested by Giorgio Agamben as a new model for international relations. With aterritoriality, Agamben questions the trinity of the nation, the state, and the territory, and proposes a vision of "political communities dwelling in the same region and in exodus one into the other." This theory decouples nation and territory and instead recognizes that a vibrant communal life is possible without the exclusive right to land as a defining element.[9]

The basic question that emerges from a legal-judicial, yet practical, point of view is, How can such deterritorialized states exercise jurisdiction over their citizens? One answer lies in the notion of personal jurisdiction. Applying jurisdiction to people, rather than to territory, opens the way for more than one jurisdictional entity existing in parallel in the same territory. Before approaching the question of how implementation of personal jurisdiction can be envisaged, it may be useful to ask whether there are any historical precedents for parallel jurisdiction in other parts of the world.

Even a brief overview provides evidence that such precedents exist. Before the nation-state became the norm for organizing political, economic, and legal power at the end of the Middle Ages, Europe was dominated by several judicial systems existing side by side. In addition to the political power often exercised by kings, princes, and noblemen, there were separate jurisdictions for separate categories of people and for different functions in society. The church had jurisdiction not only over its own servants, but also over certain aspects of life for all individuals; the guilds had their own jurisdiction over their members; and so did educational institutions such as universities.

In other parts of the world, different legislative systems existed side by side for long periods, and in some areas they still do. In the Ottoman Empire the different religious communities—Muslim, Christian, and

Jewish—had independent jurisdiction over family, land, and personal status matters.[10] This is still the case in many countries today, including Egypt, Lebanon, Syria, Iraq, Jordan, Israel, and territories under the control of the Palestinian Authority.

The fact that shari'a and ecclesiastical law and their respective courts exist today in Israel alongside the state's territorially defined secular law is a case in point. Although the application of shari'a and ecclesiastical law is currently limited to the realm of personal status (family law),[11] this limited application suggests that a coexistence of Palestinian and Israeli law within the same territory is plausible and not merely a theoretical possibility.

We can also look at Europe's current legal environment as evidence that legal pluralism is workable in the real world, with EU legislation stacked on top of Europe's national legislation. In addition, different "supranational" entities exercise authority over certain state functions. These functional layers of supranationality also cover different geographical areas. For example, while the Economic and Currency Union binds one group of European states, the Schengen Agreement dealing with immigration and borders unites a somewhat different group of states in different ways.

To return to Israel and Palestine, consider Jerusalem and the Old City. Although the structure of parallel states, or in this case maybe parallel cities or city administrations, is not present, Jerusalem is a municipality ripe for the implementation of a Parallel States system. There is a defined territory where Israelis and Arab Israelis live side by side with no walls or state borders. Religions exercise their own form of "sovereignty" over holy sites in the Old City alongside one another. The city, while not without serious problems and complications, simultaneously offers evidence that a Parallel States structure has potential and also affords a perfect opportunity to test such a structure.

This overview shows that legal pluralism is not a new invention. Neither is parallel jurisdiction, whether in Europe or in the Middle East. It might be argued that a Parallel States structure, with two states covering identical territory, stretches the existing examples of parallel jurisdiction. However, there is not one single formula for parallel jurisdictions, and this one can take whatever form is found to suit the parties best. The parallel jurisdictions could cover the whole geographical area or only part of it; they could cover all functions of society or only some of them. There is no obvious definition of what such a structure would look like, and the practical consequences—not least those in the legal field—would differ greatly depending on the basic assumptions of the system.

There will surely be differing points of view on the possible legal arrangements of a Parallel States system. Therefore, before continuing to specifics, it is appropriate to take a closer look at some of the basic assumptions of the Parallel States Project (PSP), so as to begin discussion as much as possible from a common understanding of the ideas.

## BASIC ASSUMPTIONS

The objective of this study is to provide material for discussion by introducing new and hopefully provocative ideas, and to stimulate others to think outside the box, not only regarding the Israeli-Palestinian conflict but also for other cases of conflict. Our goal in this chapter is to explore how the basic principles of parallel sovereignty could play out in a legal environment. The possible parameters are too multifarious to allow a detailed presentation of any one possible version of a Parallel States legal regime as the most suitable or viable way of creating such a system. We will discuss the basic parameters and how the general principles may work; identify some of the most serious problems that may arise, their elements and effects; and define which questions need to be answered in order to address those problems.

The theoretical notion of parallel sovereignty is the primary underlying assumption that frames this discussion. This idea flows from the evolution of the concept of sovereignty that took place between the creation of the modern nation-state and the introduction of the notion of divisible sovereignty as discussed earlier in this volume by Jens Bartelson and Peter Wallensteen. Parallel sovereignty can be implemented in a number of different ways, and a Parallel States structure is a logical translation of the concept into the domain of state architecture.

Such a structure involves two parallel sets of state institutions that exercise authority over the same geographical area. In theory, it features parallel legislative, executive, and judicial branches. The main pillar of this structure is that its authority is not exercised primarily over the territory as such, but over the respective citizens of the two states themselves, regardless of where in the territory those citizens live.

It is important to note that this study does not describe a scenario in which two state structures will merge to become one, or two judicial systems will become one. The question here is not how to merge, but rather, how to transfer and share sovereignty or functions of sovereignty—more specifically, how two sovereign states could share or forgo elements of sovereignty between two state structures.

In such a system, where both sovereignties in principle exercise jurisdiction simultaneously over the entire territory, both states would keep their national symbols; have their own heads of state, parliaments, and governments; and exercise other executive functions, such as managing their own foreign relations. There would need to be extensive cooperation between the parties with respect to defense and security, external border management, economic policy, trade, and labor, as well as legal-judicial matters and issues of jurisdiction.

In a Parallel States structure, there would, in theory, be no territorial borders between the two states, only a common external border. However, this is a point that could be subject to modification, should the notion of separate heartlands be introduced. Such heartlands, which will be discussed later in the chapter, could limit the extent of the area subject to parallel jurisdiction. For purposes of clarity, however, this discussion will assume as a point of departure a system in which parallel jurisdiction is exercised over the whole area.

Citizenship in such a system would depend on a citizen's choice rather than where that citizen resided within the territory. The option of dual citizenship should also be considered. It is assumed here, however, that most citizens would choose citizenship with that sovereign with whom they already identified. Citizens of the two states would enjoy freedom of movement over the whole territory and the right to work and live anywhere therein.

Simply put, the starting point of our discussion is the goal of establishing one Palestinian state on all of historic Palestine, which would exist simultaneously and on the same land with an Israeli state on all of Eretz Yisrael. The question is more complicated here because we are not starting with two equal states. Rather, we have one state that has already developed an elaborate and sophisticated sovereign government system along with a judicial system—albeit without a written constitution and no final defined or delineated borders. The other side is an interim, transitional governmental entity exercising very limited functions, and without any sovereignty over parts of what is supposed to be its territory. As it is not set in stone, the definition of *parallel states* can be developed and adapted to the characteristics and limitations specific to the unique historical circumstances present here.

Clearly, developing a functioning legal-judicial system would be of primary concern. This system would need to be particularly well suited to handling claims that involve parties who are citizens of the same sovereign state as well as disputes between citizens and entities under the jurisdiction of either sovereign. Establishing a legal system that has the trust of both sides would be one of the most substantial challenges posed by the Parallel States scenario, and it is assumed that establishing such a system will be our goal.

## INTERNATIONAL LEGAL REALITIES: STATE RECOGNITION

How could one imagine that a Parallel States structure would relate to and be received by the existing international system? To better understand how the two states would fit into the context of the international community, we must consider the international standards for statehood.

There are two primary schools of thought regarding the formation and recognition of a state: the *constitutive* and *declaratory* theories. The declaratory form of recognition is set forth in the Montevideo Convention on Rights and Duties of States.[12] Article 1 provides that for a state to be recognized on the international level, it must meet four fundamental requirements: "(a) a permanent population; (b) *a defined territory;* (c) government and (d) capacity to enter into relations with other states."[13] Possession of each criterion does not, by itself, establish statehood, as many examples show.[14] Nor is lack of possession of all four criteria fatal, as evidenced by Israel's declaration of statehood and acceptance to the United Nations without having defined its borders. The fact that precedent for accepting a state with undefined borders has already been set within the very same territory should give ammunition to arguments in favor of admitting parallel states to the roles of statehood even considering their novel territorial structure.

The declaratory model approaches the issue of recognition as a "declaration" of a legal matter of fact that the entity meets the criteria that define statehood. While many scholars favor the declaratory theory, it has its critics.[15] Whether state practice supports it over the constitutive theory is unclear.[16] Furthermore, despite Article 3 of the Montevideo Convention going so far as to say explicitly that statehood is, in fact, independent of recognition by other states,[17] states are not required to recognize an entity just because it meets the convention's elements.[18] This makes it necessary to consider the second primary theory of state recognition, the constitutive form.

The constitutive theory, in contrast to the declaratory, requires that a "State is, and becomes, an International Person through recognition only and exclusively."[19] Simply put, a state is only a state on the international stage when it is recognized as such by another sovereign. Considering that states are not legally obligated to recognize another entity even if the Montevideo Convention elements are met, it would seem that the constitutive theory offers a more realistic theory of state recognition. This theory also has its support in the academic community, although in reality, common practice may be a mix of the two.[20]

In 1991, the European Community adopted a common position on what should be required of potential states before it would recognize them.[21] Those requirements included

- respect for the provisions of the Charter of the United Nations and the commitments subscribed to in the Final Act of Helsinki and in the Charter of Paris, especially with regard to the rule of law and human rights;
- guarantees for the rights of ethnic and national groups and minorities in accordance with the commitments subscribed to in the framework of the CSCE;
- respect for the inviolability of all frontiers, which can only be changed by peaceful means and by common agreement;
- acceptance of all relevant commitments with regard to disarmament and nuclear nonproliferation as well as to security and regional stability; and
- commitment to settle by agreement, including where appropriate by recourse to arbitration, all questions concerning state succession and regional disputes.

While maintaining the right to recognize states consistent with the constitutive theory, the European Community has clearly seen the utility of referencing objective factors in that process, consistent with a declaratory model.

Under the declaratory criteria, Palestine for its part has more than 11 million Palestinians worldwide, including 7.1 million in the proposed Parallel States territory and 4.2 million in the current Palestinian territory. Palestine clearly already meets the population requirement under the Montevideo Convention. The Palestinian Authority exercises governmental control over the current Palestinian territories, though subject to specifics of the Interim Agreement, and the Palestine Liberation Organization has the capacity to enter into relations with other countries as evidenced by the very same Interim Agreement signed with Israel. So Palestine also meets the governmental and capacity for entering into relations requirements. Finally, with regard to the requirement that a state have a defined territory, questions of borders clearly still persist, but such questions will be resolved—or at least the questions will change—if statehood is being sought as one state in a Parallel States system. We must also recall that Israel itself was recognized as a state without meeting the requirement of having a defined territory.

Whichever theory is given prominence, obstacles to recognition do not appear insurmountable assuming a successful Parallel States solution is developed. Under the declaratory form, the completion of a Parallel States agreement should see both Palestine and Israel meet the Montevideo Convention factors individually. Under the constitutive form, recognition would depend on the perceived validity of whatever Parallel States agreement was concluded. This, in turn, would likely depend both on whether states viewed the agreement as fairly addressing the conflict between Israel and Palestine, and on whether they viewed the Parallel States entity itself as a legitimate state structure. The Palestinian Authority's agreement to a Parallel States structure would likely address the former concerns. In sum, Palestine's possession of a permanent population, its government, and its capacity to deal with other states, combined with the theoretical boundaries of a Parallel States entity, and Israel's current status as a state, suggest that a Parallel States system is workable under the declarative form of state recognition. Recognition under the constitutive form, however, would depend more on whether other states saw the system implemented in the territory as a legitimate state structure. Regardless, the process of recognition would be an important test for a Parallel States entity.

## HISTORICAL AND POLITICAL REALITIES

### Law in Historic Palestine

To call Palestine's legal history complicated would be an understatement. Since medieval times, layer upon layer of legislation has been enacted in the territory, with some of these laws either remaining valid today or at least having a noticeable impact on the contemporary system. Considering the number of regimes whose laws remain in force, one could argue not unconvincingly that parallel jurisdiction already exists within historic Palestine. If nothing else, the current web of laws takes some heft out of any argument that a Parallel States structure will only lead to the creation of a complicated legal situation.

During Ottoman rule, which spanned from 1515 to 1917, Islamic and civil law dominated the legal scene in historic Palestine.[22] Islamic shari'a law heavily influenced the *Mejelle* (civil code), which governed much of the territory. Beginning in 1839, extensive legal reform saw European-style law, with primarily French civil-law influences, replacing shari'a law.[23] Some Ottoman legislation, such as the Land Law of 1857 and the Ottoman Civil Code, remain in effect today.[24]

After its occupation of the Palestinian territories in 1917 and the League of Nations' creation of the British Mandate for Palestine, Britain began introducing English "common law" into the Ottoman-based system, continuing until 1948 when Britain withdrew. This British law, based much more heavily on written legislation, left Ottoman laws in place but transformed the system from one of Latin-Ottoman influence to a primarily Anglo-Saxon system.[25] At the same time, the British imposed crucial changes in laws related to land tenure, town planning, and urbanization. Together, these changes, which met with resistance from Palestinian peasants even as wealthier Palestinians used them to their advantage, facilitated the capitalization of the land, the removal of Palestinians from it, and its sale to Jews.[26]

From 1948 until 1967, Jordanian rule over the West Bank saw the legal system there transformed back from an Anglo-Saxon one to a Latin or civil law system. Legislation enacted by the Jordanian Parliament, including members from both the West Bank and the Jordanian East Bank, took effect with equal measure in the West Bank and the East Bank, and the two areas became one legal jurisdiction.[27] During the same period, however, Egyptian rule over Gaza led to fewer changes there, which meant that British Mandate legislation continued to be Gaza's primary source of law.[28]

After its proclamation of independence in 1948, Israel developed a legal system of its own, comprising remnants of Ottoman law, British Mandatory legislation (incorporating a large body of English law), and, in matters of personal status, the law of the various religious communities—Jewish law, Muslim law, and Christian law.

With Israel's occupation of the Gaza Strip, West Bank, and East Jerusalem in 1967, the Military Administration was established in the territories, and existing laws were amended and modified by the introduction of Israeli military orders.[29] Since that time, the Military Administration has changed the legal environment in the territories substantially, with roughly four hundred military orders being issued in the first four years of occupation alone.[30] UN Security Council resolutions 252 and 476 called all efforts by Israel to change the status of occupied East Jerusalem invalid. Nevertheless, Israel has moved beyond military administration and applied its domestic law to East Jerusalem, purporting to have unified the city of Jerusalem.[31] This annexation is maintained today despite numerous UN resolutions and international objections.

In 1994, with the establishment of the Palestinian Authority and the signing of the Israeli-Palestinian Interim Agreement in 1995, efforts at harmonization by the Palestinian Authority coincided with the division of the Palestinian territories into Areas A, B, and C.[32] Under the Interim Agreement, the Palestinian Authority exercises authority over both internal security and civil affairs within Area A and over civil affairs within Area B. Israel maintains authority over security in Area B and over both security and civil affairs in Area C. In light of this arrangement, with respect to Area B specifically, it can be argued that elements of a parallel system already exist, though certainly not the type of arrangement that should be a goal of the Parallel States structure.

Israeli law shares many of the same influences as laws in the West Bank and Gaza. A number of laws dating back to the British Mandate are still in force today, though they have been revised and updated by Israeli lawmakers over the years.[33] Some include the Companies Ordinance, the Civil Wrongs Ordinance, and the Income Tax Ordinance.[34] After its founding in 1948, Israel enacted the Administration and Law Ordinance, which preserved all existing laws in the territory but only to the extent that they did not conflict with current or future Israeli legislation.[35] Since that time, nearly all remnants of Ottoman law have been superseded and only those English laws adopted in Israeli legislation remain as a direct connection between the Israeli and British systems.[36] However, common-law principles introduced during British rule continue to be a primary influence on Israeli lawmakers and on the evolution of Israeli law.[37]

Despite its complexity, this history of law in historic Palestine shows that while the idea of a Parallel States legal system in this territory is a novel one, Israel and Palestine's legal history has long been, legally as well as in practice, a shared one. These shared characteristics are not merely historical, as laws dealing with land and private ownership dating back to the Ottoman period persist in both territories today and both judicial systems continue to utilize religious courts in many aspects of the law. In this regard, while a Parallel States system would encounter many obstacles on its way to implementation, with the right combination of parallel and creatively harmonized legislation, Israel and Palestine's legal histories do not appear to present any insurmountable obstacles, giving the Parallel States structure the potential to take both parties closer to a resolution than either has been willing to go to date.

## Sovereignty and Jurisdiction

A basic assumption of the PSP is that parallel sovereignty is possible, and that assumes sovereignty is divisible at all. In chapter 2 of this study, "Can Sovereignty Be Divided?" Jens Bartelson discusses the theory that sovereignty is indivisible as a stubborn remnant of the sixteenth century.[38] The theory of separation of powers, launched a couple hundred years later, was confirmation of the notion that sovereignty is divisible. At the same time, the classical notion of a ruler's sovereignty was replaced by the notion that sovereignty belonged to the people, as borne out by the French Revolution. Currently, sovereignty is generally regarded as an amalgamation of legislative, executive, and judicial powers, in line with the way separation of powers is expressed in the U.S. Constitution and was originally envisioned by Montesquieu. It is generally accepted that sovereignty is vested in the state itself, but exactly how that sovereignty is divided among the three branches of government is different from case to case.

Territoriality is increasingly losing its significance in the contemporary understanding of state sovereignty, and the theory of "functional" sovereignty—sovereignty over state functions as opposed to territory—is gaining ground.[39] According to this theory, sovereignty should be linked to political and economic influence rather than to the ability to assert exclusive coercive power within geographical boundaries. Still, in many fields of law, the reach of national laws and of the power of the courts, largely perceived as coextensive with sovereignty, is still measured in terms of territory, especially in the areas of criminal law and criminal acts.

The traditional definition of separation of powers in the United Kingdom, for example, rested on the assumption that Parliament and the royal prerogative were supreme and the courts' sole function was to uphold their will. However, this definition has evolved, particularly since the Human Rights Act of 1999, potentially paving the way for a more Americanized notion of separation of powers, wherein the

Supreme Court is charged with holding the government legally accountable for its actions. It will be necessary to determine how the separation of powers would be effected within a Parallel States structure and how the governments would be held politically or legally accountable for perceived or actual infringements of rights or abuses of power.

Accepting that the question of sovereignty will involve the three dimensions mentioned above, it must be noted that once the territorial factor is not perceived as a crucial pillar in the definition of a state, each of the branches would face questions concerning the source of their sovereignty. Apart from the legislative branch, which will be discussed below, this reconceptualization of sovereignty complicates our traditional ideas of the exercise of both executive power (e.g., the role of municipalities, the scope of application of regulatory measures, how the powers of the police will be defined, questions concerning licenses and permissions) and judicial power (e.g., how to define the scope of jurisdiction of the courts of each state, whether obtaining evidence for a trial is a judicial monopoly, how to regulate risks of double jeopardy), which have traditionally been envisioned, in some way or another, in terms of territory.

The "horizontal" dimension of a Parallel States system—to which citizens and what territory is sovereignty extended—raises a plethora of legal questions, not least in the legislative field. Traditionally, laws have been applied either territorially or personally to individuals. They are normally intended either to apply within a certain territory or to regulate the behavior and activity of certain persons. In a situation of shared territory, the application of the laws of each sovereign can be exercised only on the basis of the personal jurisdiction, with the exception of laws that are shared, or at least harmonized, between the two states. Such laws could be applied universally to the territory. Jurisdiction on a personal basis, however, would be the norm in a fully implemented Parallel States system, and the exercise of the state's legislative power would thus be directed primarily toward its own citizens.

For a more detailed discussion of how sovereignty can be deconstructed, and the horizontal and vertical dimensions of sovereignty—that is to say, its extent and its functions—see chapter 3 by Peter Wallensteen. For an interesting discussion about what he calls interaction of sovereignties and how this relates to the economic field, see chapter 6 by Raja Khalidi.

*Justice and Other Basic Political Issues*

To imagine a judicial system functioning in a postconflict situation without having addressed the basic political issues equitably would be pointless. No legal system can succeed without being seen as just by the people it governs. Such a system would be undemocratic at its very core. These issues must be considered to find mutually acceptable solutions so as to build a foundation upon which to construct the political and judicial institutions of postconflict governments in historical Palestine.

Justice is, of course, a fundamental pillar of any legal-judicial system, but in the context of the Israeli–Palestinian situation, fostering it will require consideration of special historical and political realities. Justice is for the Palestinian side a fundamental concept that has to be addressed and met in any form of agreement with Israel that is aimed at ending conflict. Justice in this context means the recognition of the right of return, the recognition that a wrong has been committed against the Palestinian people, and the recognition that this wrong must be corrected. The fight for justice is thus both a consequence of, and a corollary to, the fight for the right of return.

Refugee Right of Return

The quest for return has always been the primary objective of the Palestinian struggle, often taking precedence over the aim of establishing a Palestinian state.[40] Statehood has not always been a primary Palestinian objective—for many it has remained an abstract notion in comparison to the daily struggle for survival and the quest for return. This contrasts with the other side, where for Israel and the earlier Zionist movement, state-building was always the primary objective, even long before the state was established.

Justice for those displaced in 1947–48 and in 1967 is a fundamental issue from the Palestinian perspective, and in order to resolve that issue the focus must be on justice for those displaced and not on finding a way to appease them for the sake of resolving Israel's refugee problem. Any attempt to address the conflict must not merely address the post-1967 situation, but also deal with the entire territory, including Israel of 1948, and events occurring since 1948. By doing so, and by placing the concept of justice in the center, the Parallel States solution would shift the paradigm away from the narrow frames that have characterized the so-called peace process to this point.

190 | Parallel Sovereignty in Practice

Addressing the right of return in a Parallel States scenario has basically two dimensions—on the one hand how to implement the fundamental human right of freedom of movement for all people (of both nations), along with the right to settle within the whole territory; and on the other hand appropriate mechanisms for the actual return of those refugees who wish to do so. Freedom of movement as such should not in principle present major difficulties. The right to move and to settle is a fundamental concept of the Parallel States framework, but it could of course be implemented in stages, with a gradual lifting of barriers. The concept of core areas could serve as a provisional barrier if necessary. Entry mechanisms for refugees—over time and in numbers—as well as mechanisms to deal with lost property and other compensation issues, are matters that would have to be addressed in any scenario for resolving the conflict. For a number of specific issues there are examples from other conflict situations, such as Cyprus (see chapter 3).

Settlements

Another basic political issue of both an ideological and a practical nature is that of settlements. This would in a Parallel States scenario largely be addressed by the recognition of the right for all citizens of the two states to settle anywhere in the entire territory. It is important to note, however, that such a system would not mean that all Israeli settlements could be given a legal carte blanche. Also, the question of adequate compensation for the displaced would certainly need to be addressed and resolved. However, the Parallel States structure does present an option that would not require the removal of most settlements, as long as jurisdictional issues could be resolved between the parties.

Resolutions to this jurisdictional problem have already been suggested in the years since the occupation began, in a number of proposed plans aimed at dealing with the settlement issue, mainly by introducing various formulas for extraterritorial jurisdiction. This idea was first suggested in the so-called Beilin–Abu Mazen Plan of 1995,[41] there mainly as a temporary arrangement during the implementation period, and later taken up in a similar way in the Geneva Accord.[42] Extraterritorial jurisdiction has long been a feature of the international legal landscape—it basically means the capacity of one state to exercise authority beyond its borders, normally based on prior agreement with other states. Implementing this idea could mean that Israel would basically be given the right to extend its jurisdiction to persons residing in

Jewish settlements on Palestinian territory, and that those settlements would be allowed to remain by agreement. This idea is not far from the concept of parallel jurisdiction, should that concept be combined with the notion of having distinct core or national areas for either sovereign state within shared territory. Extraterritorial jurisdiction emanating from such core areas could be a basic legal construction for a Parallel States structure. In such a system jurisdiction could, in theory, be extended to all individuals residing outside the established heartlands. Thus an Israeli, living in a settlement on the West Bank, could remain under Israeli law in areas such as tax law, labor law, family law, and at least parts of criminal law, as the case may be—obviously some types of law, such as traffic rules, would have to be tied to territory, even if they could be largely harmonized or unified.

### Borders

The Parallel States framework presumes no internal borders or territorial borders between the two states sharing the same territory—at least, not borders as they are normally envisioned between two states. The two states would have one common external border, with the possibility of developing core areas or heartlands as population centers for each sovereign state. This concept will not be posited in detail, but in brief, the heartlands are envisioned as delineated territories located within the greater Parallel States territory where jurisdiction would be parallel to a lesser or different degree. In practice, it would need to be decided whether these areas would comprise the entire territory or only smaller portions; the latter concept would mean jurisdiction in the entire territory would be Israel-centric in the Israeli heartland and Palestine-centric in the Palestinian heartland, with both sovereign states sharing jurisdiction equally in all remaining areas. Regardless of such specific arrangements, a Parallel States structure envisions free movement of people and goods throughout the territory. The Old City and greater Jerusalem would be the ideal starting point for such a project. With its lack of internal borders and competing claims of sovereignty, Jerusalem could be the Parallel States structure's testing ground.

### Land Issues and Property Rights

Land issues and property rights pose special challenges. Despite efforts to deterritorialize the conflict, questions of land and territory remain at the heart of the dispute. Even without the added complexities inherent to Israel-Palestine, traditional territorial divisions are complex, and resolving issues of disputed ownership can be difficult. The complicated history here only further complicates resolution of what is necessarily a political question in the end. The land issue will be discussed further below.

## Water

Fair allocation of water is required for a successful Parallel States scenario in historical Palestine, just as it would be in any solution. The division of water resources should be made consistent with the principle in international law stipulating that both parties are entitled to an equitable and reasonable allocation of shared water resources.[43]

### PRACTICAL REALITIES OF IMPLEMENTING JURISDICTION

In implementing and adjusting to a Parallel States system, the two parties would be likely to face considerable difficulties, often of different kinds and magnitude. The Palestinian side would not only have to extend its jurisdiction to new functions throughout the current Palestinian territories, it would also need to prepare to exercise jurisdiction over persons living in what is currently Israel. Existing Palestinian institutions, which today have only a limited functional role in the West Bank and Gaza and none within present-day Israel, would need to confront a host of challenges presented by the Parallel States structure.

Israel, for its part, has better-established institutions operating throughout the country that could, given the political will, transition more smoothly into a Parallel States structure. Israel's principal gain would be an end to conflict; however, it would also benefit from increased economic opportunity, as well as the legitimation of its authority over West Bank settlements and unfettered access to areas of historical significance for the Jewish people. The Parallel States structure, by its very nature, eliminates an issue that has to date been insurmountable—borders. It requires that answers be found to questions regarding Jerusalem and the settlements. However, resolving the issues of refugees, water, and other natural resources, particularly natural gas, will likely be equally complicated.

Assuming it is possible for two sets of political bodies to operate within the same territory, the question still remains how two separate judicial bodies can operate with parallel jurisdiction. How can parallel jurisdiction work with two or more separate sets of laws? This is a key question for the whole theoretical construct of parallel states. We have seen that parallel jurisdictions have existed side by side in specific areas, and still do within family law, for instance. But can this be extended to cover all fields of legislation, all civil and criminal law as well as national and international law?

First, it must be noted that a full set of parallel legislation is not necessary in a Parallel States system. As has been the case in many regions since the beginning of the twentieth century, such as the Nordic countries and among the EU countries beginning half a century later, a high degree of legal harmonization can take place across state lines. A general international harmonization can also be said to be taking place in several domains, the emergence of a Global Administrative Law being one example.[44] Therefore, to the extent that sets of laws could be harmonized, or better still unified, full parallel sets of laws would not be a requirement.

There could be different solutions for different categories and sets of laws. Some areas of law could be unified and some could be harmonized. In areas where international standards and norms are being adopted by countries around the world, or at least becoming more and more respected, this process would not be so difficult. This is already the case with regard to commercial law (laws regulating international transactions), and one would like to think that something similar is also taking place with respect to basic human rights.

But there would certainly be areas in which two sets of parallel laws could not be avoided. The question remains, How should this be handled? This is where jurisdiction based on a personal rather than a territorial criterion becomes necessary. Naturally, there are laws not easily transformed from a territorial basis to a personal one. This is the case when a subject's physical location plays an important role, as with, for example, immovable property. Which laws would apply to the acquisition of new property? Which legal system would apply in relation to public transportation, environmental law, and other public goods? Some of these questions may find answers through legal harmonization, but others would have to be dealt with directly.

As noted previously, civil law, and particularly family law, would most likely not present the greatest difficulties. In these fields the parties have plenty of experience dealing with multiple legal systems. On the other hand, both Jewish and Muslim law violate international human-rights norms in a number of areas, particularly regarding gender equality and other so-called "personal status" issues. In the present two states, as in most of the Middle East and North Africa, religious law often trumps normative contemporary international law when they contradict. Of course, this reality exists equally in innumerable states, in the supposedly secular West (in areas such as economic rights and capital punishment) as much as in the Islamic world (family law, *hudud* laws, etc.).

It is up to Israelis and Palestinians to decide both within and between the two societies the extent to which their separate and joint legal systems would follow international or local national or religious norms. We merely point out that creating new state structures offers the opportunity for both societies to explore, reimagine, and reconstitute their legal systems in a manner that promotes greater respect for what the international community, including the vast majority of Muslim and Jewish human-rights scholars and activists, consider to be fundamental universal rights.

Perhaps more challenging is to imagine how to implement two separate sets of criminal laws, which can overlap with differences in religious law but extend far beyond them. One basic requirement here would be two judicial bodies responsible to their respective constituencies. More on criminal law will follow.

Considering the current segregation of different towns, villages, and communities, there is reason to believe that at least initially, the vast majority of legal cases would involve people from the same constituency, and such dual judicial bodies would not be a problem. However, more difficult issues would arise when people from both constituencies were concerned in the same case, and when those cases required the contemplation of higher courts. There would then have to be a system designed to resolve clashes of laws and clashes of competences. For example, assuming that the substantive private law (contracts, torts, company law, etc.) is different in each state, in which legal system would a civil law dispute between two individuals belonging to differing states be resolved? An additional question is how judgments of one jurisdiction could be enforced in the other jurisdiction. Of course, such conflicts already arise between neighboring states (whether U.S. states in its federal system or sovereign members of the European Union), and there is little reason to assume that legal conflicts in a Parallel States structure would be more legally or conceptually difficult to resolve than in other systems.

Regarding issues of conflicts of law, some guidance may be found in private international law. To a large extent private international law deals with solving these types of problems. It is, however, to be noted that many of the traditional solutions to "conflicts of laws" are territorial in

nature. The resolution of conflicts between property laws are traditionally resolved based on where the property is located, and those between
tort laws resolved based on where the tortious harm occurred. Such solutions would need to be adjusted in a Parallel States scenario.

As a preliminary conclusion to these remarks, one can see that implementation of a Parallel States structure and parallel jurisdiction present
difficult problems, but not ones without potential solutions. The real
problems may more likely be found in the psychology of the two states
and borne out in their political interaction as a basic lack of confidence
between the two sides. Such problems are not specific to a Parallel States
scenario, but would be of particular importance to an Israeli-Palestinian
Parallel States solution because of the close relationship that would be
required for a successful implementation. To understand how such a
scenario could play out in the judicial sphere, some key areas of law will
here be discussed in more detail.

*Constitutional Law*

As discussed in other chapters in this volume, the establishment of a
parallel system of constitutional bodies, or rather, the adaptation of
existing bodies, is not so difficult to imagine. The true challenge here
would be the delineation between the competences of these bodies and
the establishment of a mechanism for resolving conflicts between them.

Further exploration of Wallensteen's division of sovereignty into a
horizontal and a vertical dimension might lead us to solutions. The horizontal dimension concerns over whom and over what territory sovereignty is extended, and the vertical dimension concerns the functions
that are to be exercised. In the horizontal dimension, the main issues to
consider are questions of citizenship and borders. Neither of these
should pose any particular problems from a legal-technical point of
view, although there are a number of issues that need to be decided
politically—issues such as citizenship and how this should be determined. The same goes for the issue of core areas, or heartlands. Over
what territory should such heartlands extend and what legal status
should they have? Should the two sovereign states have their own exclusive jurisdiction over all legal fields irrespective of each other?

Within the vertical dimension, a number of functions would be exercised in common, such as defense, security, economic, and trade issues.
Mechanisms would need to be designed for cooperation and joint decision-making in these areas. Most important, processes would need to be

established to handle and resolve disputes between the two sets of constitutional bodies, heads of state, legislative bodies, and executive bodies. Here one could think in terms of some kind of permanent negotiation mechanism—one or several joint bodies composed of high-level representatives of each state.

A key issue would be establishing administrative divisions between state, regional, and local communities. Here, several different political and administrative architectures could be imagined, and they would not necessarily have to be the same for the two states. The whole territory could be divided into regions along national lines, or into smaller units such as cities and counties, or a combination of both. Those units, according to one idea, would then decide by means of majority vote to which state they would belong. Such a vote would most likely give a result more or less reflecting the present national division, but communities of Arab Israelis—Palestinians residing in the areas inside what was declared to be Israel in 1948—might compromise that anticipated trend. Needless to say, such an arrangement has to be combined with the right of individuals to opt for a choice of their own.

*Civil and Private Law*

Much has already been said about family law, which gives us some insight into how a civil law system could be fitted into a Parallel States system. Here, a system of parallel legislation already proved itself during Ottoman rule. Modern-day Israel is also an interesting example, though with a few serious qualifications.

There are, the world over, plenty of examples of courts in one country having to apply the laws of another country. For example, inheritance laws in many countries stipulate that it is the law in the country where the deceased was a citizen that is applicable to a deceased's estate, not necessarily the law where the person in question had his or her residence. Similar rules apply to divorces, where the rules of the country where the marriage took place can take precedence over the rules of the country where the couple lives. Work is currently going on within the European Union to unify the rules of both inheritance and division of property in divorces and similar situations.[45] Some of the principles mentioned above may be codified at the European level.

Considering the similarities between commercial transactions in different societies and the influence of international norms, commercial and business law are two areas that show much potential for economic cooperation between the parallel states. The concept of choice of forum is already essential to any commercial transaction, both within and across borders.[46]

The area of tax law occupies a central position in any state, and a Parallel States system would be no exception. Questions of where individuals and companies should be registered and taxed would have to be resolved. For individuals, this would hardly present major problems, but for companies, tax law would have to be carefully crafted so as not to create major imbalances. There is an obvious risk of a race to the bottom, particularly if companies are given the free choice where to be registered and where to pay taxes. At the same time, the more popular a state is in this regard, the more income it would bring in. Over time, this element of competition could prove an interesting incentive for good governance.

Without attempting to answer all the questions that arise in this area, it seems plausible to assume that there are technical solutions to many issues, and that civil law as such would not present a major obstacle to the introduction of parallel jurisdiction.

## Land and Property Law

The issue of land and property rights is arguably the most complex one facing the Parallel States concept. Because territory and land are the essence of the conflict and have been its focus for so long, and many de facto alterations have been made by Israel, whose de jure status has not been recognized by any other party, and are deemed to infringe upon international law as they fall outside a proper legal framework—consider the significant amount of land changing hands illegally—it seems almost impossible to imagine a legal framework that could correct and regulate both past and present conflicts over land. Here a colossal political effort would need to be undertaken—in any peace scenario, not just in a Parallel States structure—and most likely as part of a comprehensive settlement that sees the end of conflict, and of claims for compensation and restitution.

It should, however, be borne in mind that this particular conflict is not unique in all respects. As has been pointed out by Wallensteen, all protracted and comprehensive conflicts result in refugees leaving their homelands. What makes this case particular is the deliberate strategy to provide space for a new population, thus intentionally creating a refugee population that is displaced and forcibly removed. As a consequence, resolution of the Israeli-Palestinian issue will require the parties to answer tougher political questions than many similar situations. Resolution of these political questions must necessarily precede attempts to resolve the situation by legal means.

When it comes to technical-legal mechanisms, some guidance may be taken from other conflict situations, including those in Bosnia and Cyprus. In Cyprus, for instance, there was a clear distinction made between property rights and residency rights. One idea here is the institution of a property rights commission to evaluate claims, and find appropriate solutions between the restoration of rights and the use of compensation to satisfy claims.

But the issue of property rights within a Parallel States scenario goes further. It involves designing mechanisms not only for land registration and restoration of rights to its rightful and proper owners, but also for land and property purchases and land administration. Land laws would have to be harmonized and a special institution would most likely have to be set up to deal with the issue. It should be noted that land laws in Israel and the Palestinian Authority–administered areas are already similar, both having the Ottoman land registry and British Mandate registry as influences. A unified land registry or a high degree of cooperation and exchange between separate registries would be inevitable.

An important question is of course how the issue of public lands is going to be dealt with. It could be argued that all the state land currently held by Israel should be subject to distribution in a Parallel States scenario. Here a joint planning commission would seem an appropriate mechanism to set up. One idea could be that cities and larger villages are given control over land in their immediate vicinity, in order to preserve some level of ethnic and cultural uniformity or at least control over the way the land is developed.

It is probably not meaningful at this stage to carry a discussion of land and property rights much further, at least not before the more basic political questions are identified. Further issues, though, will include the geographical extent of the two state structures, such as whether potential heartlands should cover the entire territory collectively or only parts thereof, how those areas should be defined, and what and how jurisdiction would be divided between them.

## Criminal Law

Criminal law is an essential segment of public law, and at first sight it would seem that its enforcement could suffer greatly if taken on by a parallel legal code. Criminal law is essentially territorial in jurisdiction, but in theory, it could also follow the accused, as is the case in international extradition treaties. Depending on the final definition of a Parallel States structure, legal solutions to divided authority in criminal cases would differ.

The ideal situation concerning criminal law, as well as other areas of law, would be if the laws could be unified or at least harmonized. But because of the cultural differences involved, this is hardly to be expected. Such laws would most likely vary between the two states. A basic principle could be that citizens of a state should be tried according to the laws of that state, regardless of where a crime was committed within the shared territory.

Complications would, of course, arise in cases where a crime involved citizens of both countries. A "normal" choice would be to follow the laws of the location of the crime. But if the two legal systems covered the whole territory and the crime took place within the shared territory, other rules would have to be agreed upon regarding which law to apply and which court system to use. Most likely both court systems would have to be equipped to deal with the laws of both states. At the top of both court systems there could be a joint Supreme Court as a final recourse.

As for the general maintenance of law and order, there most likely would have to be two separate police forces and clear rules for their respective operation, right to intervene, and cooperation with each other. A joint "federal" police force could be set up. It might be worth noting that cooperation between the current Israeli and Palestinian police forces, though controversial, has been deemed successful. Such issues are further discussed in this volume in the chapters on security.

## Human Rights and Gender Issues

The preceding discussion has focused on key aspects of the possibilities and the mechanisms of fusing two legal systems into a new one that has in many respects an almost revolutionary character. Thus a number of substantive issues, no matter how important, such as human rights and gender equality are not dealt with extensively as such. As regards human rights, the argument can be made that a Parallel States structure, insofar as it can be seen as a bottom-up construction, to a large extent is founded on basic human rights, and thus it inherently incorporates a human rights perspective. The same goes partly for gender equality. In a Parallel States vision, close attention must be paid when discussing implementation, to avoid the risk of affecting the existing (from a gender perspective already highly unsatisfactory) situation in a negative way, not least considering the role of religiously based legislation in the discussion.

Even if a Parallel States vision, as a conflict resolution mechanism, is aimed at improving the situation for all people in the region, it must be recognized that it is dealing with the constitutional framework rather than the material contents of the legislation. Thus, even if it deals with issues such as the relation between religious law and state law in each society, it is not primarily aimed at influencing the legislation's contents as such, but focuses on the framework within which these contents can be dealt with.

What would happen with the present position of religious law concerning issues related to personal status would in principle be up to the legislative bodies of the respective sides to decide. The Parallel States vision is not designed inherently to challenge social and religious legislation and issues in their contents, however important those may be. Rather, it should be seen as a way of erecting a new legal system within which change is possible.

That being said, neither is a Parallel States structure aimed at preserving the existing balance of power in the societies. Its ultimate goal is to establish two democratic states, and this goal by necessity contains the ambition to address human rights and gender issues. Gender equality is both a goal in itself and a precondition for long-term, stable democratic development. And democracy, peace, and stability are at the same time necessary preconditions for successful attainment of gender equality and respect for human rights.

However, the Parallel States framework also represents a mechanism for change, and thus offers the possibility of introducing new and materially different legislation. Moreover, the process is foreseen to involve an international component, which means that there would be opportunities for influencing the situation by bringing international norms to the forefront in the process of change. With international norms and standards thus more present as standards and benchmarks for the two societies' legislation, new possibilities should open for a modernization and mainstreaming of their legislation also in regard to human rights and gender issues.

## CONCLUDING OBSERVATIONS

It is hardly possible to formulate any definite conclusions on the basis of this brief and general overview regarding the potential legal-judicial landscape of a Parallel States structure. This is especially true when only a handful of the legal issues involved have been mentioned and summarized. Some very general observations may nevertheless be made.

First, it is obvious that the entire construct of parallel states is politically and legally complicated and adds complexities to an already difficult judicial situation. Second, we can return to the basic question initially posed: is it at all feasible to construct a legal-judicial system based on the principle of parallel sovereignty? This question may most likely be answered in the affirmative. It is arguable whether such a system would be too complicated to be practically or politically feasible, but that remains another matter. There does seem to be considerable evidence that parallel systems have functioned in Palestine for centuries, during Ottoman times and later, and even in some respects into the present day. Even if no definite answer to the question of a Parallel States structure's feasibility flows from the foregoing overview, one may still justify the effort of discussion by referring to the obvious need for additional creative thinking in addressing the current stalemate that continues to mar the Israeli-Palestinian question.

A final observation is the clear need to focus on the political dimensions in the first place, and to recognize that the legal questions must follow the political ones. As one of the lawyers participating in the project's discussions put it, "give the lawyers a politically determined definition, and they will come up with an appropriate legal solution."

## NOTES

1. In this respect, a Parallel States solution approaches the conflict from a fundamentally different direction than do current efforts at a two state-solution, which are based on the principle of land for peace as enunciated in the 1993 Declarations of Principles.

2. Palestine Liberation Organization (PLO), Negotiations Affairs Department, *Territory Non-Paper* (May 2010), available at www.nad-plo.org /userfiles/file/Non-Peper/Territory%20Non-Paper%202010.pdf.

3. The World Zionist Organization, *Lexicon of Terms*, "The Knesset," available at www.knesset.gov.il/lexicon/eng/wzo_eng.htm (last visited October 4, 2012).

4. See Mark Tessler, *A History of the Israeli-Palestinian Conflict* (Bloomington: Indiana University Press, 1994), for discussion of an alternative proposal for Jewish settlement in Great Britain's East African colonies.

5. PLO Negotiations Affairs Department, *Territory Non-Paper*.

6. PLO Negotiations Affairs Department, *Territory Non-Paper*.

7. See generally Judah Magnes, "Toward Peace in Palestine," *Foreign Affairs* 21 (1943): 239; Martin Buber, *Paths in Utopia* (1946; in Hebrew).

8. Adi Gordon, review of *Between Zionism and Judaism: The Radical Circle in Brith Shalom, 1925–1933* by Shalom Ratzabi, *Jewish Quarterly Review* 94, no. 2 (2004): 422–27.

9. Giorgio Agamben, *Homo Sacer: Sovereign Power and Bare Life*, trans. Daniel Heller-Roazen (Palo Alto, Calif.: Stanford University Press, 1998).

10. Including marriage, divorce, inheritance, adoption, *waqf*, and trusts.

11. Israeli Ministry of Justice, www.justice.gov.il/MOJHeb/BatiDinHashreim/ (last visited September 27, 2012).

12. See generally Montevideo Convention on Rights and Duties of States, available at www.palestine-studies.org/files/montevideo.pdf.

13. Montevideo Convention, Article 1, supra n. 6; emphasis in original.

14. Ian Brownlie, *Principles of Public International Law,* 5th ed. (Oxford: Clarendon Press, 1999).

15. See William Thomas Worster, "Law, Politics, and the Conception of the State in State Recognition Theory," *Boston University International Law Journal* 27 (Spring 2009): 115, 119.

16. See Worster, "Law, Politics, and the Conception of the State"; Malcolm N. Shaw, *International Law,* 5th ed. 369 (Cambridge: Cambridge University Press, 2003), 369.

17. Montevideo Convention, Article 3, supra n. 12.

18. See Worster, "Law, Politics, and the Conception of the State," 119, supra n. 15.

19. See generally Lassa Oppenheim, *International Law: A Treatise,* 8th ed., ed. Hersch Lauterpacht (London: Longman, 1955).

20. *See* Worster, "Law, Politics, and the Conception of the State," 120, supra n. 15.

21. European Community, "Declaration on the 'Guidelines on the Recognition of New States in Eastern Europe and in the Soviet Union,'" *International Legal Materials* 31, no. 6 (December 16, 1991): 1485–87 at 1485.

22. See Hiba Husseini and Diana Buttu, *The Legal and Institutional Structure of the State of Palestine: The Case for a Hybrid Legal System,* report presented to the British Foreign Office (2008), 31–32.

23. Viktoria Wagner, *Palestinian Judiciary and the Rule of Law in the Autonomous Areas* (Jerusalem: PASSIA, 2000), 30.

24. See Wagner, *Palestinian Judiciary.*

25. See Husseini and Buttu, *Legal and Institutional Structure,* 32–33, supra n. 21.

26. For a detailed discussion of the changes in land tenure and urban planning, and Palestinian resistance, see Mark LeVine, *Overthrowing Geography: Jaffa, Tel Aviv, and the Struggle for Palestine, 1880–1948* (Berkeley: University of California Press, 2005).

27. Wagner, *Palestinian Judiciary,* 36–37, supra n. 13.

28. Al-Mustakbal Foundation for Strategic and Policy Studies, Report presented to CIDA on the Palestinian Authority Justice Institutions (2010), 3–4 (unpublished report on file with author).

29. See Kathleen Cavanaugh, "The Israeli Military Court System in the West Bank and Gaza," *Journal of Conflict and Security Law* 12, no. 2 (2007): 197, 200; Brigadier General Uri Shoham, "The Principle of Legality and the Israeli Military Government in the Territories," *Military Law Review* 153 (Summer 1996): 245, 251–52.

30. See Raja Shehadeh, *The Law of the Land: Settlements and Land Issues under Israeli Military Occupation* (Jerusalem: PASSIA, 1993).

31. See UN Department of Public Information, *The Question of Palestine & the United Nations: The Status of Jerusalem* (March 2003), www.un.org/Depts /dpi/palestine/.

32. Al-Mustakbal Foundation for Strategic and Policy Studies, *Developing a Palestinian Roadmap for Legislative Reform in the Business Sector* (September 26, 2006), 19, available at www.almustakbal.org/publications/Palestinian%20 Legis%20Roadmap%20English%20Final%20March%2007.pdf; *The Israeli-Palestinian Interim Agreement on the West Bank and the Gaza Strip,* (September 28, 1995), available from the Israel Ministry of Foreign Affairs at www .mfa.gov.il/MFA/Peace+Process/Guide+to+the+Peace+Process/THE+ISRAELI-PALESTINIAN+INTERIM+AGREEMENT.htm.

33. Zvi Caspi, "Introduction to the Legal System," in *Israeli Business Law: An Essential Guide,* ed. Alon Kaplan (The Hague: Kluwer, 1999), 9.

34. Caspi, "Introduction to the Legal System," 9.

35. Caspi, "Introduction to the Legal System," 9.

36. Caspi, "Introduction to the Legal System," 9.

37. Caspi, "Introduction to the Legal System," 9.

38. See generally Jens Bartelson, "On the Indivisibility of Sovereignty," *Republics of Letters: A Journal for the Study of Knowledge, Politics, and the Arts* 2, no. 2 (March 11, 2011), available at http://arcade.stanford.edu/rofl /indivisibility-sovereignty.

39. Marshall J. Breger, "The Future of Jerusalem: A Symposium: Jerusalem— Some Jurisprudential Aspects," *Catholic University Law Review* 45 (Spring 1996): 661, 683–84.

40. Khaled Abu Toameh, "Abbas: Palestinians Will Never Neglect 'Right of Return,'" *Jerusalem Post* (May 14, 2011).

41. *The Beilin–Abu Mazen Document* (October 31, 1995), Jewish Virtual Library, available at www.jewishvirtuallibrary.org/jsource/Peace/beilinmazen.html.

42. Palestinian Peace Coalition, *The Geneva Accord: A Model Israeli-Palestinian Peace Agreement,* available at www.geneva-accord.org/mainmenu/english.

43. UN General Assembly, *Resolution Adopted by the General Assembly on the Law of the Non-Navigational Uses of International Watercourses,* U.N. Doc. A/RES/51/229, Art. 5 (May 21, 1997).

44. Benedict Kingsbury, Nico Krisch, and Richard B. Stewart, "The Emergence of Global Administrative Law," *Law and Contemporary Problems* 68 (Summer–Autumn 2005): 15–61, available at www.iilj.org/GAL/documents /TheEmergenceofGlobalAdministrativeLaw.pdf.

45. "Inheritance Simplified under New Cross-Border EU Rules," EU Business Web site (March 13, 2012), available at www.eubusiness.com/news-eu /justice-lifestyle.fo5.

46. This is due in large part to the globalization of business law. The WTO, international arbitration, and dispute settlement mechanisms, as well as the laws governing contracts, are more international by nature than other areas of the law. The concept of choice of forum is essential in any cross-border business transaction, and is very often invoked these days even when two entities of the same nationality find that a different venue and set of rules would be more acceptable for their dealings. Choice of forum could be introduced as a new essential element to any contract made within the Parallel States territory.

CHAPTER 9

# Religion in the Palestinian-Israeli Conflict

*From Obstacle to Peace to Force for Reconciliation?*

MARK LEVINE AND LIAM O'MARA IV

Among the main concerns of participants in the Parallel States Project (PSP) has been to imagine a two-state solution that maintains a Jewish identity for Israel while addressing the Palestinian requirements both for statehood and for the preservation and development of their unique identity.[1] In both cases the link between religion and the formation of national discourses is crucial, as is religion's psychological function in shaping the contours of the identities of each and the conflict between them. It is thus clear that any discussion of parallel states must involve considerable attention to culture and religion. The Israeli-Palestinian conflict may have its origins in a nationalist conflict over land but it has been significantly "culturalized," and this is nowhere more obvious than in the religious rhetoric on both sides.

Questions have been raised about how parallel sovereignty would address the relation between religion and territoriality in the two nationalist discourses; and about how, in a post- (or at least non-) territorial division of sovereignty, these two powerful religiously grounded identities could allow space for a common, officially secular public sphere. It is difficult at this early stage to talk about a religiously grounded sovereignty in the Jewish-Israeli and Palestinian Arab context that would be "post"-territorial. What's more, assuming this issue *could* be addressed, the complexity of organized religious institutions within a Parallel States framework requires far more consideration than it has yet received.

What does seem clear is that in any postconflict arrangement, spaces that are shared by the two national communities would have to be "secular," at least officially. We place the word in scare quotes because the notion of a "secular" space that is free of religious symbolism, meaning, or power (public, private, or political) has been problematized by scholars in recent years.[2] Nevertheless, at the level of politics and everyday life, there is an equally clear need for common spaces where religious particularities, prejudices, and ideologies will not interfere with peaceful and even productive contact and coexistence—both within and between the two ethno-religious communities.

By understanding the changing and in many ways more prominent role of religion—particularly on the Jewish side—in the territorial struggles at the heart of the Israeli-Palestinian conflict, we can better appreciate the bridges that must be built before a Parallel States structure could be implemented. At the same time, only by appreciating the unique concerns of the different constituencies can their needs be addressed, and religious belief—Jewish, Christian, and Muslim alike—potentially become a more positive force for peace and justice in this tortured landscape.

## RELIGION AND NATIONALISM

To one degree or another, religion underlies a great many ostensibly secular identities and ideologies globally, particularly modern national ones.[3] Where some analysts posit the premodern (in this case, religious) ideology reinforcing and structuring the modern (in this case, national) one, a Parallel States perspective sees these discourses more holistically, with the two more implicately related and each playing an equal role in generating and shaping the other.[4] Understanding and accounting for the hybrid nature of these identities—that is, the fusion of simultaneously overlapping and contradicting nationalist and religious discourses—must be at the core of any Parallel States enterprise, precisely because under current conditions the merging of religious covenant and secular project has produced political identities that brook no compromise.

Of the many religious subgroups within Israeli and Palestinian societies, four are most relevant for a Parallel States analysis: the Palestinian Hamas, the Israeli settler movement, the Palestinian Kairos movement, and the Israeli Haredim (ultra-Orthodox). Each of these groups has shades of complexity that make generalization difficult. It is well known that Hamas and the settlers have contributed directly to the violent hostility. What is less known is that both movements have laid out visions of the future that could include coexistence between the two peoples. The Kairos initiative undertaken by Palestinian Christians is almost entirely unknown. And the radicalization of the Haredim and their increasing nationalism is little known outside of Israeli sociology departments.

## NATIONALISM AND ISLAMISM IN PALESTINE

Islam has been a central component of Palestinian national identity since the latter's emergence in the late nineteenth century.[5] During the British era, the role of Islam was reflected institutionally in the role played by the grand mufti of Jerusalem, Haj Amin al-Husseini, as the putative leader of the nationalist movement; in the role of organizations such as the Muslim-Christian Association in shaping Palestinian political life; and in the role of religiously grounded leaders of the pre-1948 resistance, such as Izz ad-Din al-Qassam, the Syrian militant whose martyrdom in 1935 helped to touch off the Great Revolt of 1936–39, profoundly affecting the trajectory of Palestinian nationalism to the present day.[6]

While the Palestine Liberation Organization (PLO) and its offshoots beginning in the 1960s were all officially secular, religion became increasingly prominent in Palestinian political life after the 1967 defeat, as part of the broader rise of political Islam across the Middle East and North Africa in response to the failure of pan-Arab nationalist ideologies to defeat Israel. The rise of political Islam was enhanced by the spread of the Salafi doctrine and influence, mainly financed (through mosques, universities, etc.) by the oil-rich Gulf regimes after 1973. Finally, the success of the Islamic Revolution in Iran inspired militants in Palestine and beyond; some groups in Palestine have received steady financial, moral, logistical, and military support (indirectly, through Iran's relationship with Hezbollah) since the Khomeini period.

Hamas, the Islamic Resistance Movement *(al-Haraka al-Muqawama al-Islamiyya)*, reflects the ambivalent coincidence of religious and nationalist discourses in Palestine. The movement's roots lie in the Palestinian Muslim Brotherhood, which founded a Palestinian branch with Husseini at its head in 1935. The movement was divided, however, during the two decades between 1948 and 1967, with the Gaza and West Bank branches having very different experiences under Egyptian and Jordanian rule.

During the first two decades of the Israeli occupation, the Palestinian Brotherhood worked to build its infrastructure and organization within Palestinian society, "preparing the liberation generation" along a cultural-educational model.[7] The goal of such preparation was "to launch a comprehensive effort at cultural renaissance designed to instill true Islam in the soul of the individual and, following that renaissance, to embark on the path of liberation."[8]

The latter words are drawn from a book titled *Signposts along the Road to the Liberation of Palestine (Ma'alim fil-tariq ila tahrir filastin)*, a clear allusion to the activist-militant philosophy of Muslim Brotherhood ideologue Sayyed Qutb, which was itself based on a strongly cultural politics.[9] The organization emerged directly from the Mujamma' al-Islami (Islamic Center, Gaza), which was established by Hamas founder Sheikh Ahmed Yassin in 1973 and provided a network of social services that functioned as a parallel system to the meager (or absent) Israeli occupation services.[10]

The center's focus on religious and social activities allowed it to garner public support without appearing to threaten either the PLO's hegemonic position among Palestinians or the Israeli occupation authorities.[11] So successful was this strategy that the Israeli intelligence services secretly funded the movement—including, in its earliest days, Hamas—as a way to counterbalance Fatah, whose explicitly nationalist agenda was perceived to be a more direct threat to Israeli control of the Occupied Territory.[12]

Hamas itself was formed in December 1987 by members of the Brotherhood who wanted to take a more activist stance against Israel. It was born amid the political chaos of the first Intifada, and the interplay between nationalism and Islamism help to define the movement. Its jihad and public-service activities grew in parallel, with several militant and intelligence-security arms emerging concurrently with an expanding network of services. Both operated within a complex dynamic, with an internal (Gaza-based) and an external (Syria-based) hierarchy; these have not always agreed on policy.[13]

The militant piety of the Muslim Brotherhood, Islamic Center, and then Hamas, a combination of social services provision, educational outreach, religious coercion, and violence—primarily against Israelis, but also against Palestinians—has been a defining feature of Islamist politics in the Occupied Territory ever since. At the same time, the Brotherhood-Hamas lineage is not the only one in Palestine. The Palestinian Islamic Jihad in fact emerged almost a decade before Hamas as a militant, Iranian-inspired splinter from the Brotherhood, while more recent hard-core al-Qaeda–inspired groups such as Ansar al-Sunna and the Mujahideen Shura council have taken root in Gaza and more broadly in the Occupied Territory.[14]

### A New Theology of Resistance

The description of Palestine's status in Islamic law is of crucial importance to understanding Hamas's views. From its founding Charter (Article 11), the movement declared that "the land of Palestine has been an Islamic *Waqf* throughout the generations; and until the Day of Resurrection, no one can renounce it or part of it, or abandon it or part of it." Elsewhere Palestine is declared to be "holy in its entirety."[15] This understanding of Palestine as a *waqf* (a sacred endowment), and an inalienable one at that, sacred in whole, was in fact a striking innovation without historical basis in Islamic law or theology.

Hamas's justification is grounded in a historical understanding of the importance of Jerusalem and its environs, an idea built up in the wake of the Crusades and of Mamluk propaganda.[16] But Hamas departs from this well-established position by claiming that the entirety of Palestine is similarly holy to Islam. Their argument appears designed to counter the Jewish halachic (legal) claims to religiously grounded sovereignty over Eretz Yisrael, which is in turn based on an argument that the land was given to Jews by God in an inalienable covenant. The *waqf* notion, thus expanded, provides an Islamic analogue to this covenant.

Yet these claims mark an innovation in the understanding of *waqf* land as, in essence, both holy and inalienable, neither of which had previously been considered essential or even typical features of *waqf* land. They also mark a departure from earlier justifications for Palestinian claims to Jerusalem, which did not use such Islamic legal arguments as part of their rhetoric. In short, Hamas's identity discourse reflects a broader nationalization and territorialization of the movement's pan-Islamic ideals. At the same time, such discourses are in fact a common response to the perceived lack of security—economic, political, territorial, and even "ontological"—associated with the onset of contemporary neoliberal globalization, which became the dominant hegemonic order in Israel-Palestine by the 1980s.[17] However normalized (and from a political and diplomatic perspective, hardened and inflexible) the innovative integration and synthesis of religion and nationalism expressed by Hamas has become, it potentially offers a crucial opening for consideration of a

Parallel States–inspired political solution by ostensibly militant, religiously inspired Palestinians, the implications of which will be discussed in the conclusion.

## Culture, Nationalism, Globalization, and Jihad

Hamas has from the start articulated a uniquely inflected religious and nationalist discourse, one that has territorialized militant Islamist politics and ideology in a much more concrete and explicit manner than the ideologies of most other militant Islamist movements in the Muslim world. This facet of Hamas's ideology and practice is, not surprisingly, the part that has received the most attention from analysts. Yet Hamas also has a powerful cultural discourse that is important to understanding both its policies and its potential reactions to a Parallel States discourse.

Because of its specifically religious grounding, whereas the PLO has long focused almost exclusively on "national liberation" as its raison d'être, Hamas from the start had a broader agenda, describing itself as struggling to defend the "Muslim person, Islamic culture, and Muslim holy sites."[18] Its nationalist concerns are thus inseparable from its approach to Islam, and the organization has made no secret of its desire to establish an explicitly Islamic polity.

In this sense, it also becomes possible to see Hamas as a cultural response to the globalized Oslo vision of a "New Middle East" (with Israel naturally as its cultural as well as economic engine), which excludes Palestinians from its scope no less than the more explicitly nationalist vision of traditional Zionism.[19] Like other Islamist movements, Hamas has feared the "cultural invasion" at the heart of the neoliberal paradigm reflected in Oslo's "New Middle East" discourse as much as the more concrete impact of the occupation,[20] calling for a "cultural struggle" to establish *"Falastin Islamiyya min al-bahr ila al-nahr"* (an Islamic Palestine from the sea to the [Jordan] River) while at the same time attempting to rally Christian Palestinians around a common set of social and political goals.[21]

What is crucial about this "cultural turn" by Hamas is that it bears a close resemblance to the cultural critique of Orthodox Jewish groups within Israel. Potentially, despite their mutual antipathy at the level of nationalist discourse and even religious chauvinism, the cultural politics of groups like Hamas broadly mirror those of conservative Israeli Jewish forces.[22] On the other hand, both the socially conservative, highly patriarchal, and authoritarian tendencies of these movements and their records of corruption when in positions of political power suggest a low likelihood that they could work to build a new social and political consensus in a state that doesn't cater to their narrow religious, economic, and political needs and ideologies.[23]

## FROM ZIONIST NATIONALISM TO JEWISH FUNDAMENTALISM

Before the rise of Zionism as a nationalist ideology, almost all Jews believed that a return en masse to the Holy Land (never mind the reestablishment of Jewish sovereignty there) was neither possible nor permissible before the coming of the Messiah. In this sense, Zionism was a radical challenge to existing Jewish theology, and it took decades—and to some extent the Holocaust and the "miraculous" victories of 1948 and 1967—before a clear majority of Jews around the world adopted a Zionist worldview.

The parents of Zionism were not Judaism and tradition, but anti-Semitism and nationalism. The ideals of the French Revolution spread slowly across Europe, finally reaching the Pale of Settlement in the Russian Empire and helping to set off the *Haskalah,* or Jewish Enlightenment. This engendered a permanent split in the Jewish world, between those who held to a halachic or religious-centric vision of their identity and those who adopted in part the racial rhetoric of the time and made the Jewish people into a nation. This was helped along by the wave of pogroms in Eastern Europe that set two million Jews to flight; most wound up in America, but some chose Palestine. A driving force behind this was the Hovevei Zion movement, which worked from 1882 to develop a "Hebrew" identity that was distinct from Judaism as a religion.[24]

It is well known that many early Zionist leaders were avowedly secular, even atheists. Yet despite their overt attempts to separate Zionism from its Jewish religious roots, it was inevitable that the two components of identity would not long remain separate in practice. Later Zionist leaders came to understand that the only way to secure economic viability for the fledgling Jewish *yishuv* (community) in Palestine was through the "conquest of labor" *(kibbush ha'avoda)* and the "conquest of land" *(kibbush ha'karka),* which radicalized Zionism into a "militant nationalist movement."[25] In furtherance of their goal—a total segregation of Jewish and Arab societies—these leaders increasingly used religion as well as ethnicity as markers of separation.

While historical Judaism was increasingly used as a broad marker to justify the rights of Jewish immigrants to live in, and have sovereignty over, Palestine in the pre-1948 period, there was as yet no specific set of theological arguments to justify the forcible expropriation of land. This is not surprising in practical terms, as Jews did not yet have the ability to do so, and much of the 1948 territory of Israel was, in Theodor Herzl's words, "secular" or "profane" land (at least compared to Jerusalem and the West Bank, which came under Israeli control in 1967). Few, if any, Zionist leaders bothered to make a religious case for Jewish sovereignty in Eretz Yisrael.

Things changed when Israel conquered the remainder of Jerusalem—including the Western Wall, Judaism's holiest site—and the West Bank and Gaza during the 1967 war. This event was experienced by many Israelis and Jews more broadly as an event of extreme religious significance. Not only had the war delivered the very heartland of biblical Israel and the Kingdom of Judah, but it came at a time when many Israelis feared that the existence of their state was in jeopardy. The swift victory against three Arab armies was perceived as an act of divine Providence, and it was in this moment that religious Zionism was born. Its defining feature was not the establishment of a Jewish nation-state, but rather the retention and settlement of the whole of Eretz Yisrael, in line with the covenants that God made with their forebears.

It has long been a commonplace to argue that the 1967 defeat profoundly reshaped Arab politics, helping to inspire and enable the rise of Islamism throughout the Middle East (especially with the huge spike in oil prices after the next regional war, in 1973). Its impact on Israeli politics and Jewish religious expression in Israel was just as profound, and equally religiously grounded. The 1967 war changed the contours of Israeli society by encouraging the growth of what Ehud Sprinzak terms "Zionist fundamentalism." By the 1980s this trend had become "the most dynamic social and cultural force in Israel."[26] Like its Islamic counterpart, Jewish fundamentalism was a reaction against globalization and the secular orientation of early Zionism, and a "search for wholeness in a materialistic world," at the same time that it responded to territorial imperatives after the conquest.[27]

The "reopening of the frontier" that occurred with the conquest of the West Bank and Gaza helped to recharge a somewhat moribund Jewish nationalism, at the same time that a new Israeli-born generation was coming of age for whom Labor Zionism held less attraction. In addition, many of the Middle Eastern Jews who had immigrated in the two decades following 1948 held decidedly more religious and messianic beliefs. Control over the Occupied Territory was further entrenched by the Israeli victory in the 1973 war. It was out of this combined milieu that Gush Emunim (bloc of the faithful) was born in 1974. The new movement represented a far bolder, more assertive religiosity in the service of nationalist goals, even as it frequently flouted the state's authority in furtherance of its religious ambitions.[28]

The ideological roots of Gush Emunim were derived from the writings of Avraham Yitzhak Kook, a spiritual father of the Revisionist Zionist movement, and his son, Zvi Yehuda Kook. Both men argued that Zionism, even that of secular Jews, was actively contributing to the redemption of the Jews; because of this, religious Jews should work with their secular compatriots to resettle and retain the land. While their views of Palestinian Arabs and their rights to the land were in fact fairly complex, the movement that grew out of their ideas was much less so.[29] By the early 1980s Gush Emunim comprised ten thousand to twenty thousand activists, and the movement's development helped reignite the flame of maximalist Zionist nationalism at a moment of significant stress to Israeli society.

Their fusion of secular and religious Zionist ideologies and beliefs gained them popularity across the spectrum of Israeli politics, once again uniting Labor and Revisionist Zionism in a shared focus on permanently settling as much of Eretz Yisrael as possible.[30] It is worth noting, however, that while it has taken a hard line against any relinquishing of territory to Palestinians in exchange for peace, and has advocated dismantling the Palestinian Authority and "sending the PLO back to Tunisia," the Gush did not advocate "transfer" (ethnic cleansing) as some of the racist parties did, and unlike the ultra-Orthodox parties it did not advocate a religious state (at least initially).[31]

Naturally, the main arguments used by the settler movement for claiming all of Eretz Yisrael and the surrounding territories as belonging to Jews is rooted in the Bible, numerous passages of which provide the sometimes conflicting borders of the territory "promised" to the Children of Israel by God.[32] Of course, these passages, and the desire to return to the Holy Land, have always been part of Jewish theology. Yet while they provided the broad imaginary contours and historical justifications for Zionism, traditional historiography has long described the Zionist movement as arising against the grain of so-called "traditional" Jewish theology as a largely secular movement.

Such a view is problematic in many respects, not least because of a facile dichotomization of "secular" and "religious" motivations and arguments. However, it is true that while Zionism has a clearly religious historical core, in the pre-1948 era and even until 1967 most religious

Jews were not Zionist, and in fact saw the movement as a violation of the prohibition on Jews regaining sovereignty over "the Land" before the return of the Messiah. The crucial turn engaged by religious Zionism was precisely to argue that, far from violating the divine command, settling the land and establishing a state were crucial tools in bringing the Messiah, making Jews, for the first time in their history, the agents of their redemption. With the conquest of the biblical heartland of Jerusalem and the West Bank in 1967, this ideology became the heart of National Religious Party Zionism and of the increasingly religiously grounded settlement movement through to the present day. It also served as a mediating point linking theologically anti-Zionist ultra-Orthodox Jews to their nationalist coreligionists, leading to a de facto Zionization of Haredim in the past two decades, with profound effects on Israeli politics and the future of the Oslo-grounded two-state solution.

For its part, as the settler movement became more militant and controlled more territory, it became more integrated into the formerly staunchly secular Israel Defense Forces (IDF), with special units set up for Orthodox Jews. Not surprisingly, its theology veered toward that of militant Islamist ideologues such as Sayyed Qutb and contemporary Salafi thought, including justifying the murder of leaders such as Prime Minister Rabin if they were accused of putting Jewish values or laws in danger.[33] Taken together, these changes reinforce the belief that an Israeli state so compromised by settler ideology and religious nationalism will be unable to take decisions that would uproot any significant number of settlers.[34] The question becomes, How does this reality affect the kind of solutions that could achieve the core goals of the two states?

The inability of the state to act against settler interests is more than amply attested by the 2013 Knesset elections, which saw the meteoric rise of a new settler party—Jewish Home—that is committed to annexation of the West Bank. The appearance of another settler party would not in itself be significant, were it not for their astonishing fourth-place showing with twelve seats, and for the fact that high early polling for the party caused Likud–Yisrael Beiteinu chairman Binyamin Netanyahu to veer sharply to the right. Netanyahu stated flatly that not a single settler would be uprooted, and that in fact the settlements would be expanded. Further, he reinitiated planning for the E1 zone linking Jerusalem to Ma'ale Adumim—a settlement placed there neatly bisects the West Bank, making a contiguous Palestinian state nearly impossible. The new electoral calculus makes a two-state solution even less probable.

## The Land and the Book: A Paradox in Israeli Haredi Identity

As we have already mentioned, one of the most important dynamics behind the growth of religiously grounded, territorially maximalist national identities is the Zionization of the Haredim, whose ideological-political transformation is one of the most interesting cultural transformations in Israel-Palestine. Long caught in an ideological limbo—living in the Holy Land yet living as if they were still in *goles* (exile)—in many ways the ultra-Orthodox seemed to ignore the state and it them. Such a characterization would in fact be far wide of the mark. In reality, the Haredim have been crucial players in Israeli politics since the establishment of the state. Today, they have become a—and in some ways *the*—central element in the deepening and expansion of the occupation in the West Bank.[35]

Despite their important role, the Haredim either frequently remain invisible in the extensive literature on the Israeli-Palestinian conflict, or are discussed primarily in terms of their drain on the Israeli economy or historic willingness to support land-for-peace formulas because of their ostensible theological opposition to a sovereign Jewish state in the pre-Messianic era. In contrast to these assumptions, the reality is that ultra-Orthodox Jews, who have by far the highest birthrate in Israel and Palestine, have become increasingly associated with the politics of the maximalist right. Indeed, the theological and practical devotion to "the Land" has encouraged the new generation of Haredim to support extending and maintaining its Jewish character in readiness for the coming of the Messiah.[36] This ideology is more closely associated with religious Zionism, and while it is still repudiated by most Haredi scholars, it does represent the attitudes of the younger generation.[37]

Moreover, as a conformist society, they tend to vote as a bloc in elections. This has given them power beyond their numbers for decades, as they have proved to be vital participants in coalition governments, but once paired with their population growth—now about 10 percent of the total and rising fast—Haredim become one of the most important demographics in Israeli political life. Their current interests extend far beyond securing scarce funding for their intensive education system or avoiding military service, which in fact more of them now willingly perform. Indeed, the two largest settlements in the West Bank are Haredi-only cities, while their settlements as a whole are growing faster than any other.[38] This makes them active players in the policies of occupation. It has been argued that they live in the Occupied Territory only because of subsidies, but this is contradicted by much recent Israeli scholarship on changes within their self-conception.[39]

The reasons for this increasing identification with the state can be found in contemporary, nationalist interpretations of traditional Judaism. In this way, the Haredim echo the sort of evolution seen in Hamas's version of Islam. Ultra-Orthodox Judaism retains a deeply felt distinction between Jews and non-Jews that was once characteristic of the faith but has been largely lost in secular Jewish culture. The Haredi approach to Judaism is at once conservative and highly innovative, isolationist and interventionist.[40] And the generally chauvinistic character of Haredi theology, politics, and cultural identity creates a natural sympathy with conservative Zionist parties. Indeed, the overlaps among religious chauvinism, religious nationalism, and political nationalism are increasingly extensive in Israeli political culture as the occupation continues.[41]

The expanding political power of the Haredim is best exemplified by the meteoric rise of the Shas movement and their willingness to endorse the nationalist-territorial agenda of the Zionist right. The party has been a major player in this dynamic almost since its inception. And yet Shas takes its name from a double acronym: For *Shisha Sedarim* (another term for the Talmud) and for *Shomrei Torah Sephardim* (Sephardic Torah Guardians). Both of these acronyms hint at the movement's paradoxical identity: at once Zionist and non-Zionist, Mizrahi and Western, sectarian and integrationist toward Israeli society at large.[42]

Shas's natural constituency is a conglomeration of ethnicity (being a Jew of Middle Eastern or North African heritage), of class (being from a working-class or poor background), and of religion (being traditional or ultra-Orthodox in observance). As such, it draws from a much wider spectrum of Israeli society than might be expected of an explicitly Haredi party. Before the influx of Jews from the former Soviet Union, those of Mizrahi (eastern, "oriental") descent made up approximately half of the Jewish population of the state. And yet they suffered a perennial discrimination at the hands of the Ashkenazi elites. Having a Middle Eastern cultural heritage was stigmatized in Israeli popular culture, leading many to suppress it and others to simmer in resentment. This, not coincidentally, was a major factor in the rise of the Zionist right in 1977, as Menachem Begin exploited the ways in which the Labor Party had marginalized Sephardic and Mizrahi Jews.

The party's rise to power in the 1999 elections, when it won seventeen seats, forced it to orient itself toward a national, if not explicitly nationalist, audience, and address larger social issues like poverty and inequality. By 2002 Shas had clearly moved more firmly into the right-wing camp, as epitomized by the visit of spiritual leader Yosef to a Jewish settlement in the West Bank and the praise that he heaped upon the residents there, after a decade in which the party had reliably supported the Oslo process.[43] For its failure to offer such a discourse or to focus the government's attention on Mizrahi issues, the party lost six seats in the 2003 elections.[44]

A decade later, in the 2013 Knesset elections, Shas's support remained steady at eleven seats, and once-tepid support for the peace process had become a distant memory as the link between social justice and making peace with Palestinians lost whatever salience it had previously.[45]

## The Ultra-Orthodox and the Hilltop Youth

The rise of Shas and the Zionization of the Haredim are not the only interesting phenomena in Israeli ultra-Orthodox culture. Of arguably greater significance has been a movement from the opposite direction: specifically, the growing trend of settlers, especially younger ones, adopting aspects of Haredi religious practice. This adds a new dimension to the nationalist awakening in the ultra-Orthodox community: not only are some members looking beyond sectarian issues, but some explicitly sectarian populations are moving into their cultural milieu.

This is in many ways epitomized by the "Hilltop Youth." These young settlers, who are known for creating illegal outposts on hilltops near Palestinian villages, have adopted many features of the Haredi life, from their turn toward mysticism (drawing on the Hasidic tradition) to their commitment to maintenance of all the *mitzvot*. In addition, they share with several branches of the ultra-Orthodox community an indifference or even hostility to the Israeli state, which is viewed increasingly as illegitimate because of its willingness to relinquish land to Palestinians and on account of its endorsement of a largely secular ethos.

For many young settlers, who have de facto sovereignty in the West Bank, the larger political arrangements matter less than remaining on the land. They increasingly avoid military service and have little or no respect or loyalty to the state (this despite receiving weapons training from the IDF, and army protection for their aggressive provocations). As one Hilltop Youth, the son of one of the founders of Yitzhar (which is among the most militant settlements in the West Bank), explained, the Israeli army is viewed as "little more than a UN-type presence, [there] . . . simply to maintain the peace" between settlers and Palestinians. What comes through clearly is that, if forced to choose between Israeli society and fighting for the land, there is no question where the loyalties of David and his cohort would lie.[46]

Unlike the Hilltop Youth, most Haredim moved into the West Bank for practical reasons. Housing was much more affordable, being heavily subsidized, and the settlements offered them a standard of living they could not hope to achieve within Israel proper. Further, the big Haredi settlements are a shorter distance from Jerusalem and many holy sites (tombs and the like) than most places within Israel. Nevertheless, once in the West Bank these populations have a vested interest in remaining there and retaining their privileged status. This has the effect of aligning them ever more closely to the Zionist right and its obstructionist policies regarding the Oslo process. And with eighteen seats in the 2013 elections (up two from 2009), the votes of ultra-Orthodox parties continue to pose an existential threat to any peace settlement with the Palestinians.

What we have witnessed in the past few decades is the evolution of a distinctive yet complex and plural Haredi Jewish identity in Israel that, despite theological opposition to Zionism per se, has bound the ultra-Orthodox ever more tightly into the national fabric and has made them natural allies of the Zionist right. As the nature of Israel's population changes and becomes more devoutly religious, so too does the nature of the conflict become religious in character. But as the case of the Hilltop Youth makes clear, the emerging identities can also open new areas of potential coexistence, as traditional expectations and allegiances to the state are transformed in unexpected ways by processes that at first glance could be expected to strengthen them.[47]

## "BLESSED ARE THE PEACEMAKERS": CHRISTIAN PALESTINIANS UNDER OCCUPATION

Palestinian Christians have long complained of being double victims of the Israeli-Palestinian conflict, as they are marginalized within their own Palestinian national community on top of the oppression suffered under the occupation. While Islamist politics in Palestine has tended to concentrate on militant violence, Palestinian Christian clergy have been at the forefront of developing a theology of liberation based on a more inclusive rather than exclusive understanding of God and God's relationship with the peoples inhabiting the Holy Land.

This idea is taken up by Palestinian priest Naim Stifan Ateek, who notes that the Bible is suffused with the contrast between "universalism and particularism—whether God is *in*clusive or *ex*clusive in divine love for human beings. The Bible is a record of the dynamic, sometimes severe, tension between nationalist and universalist conceptions of the deity."[48] Christian theology has long taken the universalist interpretation, of course, but Ateek brings this up as a potent question in specifically *Palestinian* Christian theology, where the history of national struggle has blurred the message of Christ and its relevance to those seeking justice in Israel-Palestine.

Ateek and other Christian activists focus their actions on well-known New Testament admonitions that place peacemakers among the most beloved "children of God."[49] In fact, justice can come only through peace and reconciliation between the two peoples on the land. Against the militant-nationalist approach to Judaism, he draws a parallel with the Zealots of the first century C.E. That faction argued for the "absolute sovereignty of Yahweh over Israel," and for a stance that brooked no compromise with a non-Jewish population on the land. He observes that the Zealots "succeeded in attracting . . . the loyalty of many Jews and temporarily gaining the upper hand over Rome, but eventually led their nation to destruction."[50] Could this be a parable for the modern state?

Ateek also makes use of the "prophetic imperative [that] arises out of the Church's conviction that the active promotion of justice is not outside its purview and competence."[51] His call is, therefore, aimed principally at other Palestinian Christians, who he hopes can set aside their sectarian differences and forge a common strategy for peaceful confrontation. His argument to the churches is that they might accept, as a basis for peacemaking, the following three theological propositions: "God's continuous action and involvement in history; God's love for the whole world; and God's concern for justice, mercy, and peace in the world."[52]

In a similar spirit, the group Kairos Palestine speaks out against Christian groups who would seek to legitimize the Israeli occupation as God's will. (In this they target the Christian Zionists, and in particular the Christian right in America.) They argue that "the military occupation of [the] land is a sin against God and humanity" and should be opposed by Christians everywhere, "because true Christian theology is a theology of love and solidarity with the oppressed, a call to justice and equality among peoples."[53] Kairos Palestine has also brought together other Christian denominations to publish detailed indictments of the occupation, from the Separation Wall to settlements to Jerusalem,[54] and argues that since the land "is God's land therefore it must be a land of reconciliation, peace and love."[55]

Not surprisingly, the group's writings also argue strongly against the use of religion to foster violence, saying, "Any use of the Bible to legitimize or support political options and positions that are based upon injustice . . . transform[s] religion into human ideology and strip[s] the Word of God of its holiness, its universality and truth."[56] While they limit themselves to referencing the Bible, this is equally true for the Qur'an and the Torah. The use of these documents, part of the heritage of humanity, to incite hatred and perpetuate injustice robs them of their sanctity. Kairos Palestine issues a call to the other Abrahamic faiths, "with whom we share the same vision that every human being is created by God. . . . Let us . . . rise up above the political positions that have failed so far and continue to lead us on the path of failure and suffering."[57]

It is worth noting that neither Palestinian society as a whole nor the Christian community has embraced a turn-the-other-cheek idealism. Indeed, the calls for social justice that emanate from the clergy can be endorsed by the most ardent Hamas supporter and the most committed secularist, but the path of nonviolence is still hotly debated in the public sphere. In addition, the church in Palestine represents a small and ever-shrinking proportion of the overall population. Today a mere 2 percent of the West Bank is Christian. Three times as many Christians live within 1948 Israel as live within the Occupied Territory. More than likely this means that, for all the idealism and vision they show, the Kairos Palestine statements are likely to have little effect.

## ADDRESSING QUESTIONS OF GENDER THROUGH THE PARALLEL STATES STRUCTURE

This chapter has been trying to bring religion and religious culture into what is on the surface a fairly dry, legalistic debate. Searching for a way out of the quagmire of endless Israeli-Palestinian negotiations has led some courageous scholars to suggest the impossible—two legal entities sharing a common spatial reality, with a host of unique institutions necessary to create a neutral space between the two national groupings. This approach has potential to break the deadlock that a territorial mind-set has imposed on the negotiators, for neither side can fully cede its historic claim to the totality of the land, and a means of sharing it presents a near-ideal set of circumstances to those who have built their religious identity upon issues of territoriality.

But what of those whose religiosity is not so defined, and for whom other concerns are greater than control of the land? As in most countries of the region, citizenship in Israel and Palestine is profoundly gendered and in ways that are enmeshed with the sectarian distribution of power as well. Such gendered-cum-sectarian specifications of citizenship have made it very difficult to have any "universal national subject" above and beyond religious and gender or sexual differences.[58] In most countries, the state has itself been complicit or determinative in the construction of patriarchal categories and institutions. Indeed, as Kathleen Staudt has powerfully expressed it, summarizing the weight of theorizing on the issue, "states [historically] have been the organized bastions of men pursuing men's interests."[59] The question then becomes, Can a Parallel States structure escape these dynamics?

Territorial considerations have little bearing on traditional constructions of sex or gender identity, and women and family law have requirements very different from those of the state. The situation as it exists today under Israeli control has empowered some of the most conservative elements in both societies, by removing family law from the purview of the secular legal system. Issues of family status are exempted from the Women's Equal Rights Law and, as in the Mandate period, "religious communities (Muslim, Christian, Jewish) retain . . . their own courts for matters of personal status."[60] Within Orthodox Jewish courts, for example, women are at a distinct disadvantage, "because the judges . . . *(dayanim)* are exclusively men, and only the testimony of men is admissible in them."[61] Ideals of the secular state are irrelevant here, as "the rules of Orthodox Judaism . . . are not bound by the principle of equality or by other precepts of Israeli civil law."[62]

The situation of Islamic law in Israel is in some ways even more complex. Palestinian shari'a has become progressively "Israelized" since the creation of the state—a de facto harmonization that owes both to the absolute dominance of Israeli laws and to the shared legal culture that predated 1948. The Israeli government implements a specific vision of the shari'a through a publicly funded court system whose roots go back to the Mandate period.[63] As in most Muslim countries, these laws set women at a distinct disadvantage (that neither the Israeli nor the Palestinian government or criminal justice system takes seriously violence against women or honor killings is an equal cause of concern, but this owes as much if not more to a lack of enforcement as to a lack of legal penalties on the books for such violence). The "twin-track" secular and religious system of law presents numerous problems—from how to reconcile mixed marriages to the incompatibilities with international law or even with the norms expressed in most basic laws of the two societies, which officially respect religious freedom and freedom of belief broadly but do little to protect those with minority views or those who are victimized because of their beliefs or gender (for example, the persecution of Shiʻa or the diminished rights of women).

The dynamics in Palestinian society in the West Bank and Gaza are equally problematic, with Hamas-ruled Gaza in particular witnessing significant gender-based oppression. The situation is bad enough that scholars, commentators, and activists alike routinely describe Palestinian women as facing two simultaneous struggles—against the occupation, and against patriarchy and oppression within their own societies.[64]

Much of this volume has been occupied with legal issues, and it is here that religion presents a substantial challenge; if a Parallel States solution is to be hoped for, issues of family status will need to be addressed in ways that accord with international legal norms while still remaining acceptable to those keeping a traditional lifestyle. This is a more difficult circle to square than it might appear. Western societies have long been accustomed to a fully secular legal space within which family law is to be adjudicated, though individuals of course retain the freedom to seek religious solutions to their needs in parallel. In the rush to see Israel as a progressive, Western polity, commentators have generally overlooked the degree to which it resembles its Arab neighbors in preserving a space for religious law to trump the secular. (In fact, several Arab states are considerably more "Western" in this regard—Tunisia, for example.)[65] This is not to say that Israelis have not long chafed at this hybrid regime; several political parties have fought over the years to change it, without success.[66] The fractious nature of coalition governance has meant that Orthodox parties have easily retained their privileged hold on family status. In a Parallel States system, this situation could hardly continue unchecked.

Indeed, the present political structure of Israel is a substantial impediment to peace, as many authors have shown. Palestinian politics has done no better a job at encouraging a realization of society's national goals. To make the Parallel States structure palatable, many constituencies will need to be brought on board. Yet in fundamental ways, often if not largely relating to religion, the constituencies most needed to enable a Parallel States solution engage in practices that would challenge the development of states and legal systems that fully respect and implement international human-rights norms. This chapter has already shown how those with a religio-territorial stake (such as the settlers or Hamas) may be enticed to consider it. How, though, could the architects of a Parallel States framework appeal to those who have long looked to the state to enforce religious law? The authors make no claim of having the answer to this question, but it must be asked if the PSP is to achieve its end. In order to ensure smooth operation of its institutions and to guarantee the rights of each national-religious grouping on the land, the Parallel States structure will almost certainly need to adopt contemporary European norms with respect to human rights. This will require the religious courts to cede their monopolies and act only within and on individuals' private lives, much as traditional religious institutions operate today in the United States and in Europe.

This may prove a difficult sell in some quarters. For example, women in Orthodox Judaism are associated with temptation and rampant sexuality, and identified with a cult of domesticity that makes them responsible for the mundane operations of the Haredi world. In this view, "women fulfill most of their religious aspirations and gain their spiritual rewards through routine domestic tasks."[67] The sexuality of women is tightly controlled and subject to male prerogatives. As Samuel Heilman comments, "For *Haredim* nothing so much embodied sexuality as a woman. Her hair, arms, legs, and voice were enough to arouse the basest instincts. Thus, in public, on the street, in the presence of men, women had to be properly covered. Signs proclaimed this message again and again."[68] One such sign, at a street corner leading into Mea Shearim, a Haredi neighborhood in Jerusalem, reads, "To women and girls who pass through our neighborhood we beg you with all our hearts. Please do not pass through our neighborhood in immodest clothes. Modest clothes include: closed blouses, with long sleeves, long skirt—no trousers, no tight-fitting clothes. Please do not disturb the sanctity of our neighborhood and our way of life as Jews committed to G-d and his Torah."[69]

The apparent double standard is present in traditional forms of Islamic law as well, with a coded assumption that men are less able to control their sexual desires than women, and thus female sexuality must be controlled and restricted. This attitude is at the heart of both Jewish and Muslim attempts to control the manner in which women appear in and move through public spaces. In Palestinian society the precursor to Hamas and its earliest incarnation gained public notoriety in part for acid attacks on women not deemed adequately covered in public. While this attitude is not universal—or even today an absolute majority's view—in the two societies, it still represents a very large segment of society, and indoctrination into this manner of thinking begins very early, with even children enjoined to dress modestly.

Samuel Heilman quotes another sign: "Young Girl: She who wears shameless clothes, woeful are the days of her youth. Her sins are more numerous than the strands of her hair."[70] The need of men to avoid female contact and the temptations of the eyes follows a rationale similar to the one that led to the *ḥarīm* and the *ḥijāb*. Men's presumed inability to resist fantasizing about the women they see, and the danger this presents to their focus on godly pursuits, requires that women subject themselves to modesty.

These values have been transmitted to women generation after generation, and they undoubtedly affect the way that notions of gender equality might be interpreted by both women and men in these communities. In addition, the politically active within Haredi Judaism have been racing in the opposite direction for some time, seeking a much more activist state. Gerald Cromer has identified a dual strategy of withdrawal and conquest in Haredi politics, the conquest part being a slow but steady reshaping of the cultural landscape. "At the present time, *Haredi* politicians are, among other things, trying to ban pornography in public places and further restrict the breeding of pigs."[71] Needless to say, if a secular space is to be interjected and a parallel legal structure established, such efforts to enforce particular moralities will become impossible.

## CONCLUSION: FROM FOSTERING HATRED TO SERVING THE COMMON GOOD

With such ideals far from the recent experience of religion in Israel-Palestine, how can one imagine a Parallel States scenario being embraced by religiously motivated citizens of the two nations? There are several answers to this question. First, we argue that a Parallel States structure is valuable precisely because of the lack of agreement between them. Specifically, both Jewish and Muslim religious nationalist claims to the territory of Palestine-Israel revolve around the need for divinely grounded sovereignty over all the land. And it is quite easy to find encoded within the religious literature of the communities stories, arguments, and polemics that encourage and justify xenophobia, chauvinism, and violence.[72] Some groups may never be able to let go of their maximalist demands. A Parallel States scenario—by removing the linkages among the individual citizen, specific segments of the larger territory, and sovereignty—would allow both nations to imagine a sovereign community over the entire territory, but in a manner that is not exclusive of the other group's claims to the same land.

Second, a fully realized Parallel States vision would allow citizens of all three faiths to live anywhere they chose in the whole of the territory, which means precisely that Jews would have permanent access to the biblical heartland of the West Bank and Jerusalem, which is today the heart of Palestine. The covenantal promise could then be kept, but without disenfranchising and even dispossessing Palestinians, and at the same time the imagination of the territory of Palestine as a *waqf* would acquire a level of political viability it did not enjoy previously. Indeed, conversations between participants in this project and leading members of both the religious Zionist camp and representatives of Hamas produced significant interest in the concept of shared and overlapping sovereignties that would allow full movement of citizens of both states while preserving the particular character of their state.[73]

Equally important, a Parallel States arrangement could help members of all three faiths transcend the most xenophobic and chauvinistic tendencies of their identities without challenging their core ties to the land. However ironic it may seem, by removing the links among the individual, sovereignty, and the land, the core, religious-derived bond between the individual and territory becomes easier to see.

Finally, a Parallel States solution, once implemented, could provide the practical grounds from which new interpretations of Judaism and Islam could emerge. The Abrahamic faiths are grounded in a very deep ethical framework that is centered on notions of justice and the common good. These have, from time to time, served as the foundation for movements advocating freedom, dignity, democracy, and other core values that are crucial to the successful transformation of Israel and Palestine—away from cultures of occupation and violence and toward pluralism and tolerance. Social justice is an Islamic imperative, and securing the common good and "enjoining the good and prohibiting evil" are the collective responsibility of all Muslims. Similarly, one of the key roles assigned to Jews, as an obligation of their "chosenness," is securing justice and fighting oppression. Recognizing this may serve as the basis for a much more positive religious identity and praxis among Muslims, Christians, and Jews.

This kind of "project"-oriented identity, rather than the more negative and closed "resistance" identity that currently dominates the public expressions of Judaism and Islam, is important for the growing ranks of progressive Muslims and Jews within their larger religious communities. Although these movements have yet to make a significant impact inside the space of Palestine-Israel, they are slowly making their presence felt and have a crucial part to play in helping to transform the two communities within the country.[74] Movement toward parallel states may allow their ideals to gain wider traction in society, as competition over the land need no longer be a dominant factor in sociocultural identity.

One question, of course, is how to encourage such a transformation in the core religious sensibilities of Jews and Muslims (and to a lesser extent of Christian Palestinians) so that a Parallel States solution could even be on the table. Much of the work needs to be done by diaspora communities, who in many ways have fetishized—or better, idolized— the land to an even greater degree than their coreligionists actually living and dying there. However, if we were to wait for such a transformation to occur, either in the diasporas or inside the country, *before* attempting to build a different future, it might never come. In the context of a political resolution such as that proposed by the PSP, we believe that creating a public space that is "secular"—that is to say, open to a variety of views, without any particular identities, religious systems, or ideologies being given preference over others—could encourage the kind of religious transformation that would have to be at the heart of a long-term reconciliation between the two societies.

Further, we believe that the PSP's focus on the relationship between the state and the individual citizen, rather than the collective, also creates space for such a development. By changing the nature of citizenship, the Parallel States framework could encourage the creation of a public culture that would bring Jews and Muslims, Israelis and Palestinians, toward visions of a common good. Free movement, for example, would liberate citizens from the dangerous and exclusive attachment to territory that currently divides Israelis and Palestinians. And having states that are truly democratic would reinforce the positive forces of fairness and justice, and allow for greater respect and tolerance. If they had to interact and negotiate within a shared territory, Israelis and Palestinians would be forced to ameliorate their systemic inequalities and imbalances in power, which in time would open the door to genuine understanding and equality.

This is, of course, a long-term vision. As Dror Zeevi and Nimrod Hurvitz point out in chapter 4, without security at the most basic level for both peoples, any chance at broader reconciliation, at forging a truly common good, is impossible to imagine. As Rosemary Ruether ably paraphrases Father Ateek in her foreword to his book *Justice and Only Justice,* "the Israeli Jews seek peace with security, and the Palestinians seek peace with justice. Palestinians must come to acknowledge

Jewish fear and the need for security, while Israeli Jews must recognize that the only authentic security for them is through justice to the Palestinians."[75]

We believe that the Parallel States solution offers the only real possibility for attaining both security and justice for all Israelis and Palestinians—both at the national level and for the two societies' constituent groups—within the reality of sharply opposed theological visions of the land. Ultimately, the current focus on territory actually opens up space for discussions about the kind of political arrangements discussed by the PSP, precisely because such solutions remove territory from the definition of sovereignty. Pursuing a Parallel States framework, from the religious perspective at least, removes the single greatest obstacle preventing the two nations from sharing their homeland.

## NOTES

1. The authors would like to thank Charlotta Liljendahl and Leif Stenberg for their important research and comments, which helped shape the arguments of this chapter.

2. See Talal Asad, *Formations of the Secular: Christianity, Islam, Modernity* (Palo Alto, Calif.: Stanford University Press, 2003), and Armando Salvatore and Mark LeVine, *Religion, Social Practices and Contested Hegemonies: Reconstructing the Public Sphere in Muslim Majority Societies* (New York: Palgrave, 2005).

3. See, e.g., Elie Kedourie, *Nationalism* (Oxford: Wiley-Blackwell, 2006 [orig. 1960]), and Benedict Anderson, *Imagined Communities: Reflections on the Origin and Spread of Nationalism* (London: Version, 2006 [orig. 1983]). For an alternative approach see, for example, Dipesh Chakrabarty, *Provincializing Europe: Postcolonial Thought and Historical Difference* (Princeton, N.J.: Princeton University Press, 2000).

4. For the impact of religion in the formation of enduring national identities, see Juval Portugali, *Implicate Relations: Society and Space in the Israeli-Palestinian Conflict* (Berlin: Springer, 1993); Anthony D. Smith, *Chosen Peoples: Sacred Sources of National Identity* (Oxford: Oxford University Press, 2003); and Adrian Hastings, *The Construction of Nationhood: Ethnicity, Religion and Nationalism* (Cambridge: Cambridge University Press, 1997).

5. See among others Rashid Khalidi, *Palestinian Identity: The Shaping of a National Consciousness* (New York: Columbia University Press, 1996); and Mark LeVine, *Overthrowing Geography: Jaffa, Tel Aviv, and the Struggle for Palestine* (Berkeley: University of California Press, 2005).

6. Two important works exploring the role of Islam and the Muslim public spheres are Armando Salvatore's *Islam and the Political Discourse of Modernity* (London: Ithaca Press, 1998), and Michael Gasper, "Abdallah Nadim, Islamic Reform, and 'Ignorant' Peasants: State-Building in Egypt?" in *Yearbook*

*of the Sociology of Islam,* vol. 3: *Muslim Traditions and Modern Techniques of Power,* ed. Armando Salvatore (Hamburg and New York: Lit Verlag and Transaction Books, 2001).

7. Khaled Hroub, *Hamas: Political Thought and Practice* (Washington, D.C.: Institute for Palestine Studies), 27.

8. Ibrahim Maqadima, *Ma'alim fil-tariq ila tahrir filastin* (Gaza: Aleem Institute, 1994), 254–55; cf. Hroub, *Hamas,* 28.

9. For a detailed analysis of Qutb's cultural politics, see LeVine, "'Human Nationalisms' versus 'Inhuman Globalisms': Cultural Economies of Globalization and the Re-Imagining of Muslim Identities in Europe and the Middle East," in *Muslim Networks and Transnational Communities in and across Europe,* ed. Stefano Allievi and Jorgen Nielsen (Leiden: Brill, 2003).

10. Shaul Mishal and Avraham Shela, *The Palestinian Hamas* (New York: Columbia University Press, 2000), chap. 2.

11. Mishal and Shela, *Palestinian Hamas,* chap. 2.

12. For a discussion of Israel's support of the Islamic movement in the 1970s and 1980s, see Robert Dreyfuss, *Devil's Game: How the United States Helped Unleash Fundamentalist Islam* (New York: Metropolitan Books, 2005), 195–200.

13. "HAMAS—The Islamic Resistance Movement," Israel Defense Forces spokesman briefing, January 1993; available at www.fas.org/irp/world/para/docs/930100.htm. Hamas's Gaza head, Mahmoud Zahar, is considered extreme, while its West Bank head, Hassan Yousef, former head of the charity wing of al-Quds University, has spoken openly of a truce with Israel.

14. Beverly Milton-Edwards, *Islamic Politics in Palestine* (London: I.B. Tauris, 1999), 104.

15. Yitzhak Reiter, "'All Palestine Is Holy Muslim Waqf Land': A Myth and Its Roots," in *Law, Custom, and Statute in the Muslim World: Studies in Honor of Aharon Layish,* ed. Ron Shaham (Leiden: Brill, 2006).

16. F.E. Peters, *The Distant Shrine: The Islamic Centuries in Jerusalem* (New York: AMS Press, 1990).

17. Catarina Kinnvall, "Globalization and Religious Nationalism: Self, Identity, and the Search for Ontological Security," *Political Psychology* 25, no. 5 (2004): 741–67.

18. Hamas Covenant, Clauses 6, 9, and 12. Cf. Meir Litvak, *The Islamization of Palestinian Identity: The Case of Hamas* (Tel Aviv: Moshe Dayan Center, 1996), available at www.dayan.tau.ac.il/d&a-hamas-litvak.htm.

19. The phrase "New Middle East" references an idea and book of that title (Shimon Peres, *The New Middle East* [New York: Henry Holt, 1993]).

20. Sheikh Hamad Bitawi, interviewed by Hisham Ahmad, *From Religious Salvation to Political Transformation: The Rise of Hamas in Palestinian Society* (Jerusalem: PASSIA, 1994), 109.

21. Hamas leaflet no. 82, dated August 18, 1988. Cf. Hamas Charter, chap. 2, Article 9, Appendix, doc. 3; see Hamas Communiqué no. 57, stressing unity with Christians, and no. 65, thanking the Christian community for supporting Muslims martyred in 2000, as well as a special communiqué expressing anger at the occupation of a Christian church by a group of Muslim militants. A

collection of Hamas leaflets can be found in Jean-François Legrain, *Les voix du soulèvement palestinien, 1987–1988* (Cairo: CEDEJ, 1991).

22. Mark LeVine, *Impossible Peace: Israel/Palestine since 1989* (London: Zed Books, 2009), chap. 5.

23. Cf. Salvatore and LeVine, eds., *Religion, Social Practice and Contested Hegemonies.*

24. Walter Laqueur, *A History of Zionism: From the French Revolution to the Establishment of the State of Israel* (New York: Schocken Books, 2003), especially 75–83.

25. Gershon Shafir, *Land, Labor and the Israeli-Palestinian Conflict* (Berkeley: University of California Press, 1989), 89.

26. Ehud Sprinzak, *Gush Emunim: The Politics of Zionist Fundamentalism in Israel* (Washington, D.C.: American Jewish Committee, 1986), 2. Also see Robert Friedman, *Zealots for Zion* (New York: Random House, 1992).

27. Samuel C. Heilman, "The Vision from the Madrasa and Bes Medrash: Some Parallels between Islam and Judaism," *Bulletin of the American Academy of Arts and Sciences* 49, no. 4 (January 1996): 6–37.

28. Ian Lustick, *For the Land and the Lord: Jewish Fundamentalism In Israel* (New York: Council on Foreign Relations, 1988), introduction. A good early analysis of Gush Emunim is Kevin A. Avruch, "Traditionalizing Israeli Nationalism: The Development of Gush Emunim," *Political Psychology* 1, no. 1 (Spring 1979): 47–57. For the basic writings of Kook, see A.Y. Kook, *Orot* (*Lights;* Jerusalem: n.p., 1950).

29. Rebecca Kook, "Hillel Kook: Revision and Rescue," in *Struggle and Survival in Palestine/Israel,* ed. Mark LeVine and Gershon Shafir, 157–69 (Berkeley: University of California Press, 2012).

30. Ehud Sprinzak, "Gush Emunim: The Tip of the Ice Berg," *The Jerusalem Quarterly* 21 (Fall 1981). Gush Emunim first emerged as an organized faction within the National Religious Party, which took on a more messianic ideology following the 1967 War.

31. Three other right-wing parties that have emerged since the 1980s are Tzomet, Moledet, and Tehiya.

32. Cf. among others Exodus 23:31, Genesis 15:18–21, Numbers 33–34, Deuteronomy 1, and Joshua 1.

33. The best English-language analysis of the religious discourses surrounding Rabin's murder is Michael Karpin and Ina Friedman's *Murder in the Name of God: The Plot to Kill Yitzhak Rabin* (New York: Metropolitan Books, 1998).

34. For a discussion of "settler Judaism," see Michael Lerner, *Jewish Renewal: Path to Healing and Transformation* (New York: HarperCollins, 1995).

35. See, e.g., Neve Gordon and Yinon Cohen, "The Demographic Success of Israel's Settlement Project," available at www.aljazeera.com/indepth/opinion/2012/12/20121124135935526146.html

36. Gershom Gorenberg, *The End of Days: Fundamentalism and the Struggle for the Temple Mount* (Oxford: Oxford University Press, 2000), 143–45.

37. Nurit Stadler, *Yeshiva Fundamentalism: Piety, Gender, and Resistance in the Ultra-Orthodox World* (New York: New York University Press, 2009).

38. The authors know of nine Haredi settlements in the West Bank: Beitar Illit, Modi'in Illit, Ramat Shlomo, Immanuel, Matityahu, Tel Zion (a neighborhood), Ma'ale Amos, Nahliel, and Metzad. Their combined population stands in excess of 120,000 persons.

39. See, for example, Kimmy Caplan, *Be-sod ha-shiah ha-Haredi* (Jerusalem: Zalman Shazar Center for Jewish History, 2007); Kimmy Caplan and Emmanuel Sivan, eds., *Haredim Yisraelim: Hishtalvut be-lo temiah?* (Jerusalem: Van Leer Institute, 2003); and Stadler, *Yeshiva Fundamentalism.*

40. This dynamic is reflected in their use of medieval texts to support a chauvinistic view toward non-Jews. See *Shulchan Aruch,* Yoreh De'ah 158; Moses Maimonides, *Guide for the Perplexed,* trans. M. Friedländer, 2nd ed. (London: George Routledge and Sons, 1904), book 3, chap. 51, p. 385, available at http://www.sacred-texts.com/jud/gfp/gfp187.htm; and Jonah Mandel, "Yosef: Gentiles Exist Only to Serve Jews," *Jerusalem Post,* October 18, 2010. The article has since been removed from the *Jerusalem Post*'s online archive (formerly at http://webcache.googleusercontent.com/search?q = cache:lo7PBbQrvDsJ:www .jpost.com/LandedPages/PrintArticle.aspx%3Fid%3D191782+&cd = 1&hl = en&ct = clnk&gl = us).

41. A growing trend has been noted in which Haredim cast votes not for the traditional ultra-Orthodox parties, but for far-right nationalist parties. In some of the more isolated settlements, such as Nahliel, this support has reached about 50 percent, with most of that going to (the new) Herut. For some recent numbers, see www.peacenow.org.il/eng/content/ultra-orthodox-jews-west-bank.

42. Yoav Peled, ed., *Shas: Etgar hayisra'eliyut* (Shas: The Challenge of Israeliness; Tel Aviv: Yediot Ahronot Publishing, 2001), editor's introduction, 11. A detailed discussion of Shas is provided in LeVine, *Impossible Peace,* chap. 5.

43. Yoav Peled, "No Arab Jews There—Shas and the Palestinians," working draft prepared for the workshop "Ethno-Religious Movements in Israel/Palestine," University of California, Irvine, October 10–12, 2002.

44. Sami Shalom Chetrit, "Milkud 17: Bein harediyut lemizrahiyut (Catch 17: Between haredi-ness and Mitrahi-ness)," in *Shas,* ed. Peled, 21–51.

45. Cf. Yoav Peled, "Divided Yet United: Israeli Jewish Attitudes Toward the Oslo Process," *Journal of Peace Research* 39, no. 5 (2002): 597–613; Yoav Peled, "The Continuing Electoral Success of Shas: A Cultural Division of Labor Analysis," in *The Elections in Israel, 1999,* ed. Michael Shamir and Alan Arian (Albany: State University of New York Press, 2002).

46. The research for this section is derived from Moriel Ram and Mark LeVine, "The Village against the Settlement: Two Generations of Conflict in the Nablus Region," in *Struggle and Survival in Palestine/Israel,* ed. Mark LeVine and Gershon Shafir (Berkeley: University of California Press, 2012).

47. Gershom Gorenberg, *The Unmaking of Israel* (New York: HarperCollins, 2011).

48. Naim Stifan Ateek, *Justice and Only Justice: A Palestinian Theology of Liberation* (Maryknoll, N.Y.: Orbis Books, 1989), 92.

49. Matthew 5:9.

50. Ateek, *Justice,* 94.

51. Ateek, *Justice,* 152.

52. Ateek, *Justice*, 153.

53. Kairos Palestine, www.kairospalestine.ps/.

54. In one instance, it published an open letter to the world signed by a broad coalition of Christian dignitaries in Palestine, including the Patriarchs of the Greek Orthodox, Latin, and Armenian Apostolic churches, and bishops of the Coptic, Syriac, Ethiopian, Maronite, Lutheran, and Anglican churches critiquing the occupation from a variety of angles. See Kairos Palestine, *A Moment of Truth: A Word of Faith, Hope, and Love from the Heart of Palestinian Suffering*, 2009, available at www.kairospalestine.ps/sites/default/Documents/English.pdf 2.

55. Kairos Palestine, *Moment of Truth*, p. 8, sect. 2.3.1.

56. Kairos Palestine, *Moment of Truth*, p. 9, sect. 2.4.

57. Kairos Palestine, *Moment of Truth*, p. 15, sect. 8.

58. Suad Joseph, "The Public/Private: The Imagined Boundary in the Imagined Nation/State/Community: The Lebanese Case," *The Feminist Review* 57 (Autumn 1997): 71–90.

59. Kathleen Staudt, "Engaging Politics: Beyond Official Empowerment Discourse," in *Rethinking Empowerment: Gender and Development in a Global/Local World,* ed. Jane L. Parpart, Shirin M. Rai, and Kathleen Staudt (New York: Taylor and Francis, 2003), 97–111, at 100.

60. Charles D. Smith, *Palestine and the Arab-Israel Conflict,* 8th ed. (Boston: Bedford/St. Martin's, 2013), 221.

61. Gershon Shafir and Yoav Peled, *Being Israeli: The Dynamics of Multiple Citizenship* (Cambridge: Cambridge University Press, 2002), 103.

62. Shafir and Peled, *Being Israeli,* 104.

63. See Moussa Abou Ramadan, "Framing the Borders of Justice: Sharia Courts in Israel and the Conflict between Secular Ideology and Islamic Law," in *Reapproaching Borders: New Perspectives in the Study of Israel-Palestine,* ed. Sandra Sufian and Mark LeVine, 267–86 (Lanham, Md.: Rowman and Littlefield, 2007).

64. Ramona M., interview with Hitam Saafin, International Middle East Media Center (IMEMC), March 9, 2011, accessed July 24, 2013: www.imemc .org/article/60818.

65. Mounira M. Charrad, *States and Women's Rights: The Making of Postcolonial Tunisia, Algeria, and Morocco* (Berkeley: University of California Press, 2001).

66. The secular parties Meretz and Shinui (an explicitly anticlerical outfit) nearly doubled their Knesset total in 1999 by running a campaign targeting Shas and the Haredim: Reuven Y. Hazan and Abraham Diskin, "The 1999 Knesset and Prime Ministerial Elections in Israel," *Electoral Studies* 19, no. 4 (December 2000).

67. Stadler, *Yeshiva Fundamentalism,* 120.

68. Samuel Heilman, *Defenders of the Faith: Inside Ultra-Orthodox Jewry* (Berkeley: University of California Press, 2000), 308.

69. Liam O'Mara IV, photograph, Jerusalem, 2010.

70. Heilman, *Defenders of the Faith,* 309.

71. Gerald Cromer, "Withdrawal and Conquest: Two Aspects of the Haredi Response to Modernity," in *Jewish Fundamentalism in Comparative Perspective:*

*Religion, Ideology, and the Crisis of Modernity,* ed. Laurence J. Silberstein (New York: New York University Press, 1993), 174.

72. See, for example, William Nicholls, *Christian Antisemitism: A History of Hate* (Northvale, N.J.: Jason Aronson, 1995); Karen Armstrong, *Holy War: The Crusades and Their Impact on Today's World* (New York: Anchor Books, 2001); Rosemary Ruether, *Faith and Fratricide: The Theological Roots of Anti-Semitism* (Eugene, Ore.: Wipf and Stock, 1997); David Cook, *Understanding Jihad* (Berkeley: University of California Press, 2005); and Bernard Lewis, *The Crisis of Islam: Holy War and Unholy Terror* (New York: Random House, 2004).

73. These opinions were drawn from project participants, including Israeli settler leader and *Haaretz* columnist Israel Harel, who was a longtime member of this group, and interviews by several members with Hamas officials, both outside Palestine and in Gaza.

74. For a discussion of "project" and "resistance" identities, see Manuel Castells, *The Power of Identity* (New York: Blackwell, 1996). For a detailed discussion of the common good in Islam, see Salvatore and Levine, *Religions, Social Practice and Contested Hegemonies.*

75. Rosemary Reuther, "Foreword," in Ateek, *Justice,* xi.

# CHAPTER 10

# The Necessity for Thinking outside the Box

HIBA HUSSEINI

"Land for peace" was the formula on which the two-state solution was predicated when the peace process was launched in 1992. When the Interim Agreement on the West Bank and the Gaza Strip was signed in 1995, there was great promise that the Israeli-Palestinian conflict would end by the year 2000, concluding the five-year term jointly agreed to for the establishment of the Palestinian state on land occupied by Israel during the 1967 war. The famous "land for peace" formula would see Israel withdraw from the occupied West Bank, East Jerusalem, and Gaza Strip to allow for a Palestinian state. But as early as the late 1990s, there were indications that the terms and principles agreed to in the Declaration of Principles of 1993 and the Interim Agreement were susceptible to derogations. A series of setbacks has plagued the peace process, leaving it far afield from a much-needed comprehensive, satisfactory, and reasonable end to conflict. Instead, the conflict has morphed into an existential issue for both sides. The Israelis are ever fervent to maintain a Jewish state, and the Palestinians see the land on which their aspirations for a future Palestinian state lie being quickly devoured with the ever-mushrooming settlements, coupled with Israel's stronger hold on East Jerusalem.

"Land for peace" meant territorial divisibility, yet divisibility for both parties has come to signal a high cost. Thus, the long-established approach to achieving an end of claims and end of conflict through a bilateral negotiated process to reach a comprehensive settlement has been frustrated and rendered impracticable, at least in the foreseeable future. Fundamental challenges and extreme distrust characterize the two parties' relationship, making the two-state reality ever more illusory and causing the two-state solution to slip farther and farther away.

After decades of peace-building efforts, negotiations, endless bilateral talks, and numerous attempts at direct and indirect facilitation (by the United States, along with other players supporting the process including the European Union, the Arab states that launched the Arab Peace Initiative, and other members of the international community), the two-state solution has remained a theoretical construct while finding ways to actualize it has eluded all those involved. For the Palestinians, the gradual erosion of the two-state solution has stemmed primarily from the increased shift to the political right in Israel, as evidenced by the successive Israeli governments that have supported policies to expand the growth of Israeli settlements, introduced suffocating closure policies, systematically isolated East Jerusalem from the West Bank, decoupled the West Bank from the Gaza Strip, and in general fostered the ever-deteriorating physical conditions on the ground. The Palestinians have concluded that the situation has gone too far to permit a reasonable territorial division. Furthermore, they have seen that Israeli vested interests, be it over Jerusalem, settlements, security, borders, or the Jewish state notion, and their strict position on the right of return of refugees, among others, have rendered divisibility unfeasible.

Meanwhile, the political stalemate has been very costly for the Palestinians, as they continue to live through occupation, experience restrictions on movement, and suffer declines in economic development. Among Palestinians, the impact of the conflict has manifested itself and culminated in a serious political and ideological schism between Fatah and Hamas, thus dealing the peace process yet another blow. It has also created a tension between resistance and statehood, leaving a serious and almost irreversible rift between the Gaza Strip and the West Bank, as the means and goals of the struggle are now divided between the different components of the Palestinian national movement. To ameliorate this dilemma, a national Palestinian consensus is required; Hamas must be brought into the political process in a manner that it can accept and that others can live with. The Hamas dimension poses a dichotomy within the Parallel States idea. On the one hand, Hamas will find the concept intriguing because it presumes that all the land is open and not divided. On the other, sharing the land and sovereignty constitutes a negation of its ideology.

## DIVIDING SOVEREIGNTY

The challenges facing the two-state solution are formidable and have caused all concerned to experience fatigue from engaging in an endless process. So it is perhaps timely to address the issue of sharing the land in a totally different way. Rethinking the "land for peace" formula has become an urgent necessity. The manifestation of such a fresh approach is being considered by the Parallel States Project. The PSP provides a much-needed *novel* way of thinking about the conflict and an opportunity to explore ideas and solutions from a different vantage point.

The focal tenets of a Parallel States structure involve the decoupling of state and territory and a reconceptualization of sovereignty, from the conventional notion of geographic authority to an emphasis on the relationship between state and citizen. Accordingly, Palestine and Israel would both be sovereign over the entire territory, with certain functions jointly administered; both would exercise partial sovereignty in the sense that certain functions would be at least partly governed by internationally accepted norms of different kinds.

Reconceptualizing sovereignty in a conjecture that envisages both states sharing the same land may be the freshest and most creative approach at hand. The two states would exist on the same territory without divisibility of the land. Ironically, this is the current de facto situation today. Hence, in some ways the Parallel States solution would only envision formalizing the status quo. However, the presumption, of course, is that under a Parallel States structure, the occupation would end, the right of return of refugees would be dealt with, Jerusalem would remain open, and the borders of the two states would be clearly identified and delineated.

Here it must be noted that over decades, the identity of Palestinians in the Occupied Territory and Israel has been shaped by the ongoing systems of discrimination, apartheid, and institutional inequity imposed by Israeli occupation, policies, and practices. The constant need for Palestinians to defend themselves in the face of such systems has added unique dimensions to the conflict, which must be addressed if Palestinians are to heal, to reconcile with Israel, and to enjoy lasting peace. A recent report released by the civil society research center BADIL highlights the plight of the Palestinian Arab minority in Israel, the status of whom in reality amounts to second-class citizenship—or, as described by the report, a "probationary" citizenship. The report emphasizes the stark disparities between life in Israel as a Jew and life in Israel as a Palestinian Arab.

The BADIL report outlines the palpably discriminatory message to Israel's non-Jewish citizens that permeates every aspect of life, from the demand to pledge allegiance to the state of Israel to the lopsided legal framework underpinning the Jewish state. As long as Palestinian Arab citizens of Israel feel that they are seen as the Trojan horse by their fellow Jewish citizens, they cannot reach their full and equal potential as citizens. Under the current system, Palestinians see their culture, history, and land disappearing from the Israeli-Jewish physical reality and discourse. The Parallel States solution would revive and reinforce both cultures and histories without requiring that one or the other be ruled out. Pursuing this course would allow those Palestinian Arabs currently suffering identity-jettison because of the destructive practices of Israel the opportunity to opt to become a citizen of the Palestinian state and enjoy fulfillment of their human rights at the same time as it would allow Israel to apply the laws and procedures it wishes to its own population.

Thus, when we discuss the Parallel States structure as providing an alternative to the "land for peace" formula by proposing a shared land based on parallel sovereignty, it is not merely an approach based on human rights rather than territorial separation; it is one that offers crucial new contours of identity for citizens like Palestinian Israelis, who have one foot in each nation and yet currently find it hard to be fully embraced by either. In short, it allows for a reterritorialization of a Palestinian identity that has for so long been deterritorialized, but without deterritorializing the Jewish identity that has so long oppressed it.

The Parallel States construct anticipates, to a large extent, the protection of both sides' identities, in a paradigm that sees both states maintain their own national symbols, their own executive and legislative bodies, as well as their own foreign policy and foreign representation. There would be an option to enter into a defense union, a customs union, and a shared labor market, and to manage external borders on a mutually cooperative basis. Such ideas are not so difficult to imagine considering that there is already a single currency for both Israel and Palestine, not to mention the fundamental intertwining of the two economies and the numerous agreements that see mutual legal assistance in certain areas between the two sides.

For Palestinians, sovereignty and territory are synonymous. A territorial division with defined borders would give the Palestinians the exclusive sovereignty they have long yearned for on their territory, but only over a fraction of that territory. In light of the intractability of the issues as discussed above, the Parallel States structure provides the formula that comes closest to achieving the full aspirations of Palestinians in the foreseeable future. Palestine would be sovereign over its people in all the territory. However, certain functions would be jointly administered with Israel, for example, the borders.

In today's world, the notion of states without borders is not so alien—there are several "borderless" examples, with the European Union just one vision of a practically borderless area. In fact, as the traditional sovereignty associated with borders has slowly been eroded, the modern-day trend is to share borders jointly.

Today, Palestine is deprived of any real sovereign powers. As long as the two-state solution remains illusory and Israel is in control of the territory and the borders, Palestinians cannot and will not be able to exercise any sovereign powers. At best, they exercise nominal powers over certain limited functions. Sharing sovereignty within the context of a Parallel States structure would give the Palestinians the sovereignty that they have long looked to enjoy in a viable Palestinian state. Palestinians would gain by sharing sovereignty—in contrast to Israel, which would have to surrender some of the exclusive sovereignty it enjoys today.

## THE RETERRITORIALIZATION OF IDENTITY

As already noted, the Palestinian consensus and the Palestinian sense of identity have been left insecure and considerably fragmented as a result of the conflict and of Israeli practices and policies. Nevertheless, the Palestinian sense of identity and security is indelibly attached to the land, to self-determination, freedom, and sovereign rights. While Palestinians remain steadfast on these inalienable rights, the prolonged conflict with Israel and physical-geographical discontinuity between the West Bank and Gaza have, indeed, chipped away at the fabric of national consensus on the traditional formula for the two-state solution: "land for peace." Perhaps it is an opportune time to reconsider this approach and build consensus around turning the fragmentation to another positive formulation—building a solution to the conflict that is decoupled from the land and territory—because the Parallel States solution can make more land available to the Palestinians. Such a decoupling would not affect the definition of the Palestinian identity; rather, it separates the land from the identity.

To move toward such a vision, Palestinian national consensus would have to be reconfigured. This would no doubt prove to be a challenge because of the current internal ideological and political divides. However, the Parallel States structure, again, can offer a unique opportunity because the "entire" territory would be open to be shared, thus reducing, to a large extent, the inherent sense of grave compromise over the land that Palestinians have always felt. While under the Parallel States model, in theory, all land is to be shared by either side, the reality on the ground would persist for generations to come, thus limiting choices. So, for example, initially land that might present itself as a potential new opportunity for Palestinians to expand inside Israel might include areas that have limited or no religious attachment to Judaism. This formulation might then present a break from the current reality of the negotiations, which has shrunk the Palestinian claim to the 1967 demarcation. The Parallel States solution offers more and "other" lands. So a novel identity definition to the "other" lands would become available to the Palestinians.

Another reason why such thinking might prove attractive during this stalled period stems from the increased tilt to the right by religious and ideological groups in Israel. These groups might, perhaps, be willing to detach and part with lands that bear no or limited religious significance, and thus a greater portion of the land would open up and present an opportunity to become territorialized by Palestinians.

## RELEVANCE TODAY OF THE PARALLEL STATES CONCEPT

As mentioned in other chapters, today, technology and globalization have changed the way we perceive our socioeconomic, political, and social welfare. The same can be said of even inherent national issues such as legislative and jurisdictional powers. States have started rethinking these traditional concepts of legal norms within the context of globalization. How states assert their legislative, executive, and judicial powers in a nonexclusive system has also been reconsidered in the modern-day example of statehood. In that respect, the Parallel States structure offers Palestine an opportunity to consider how it would define jurisdiction over property and persons—for example, jurisdiction over foreigners. It would have to determine how its laws, within a sovereign state, would be applied in the context of shared territory. Such profound considerations would also have to occur in respect to how the police and judiciary would exercise their powers, and how rules of citizenship would be decided.

In the context of legal systems, Palestinian and Israeli private laws have similar roots, but they diverge in most other respects. So it would become most relevant to assess how disputes between two individuals belonging to separate states would be resolved, bearing in mind that many of the traditional solutions offered by the discipline of "conflict of laws" are territorial. It would be imperative to have these traditional principles adjusted to the Parallel States construct.

## MANAGING PALESTINIAN SECURITY

From a Palestinian security perspective, as mentioned in other chapters, shared territory poses a dilemma because since 1948, Palestinian loss of land has been synonymous with lack of security and a *nakba* (catastrophe) to its group identity. Since then, the realities faced by Palestinians comprise disposition, displacement, dispersal, occupation, daily humiliation, deeply felt trauma and a group identity in crisis. Contrary to popular propaganda, the Palestinians have security concerns that are equally serious as those of the Israelis, amounting to an existential crisis and group identity crisis. The security threats are not limited to the Palestinians in the Occupied Territory. Rather, they include Arab Israelis inside Israel, Palestinians in refugee camps, those present in neighboring states, and those in the diaspora. Palestinian security needs to take the form of economic development; freedom of work, movement, and residence; control over borders and natural resources; as well as protection of the diaspora.

In addition to this security dimension, the Palestinian situation entails a need for dignity, equality, and justice, in particular the issue of return and full recognition of the right to return. The latter is in essence a matter of moral bearing but can also be interpreted as an indispensable security need. The Parallel States structure would offer another creative approach to the security issues raised here and in other parts of this book. Security, which has been a core determining factor in the conflict, may, through the Parallel States model, be considerably deflated and reduced to its actual size. More important, the Parallel States structure turns security into a mutual concern of both the Palestinians and Israel in equal measure. Although this might be difficult for the Israeli side to perceive at the outset, both sides would become more secure—each in their own right. As Palestinians started to experience the freedoms they have long sought to enjoy and to have their concerns and rights redressed, alienating Israelis through security threats would no longer be a goal. By the same token, Israeli motivation to take measures to secure themselves at all costs from the Palestinians would be eliminated because the underlying causes for the security threat would have been eliminated. Thus, the Parallel States model presents an opportunity to achieve the security that both sides crave.

That said, for national security to be achieved, Palestinians should be enabled to guarantee their own ethno-national survival, to remain on national soil, and to be free from foreign rule. To ensure the well-being of the people, the refugee problem must be fairly addressed and resolved. Palestinians must be able to maintain an authentic and independent representation that articulates their demands and provides for their moral and material needs. To the extent that the Parallel States structure can address these issues in some form, it might be a plausible option. If reterritorialization is adopted with respect to the land, Palestinian security concerns might be alleviated or, at least, addressed in a manner that offers alternatives and options. Again, the issue of land and security would, within the context of the Parallel States structure, shrink to more manageable dimensions, to the point that it can be more effectively dealt with. Loss of land has caused Palestinians insecurity, loss of dignity, despair, and injustice. The Parallel States structure with its creative reterritorialization would open doors to redress these grievances and help restore much-craved security.

In addition to the insecurities mentioned in the previous paragraph, other Palestinian liabilities include, as mentioned in other chapters, their inability to acquire an independent, cohesive, and conventional self-defense capability; their structural disadvantage compared to the Israelis; their geostrategic constraints and lack of territorial depth; and the lack of physical continuity between the West Bank–Jerusalem and the Gaza Strip, which has caused political and psychological bifurcation within the Palestinian polity. These security dimensions must be addressed by the Parallel States structure, and it may very well be that the framework *can* address them in some respects. Certainly, the contiguity issue may be handled with the introduction of reterritorialization, and the same might be true of territorial depth.

On the other hand, the Parallel States framework requires that a Palestinian state have strong leadership with decision-making powers to ensure its national security. For a Palestinian leadership to succeed, it would need legitimacy, flexibility, free elections, national representation and statehood, consensus, a mix of centralization and decentralization, and domestic order. The Parallel States structure must consequently be able to provide, or at least facilitate, these minimal requirements, because reterritorialization would not be able to address them.

All in all, the security dimension is most complex from a Palestinian perspective. However, considering the fact that the state of Palestine is likely to be dematerialized, even reterritorialization would not restore the evident imbalance of power with Israel.

## LOOKING AT A PARALLEL STATES ECONOMY

The Palestinian economy, as mentioned in other parts of this book, has been totally distorted by imbalances created over the past seventy years by virtue of its utter dependence on the Israeli economy. The structural disparity in relations between the two economies is stark. The Israeli economy is large, advanced, and rich, while the Palestinian economy is small, underdeveloped, landlocked, poor, and nonsovereign.

Both states would inevitably have to contend with major structural economic and trade imbalances from the outset. On the other hand, it is noteworthy that the Parallel States solution would not be too far-fetched on the economic level because the Palestinian economy already shares with Israel the same fiscal, trade, monetary, and macroeconomic regime. Further, the Parallel States structure and its ensuing reterritorialization would also pave the way for the Palestinian and Israeli economies to share another aspect that is key to economic growth—the consumer market—thanks to almost impermeable barriers to freedom of movement and access to goods and services. Having open borders between the two states through reterritorialization could only serve to benefit both states, whose products would have access to wider and more diverse markets.

Additionally, in the context of shared markets, perhaps a more significant consideration with respect to the idea of Palestinian reterritorialization is the opening and merging of the divided Palestinian markets themselves. Currently, the West Bank, Gazan, and East Jerusalemite markets have little or no access to one another, nor indeed to other Palestinian communities within Israel or in the diaspora, as a result of stringent restrictions on the movement and access of goods and services. This economic severing also serves to distance, fragment, and compartmentalize these respective Palestinian clusters by location, which in turn has a detrimental affect sociologically and ideologically on the collective identity. Reterritorialization would allow these markets access to one another, which in turn would strengthen ideological links, as culturally significant produce, for instance, could be accessed more freely.

Thus, the Parallel States framework would allow for a new examination of economic prospects and the need for long-term economic convergence. Reterritorialization might just be the correct formula to enable the Parallel States economy. Reterritorialization would offer one international border, the free mobility of people and goods, and a unitary economic area with an all-embracing framework for relations. The possibility of delineating separate economic policies in some areas and joint policies in others accords well with special Palestinian development needs. The two legal systems would allow for different forms of economic legislation, resulting in differences that would take into account each economy's level of development and would be appropriate to meet their respective needs.

The establishment of a high level of economic cooperation as implied by the Parallel States structure would also provide noneconomic benefits to the Palestinians, sociopolitical externalities such as regional stability, the easing of social tensions, and the diminution of international conflicts. The same would be true for the Israeli side. However, before the Parallel States economy can be functional, certain minimum conditions would have to be achieved within Palestine. The Palestinian economy would have to build up its basic physical, institutional, organizational, and economic infrastructures, while the independence of the two economies should be kept up through a separate fiscal and trade policy, implying limitations on economic openness, at least in the near term.

The question of labor-force mobility must be cautiously considered, in order to contribute to the solution of problems of unemployment and income on the one hand, but also to prevent negative effects of economic dominance and of distorting economic structures on the other. While each of the states would maintain its own distinct economy, the framework for sharing sovereignty over territory and citizens would by necessity create a third economic space, the Parallel States economy. This economy should be determined by core principles, applicable to both parties, guiding the process of managing common or adjacent economic resources, and harmonizing national economic policies and cross-polity relations. These principles should, to name a few goals, narrow income differentials and development gaps; work toward economic integration and separate but connected development, as well as common but differentiated responsibilities; and encourage economic self-determination. A new set of parameters aimed at correcting generations of adverse Israeli-Arab economic relations must be recognized, endorsed, and pursued by all parties, including external partners.

## PLAUSIBILITY OF THE PARALLEL STATES SOLUTION

The Parallel States structure presents its own challenges and pokes at the conventional wisdom, just like any other theoretical model. It asks two nations and two states to shed a seventy-year-old conflict, which has been marked by bloodshed and a strong ideological divide. Palestinians are strongly tied to their ancestral land. The refugees desperately want to express their right of return to that land, and all Palestinians want to move freely and to have access to worship at their holy sites, especially in the Old City of Jerusalem. If they shared the land in the context of a Parallel States structure, they would be giving up exclusivity and absolute control. Many would find the framework in this sense problematic.

The Parallel States structure proposes that the Palestinians abandon ways of thinking that have shaped their approach to nationhood since the onset of the conflict, and skip many stages of national expression built around exclusive territorial definition and sovereignty. Consequently, it presents them with the challenge to bypass conventional notions of independence and the customary norms of international law. According to this model, they would share the land and have joint administration over certain functions with Israel. It would be a very large leap into the future.

However, Palestinians would have to weigh continued waiting to divide the land with Israel while risking that their share of the pie will continue to get smaller and smaller—not to mention that any such division would bar them from much of historic Palestine. These considerations should be viewed in conjunction with the ongoing threat to Palestinian identity and its attachment to territory. Thus, they may want to critically contemplate and consider adopting an option like the Parallel States solution, wherein the whole land would be shared on a nonexclusive sovereign basis. The Parallel States structure is a conceivable alternative that ought to be seriously considered, since it promises to provide the political, economic, and security welfare and prosperity that the Palestinians have long and desperately desired.

# CHAPTER 11

# Parallel Lives, Parallel States

*Imagining a Different Future*

EYAL MEGGED

"We are not going to get rid of them. They will continue to live around us and in our midst."[1]

I wrote those words to open an article for *Haaretz* on the Parallel States plan as the 2013 Knesset campaign was drawing to a close. The sentiment was expressed in response to a comment by Israel's newest political savior, former newsman Yair Lapid, in a rally for his Yesh Atid (There Is a Future) party on October 29, 2012. "We have to get rid of the Palestinians," he declared when asked about his peace plan.[2] *Lhipater*—to expel, get rid of, dispose of. There is no ambiguity in the word he chose. Nevertheless, of course, people immediately began to "explain" his intention—"What he means, of course, is not that . . . "; "He doesn't really want to expel them; he means we have to get rid of the demographic threat"; and so on. Indeed, Yitzhak Rabin used similar language—he spoke of a desire to "divorce" the Palestinians, the centerpiece of Labor Party rhetoric at the start of the Oslo era.

But Lapid's tone remained unchanged on election night on January 22, 2013, when he declared that he would not block a Netanyahu-led coalition by forming one with any "Hanin Zuabis" (a reference to the rising star of Palestinian Israeli politics and member of the Balad Party). What do these words reflect? They reflect a racism that is both commonplace and well entrenched; no Jewish Israeli political leader has ever used Arab parties even to cement their coalition, never mind block another one. Yet his attitude is also one that is becoming even more pronounced today, when a man routinely described as "well-read" and "worldly" (and not "right wing" or "religious") can say such things as if they require no comment—and in fact it seems they do not.

Lapid's comments are just one recent incident pointing to the increasingly blatant and unreserved racism across and within Israeli society. On a radio show I was asked what I think about the football team Beitar Yerushelaim, whose supporters are known to be rabidly anti-Arab and will not allow the management to buy Muslim players from Chechnya. I responded that, as an enthusiastic football fan, I do not see this as a football problem. This racism reflects the racism of Jerusalem and of all Israel. Yair Lapid knew exactly to whom he was speaking when he said what he said.

And so, as I began writing the column for *Haaretz,* this was the first thing I thought: We are *not* going to get rid of them. Stop the illusion. And anyway, I don't want to get rid of them, because I like to live with some of them more than I like to live with some of us.

However intense the anger, hatred, and racism, the day will come when "we" will sit with "them" and discuss how to live together. That will probably happen not by choice, but by coercion, and the representatives from the two sides will not be the present ones. Those who represent us today are attached to one story alone, and quote from it only what they consider convenient.

## MOVING BEYOND SELECTIVE HISTORY

For example, I read that from the famous eulogy delivered by Moshe Dayan for Roi Rothberg—who was killed on the border with Gaza in 1956—Ehud Barak chose to quote only this sentence: "This is the fate of our generation. The only choice we have is to be prepared and armed, strong and resolute or else our sword will slip from our hand and the thread of our lives will be severed."[3]

The rest of the eulogy, which was written in the spirit of a biblical lament, did not serve the defense minister's purpose at that moment. This is the vast disparity between the leadership of our generation and that of the previous generation: ours are salesmen, mainly selling themselves, while they—despite all their blunders—were fired with a sense of mission. Even as he grieved at the newly dug grave, Dayan did not forget the other side to the tragedy and did not let his listeners forget: "Let us not today fling accusations at the murderers. What cause have we to complain about their fierce hatred for us? For eight years now, they sit in their refugee camps in Gaza, and before their very eyes we turn into our homestead the land and villages in which they and their forefathers lived. We should demand blood [for Roi] not from the Arabs of Gaza but from ourselves."

If that narrative does not speak to you, there is no chance that you will be able to breach the hate barrier. There is no reason to suspect that Prime Minister Binyamin Netanyahu is unaware of the course of history. But whereas Dayan felt the Palestinian side of the story in every fiber of his being even as he fought against it, Netanyahu is just insensitive to it. He refuses to see reality through the eyes of the other side, apparently on the assumption that seeing both sides will weaken him and us. But to be sensitive and mindful of what is happening on the other side of the fence does not mean forgoing the survival instinct. On the contrary: those who see the whole picture are assuredly more firmly rooted in reality. Certainly the chance of any two-state solution, even one based on divorce or "getting rid of" the other side, will be nil without seeing enough through the opponents' eyes to recognize their history and the justice of their claims.

Indeed, in the same period in which Dayan delivered his lamentation for Roi Rothberg, an infiltrator from the Gaza Strip murdered my grandfather in his orchard, in the dunes of Palmahim. The citrus industry had just recovered from the nadir into which it had been plunged by the world war and Israel's War of Independence. Following a lengthy period rife with despair and humiliations, during which my grandfather had to hide continuously from his creditors, buds of hope had appeared. One day, before starting to walk along the dirt trail that led to the road to Rishon LeZion, from which he always started his long journey home by foot and by public transportation, my grandfather went to start the pump engine, as he did at the end of every working day. He was killed near the dark structure that housed the well. An Arab worker nearby fled when he heard the shot, leaving my grandfather to bleed to death.

After the assassination of Ahmed Jabari, second in command of Hamas's military wing, an earlier interview with him was broadcast in which he had rejected all possibility of Jewish life in the land of Israel. "I have no problem with a Jew who lives in the United States or England," he said, "but I will fight every Jew who lives between the Jordan and the sea." It used to be to our minds only on the Palestinian side, but of course more and more we see the same discourse in Israel. For a long time I didn't like to make parallels between us and them, but now I see that we are not better than they are.

It's not merely that Israeli society has become so anti-Palestinian; at least there are reasons for this. It's the prejudice against everything that is not Jewish. We've become more closed and hostile, moving in a direction that's impossible to support—calling for the destruction of the Dome of the Rock or the expulsion of Palestinians, declaring that there will never be a Palestinian state under any conditions, and so on. People pretend to be optimistic—they say, "Look, we're not as radical as we thought" after the election because of Lapid's strong showing—but this is an illusion: if Lapid says things like the quote at the start of this chapter, then we're not in the center anymore.

Those words, combined with the deeds that have accompanied them for decades, are cause for despair. At least with Dayan and the other leaders of the 1948 generation, they knew to whom the bill was due, even if they weren't prepared to pay it. We don't even know that the bill is due anymore, never mind to whom it's owed; or perhaps more accurately, we don't care to know. Today we lack the ability to identify with the other. The impact of this disability on Israeli society is immense, the lack of ability to have pity on others, to sympathize. It's harder to imagine that maybe Israel could once again become what it used to be because I now doubt whether it ever was what we thought.

It is in this context that today we find ourselves in the midst of another chapter in this struggle. By now, everyone knows that when one launches a military operation, there is no way to predict what its aftermath will be. From the Punic Wars to the Napoleonic conquests and the two world wars, the first moves by one of the parties began with a triumphant fanfare, often followed by impressive achievements on the ground; then they continued with disappointments, and ended in bitter chagrin. On the very first day of Operation Pillar of Defense in 2012, we were informed of tremendous achievements by the air force in destroying the enemy's missile stockpiles, just as in previous operations. But amazingly, as the war went on attacks did not lessen, much less stop; on the contrary, they intensified, as though nothing had been destroyed. Moreover, one errant Israeli bomb wiped out a family, instantly turning the war heroes into war criminals.

"So, what do you suggest?"

HIDDEN MOTIVES, A NEW AGENDA?

As a first step, I begin by wondering about the hidden motives that impel our government—which we are supposed to trust implicitly—first in going to war, and second, in feeding the public falsehoods. Too often have we gone through the ritual in which extraneous considerations encourage public attention to focus on a cycle of violence that suppresses thought and fans passions. As in narrative plots, psychological motives are at work here that do not manifest themselves either in headlines or in what underlies them. Here, precisely, lies the position that should be occupied by the irresponsible eccentric known as the "intellectual," who, in contrast to commentators and politicians, eventually gets bored with thinking the same thoughts all the time.

The problem is that the practical, ostensibly acceptable ideas are appallingly limited. Time and again we chew the same conceptual cud; time and again we hear the same moldy, despair-creating solutions, which are unable to break the vicious cycle of stimulus and response— the solutions we have witnessed all our lives. As someone who is considered an "involved writer," I am frequently asked, after I voice comments of one kind or another, the question of questions: "So, what do you suggest?" I prefer to say what I dream about. I dream about a leader who embarks on peace talks more easily than he or she embarks on a military operation. Someone who is not entirely certain that the only language Arabs understand—in contradistinction to us—is the language of force. I dream of someone who is capable of fresh thinking.

This is where the Parallel States Project comes into the picture. I have been involved in the group of scholars, activists, and diplomats represented in this book since its inception more than half a decade ago. At first—and perhaps second—glance, the idea seemed fantastical (and indeed, it still does): two parallel states covering the entire territory from the Mediterranean to the Jordan River. How can we share something even more intimately when we can't manage to divide it so disproportionately? And yet there is something powerful about the idea that each state will have the right to say, "it's all mine," for it means that for the first time citizens of the two states will truly realize their sovereignty "bodily"; they will bear that sovereignty wherever they go within the borders of Israel-Palestine.

Sovereignty based on the citizen, not on the territory: the meaning of this transformation is as profound as it is still difficult for me to comprehend. This is something we have barely yet talked about among the participants in this project and this book. It is like creating a European citizen on top of and alongside one's older "national" identity; like the Pole who carries his national identity wherever he travels but now today has a European identity that is equally important. For me, such a notion of sovereignty allows for the retention of an Israeli Jewish identity while also becoming fully "Middle Eastern." I would rather have a new Middle Eastern identity than a merely Jewish Israeli identity. This is the real "New Middle East," a very different one from the version originally dreamed up and sold by Shimon Peres, Yossi Beilin, and the other architects of Oslo.

I think about the practical ramifications: all citizens of the two states would be able to live wherever they chose between the Mediterranean Sea and the Jordan River, and yet remain citizens of one or another of the two states exclusively. They would be able to vote for the governing bodies of their state and be brought to trial according to the laws of that state, and yet would share the land, completely, with the other whom for a century their people had been in a life-and-death struggle to evict. Having state-exclusivity but sharing land completely—this is the trick that makes a Parallel States plan seem simultaneously fantastical and perhaps unrealistic and yet profoundly realistic. It can help heal, or at least displace and yet heal, all the anger that swims around inside every inhabitant of this land, regardless of which side he or she lives on.

In short, a Parallel States plan helps us heal by allowing and encouraging us to share. Seven years ago, I wrote, "Coveting the same land, like coveting the same woman, creates a complex relationship. You can't help feeling close to someone who is attracted to the same things you are. Loving the same woman means that you have something in common deep down inside. On the one hand you feel close to this man, on the other you yearn for his destruction. Whatever the case, the bond created between you and he cannot be denied."[4]

Of course, in this scenario the one who is always denied choice is the woman, here the land (which in both Hebrew [adamah] and Arabic [ard] is gendered feminine). She becomes passive, without the ability to make the choice. She becomes perhaps the primary victim of the abuse, the violence, and the anger. If today we don't care about two-thousand-year-old olive trees—how can you care about the olive trees and destroy them by the thousands, as we've done?—or the landscape, which we've destroyed with giant roads and monstrous walls, how can we say we love the land? We're not talking about the same kind of love, or love of any sort anymore. The land is merely used and abused.

Perhaps in the first stage of the post-1967 settlement enterprise the settlers had this love-relationship with the land. They were really idealists and in a way—at least from our side—innocent, naively thinking that the "natives" would recognize their claims or passion to come back to the land of their forefathers. They really thought so. And it took them a long time to change. And when they did they became mere colonizers.

This brings us back to Hanin Zuabi, with whom Yair Lapid declared he'd never join in coalition to block a right-wing government. In a *Haaretz* interview, she said, "Jews don't know how to love their country." And today I can understand what she means and can agree with her. We are home; but how can we call home what we treat the way we treat this land?

## RETURNING TO OUR ROOTS

Here it's important to know whence the Parallel States idea emerged. Basically, the program sprang from the clear recognition that it is impossible to divide the land of Israel and impossible to divide Palestine, either physically or mentally. Perhaps, as Solomon would have admonished us, true love would rather share than mortally divide. Disengagement from the Palestinians carries with it no salvation, but rather the reverse, as we have seen with our own eyes since the "magic solution" concocted by Ariel Sharon for Gaza with the 2005 "disengagement." (Never mind the "divorce" that Oslo was always supposed to be.) That is why I opposed the unilateral pullout from Gaza with all my might, despite the high price I paid for crossing the political lines.

From an Israeli perspective, the Parallel States idea stems also from the desire to break the dogmatism of the "peace camp"—or should we say "peace religion"—which presupposes, in a mistake that conflicts with reality time and again, that the return of the territory conquered in 1967 will constitute suitable atonement for the sin (with or without quotation marks) that we committed in 1948. The sin has changed over time. Today it is at its heart the sin of forgetting, or of erasing what members of the previous generation saw with their own eyes before partition. And so atonement, then, is bringing back forgotten or repressed memories and confronting them. The Parallel States plan allows this to happen; indeed, it encourages and demands it. If the sin was wiping out the Palestinian reality—not only on the ground but in the memory, history, everything—then atonement is reestablishing and reimplanting that memory, as much within ourselves as allowing them to do so on their ancestral land.

Those participating in this project began from a position of hope, however fantastical: in an era in which, to evoke Marx's axiom, consciousness is no longer necessarily determined by one's being, in the virtual and simulative time in which we live—the time of computers, Facebook, Google, and the rest of the Internet, where fewer and fewer connections are material, are real—it is possible, we believe, to apply full sovereignty without territorial attachment. Our political and national identities can be realized without our possessing exclusivity over the territory.

And yet the Parallel States plan is not merely a drastic innovation; it is also a compromise between the prevailing notion of two states for two nations and a binational state. We are talking explicitly about two sovereign nation-states, each of which realizes within its own framework its aspiration for a distinctive, separate identity. Obviously, numberless questions arise, of a legal, economic, and above all security character. This book represents a preliminary—however hopefully thorough and well-executed—attempt to answer some of the myriad questions arising out of this idea.

Despite all our work and attempts to compromise, despite endless arguments and compromises and pleadings and defiance and "Eureka!" moments, many of our suggestions, never mind their details—for example, in the security realm—will inevitably shatter our illusions about the possible futures before us. That is, there really is no long-term alternative to just continuing to muddle through, to just "managing the Palestinians" while life goes on as normal and the occupation continues indefinitely. Either apartheid or a unitary state is on the horizon, likely both together, if we don't change soon.

More prosaically, it is clear that however much the Parallel States plan is based on Palestinians and Israelis living together, for the foreseeable future there will be no choice but to allot exclusive areas to each state in which military forces will deploy for every emergency (special forces, secret military assets like the Dimona nuclear reactor, and special combat units). Lions and lambs—or rather, lions and cougars—don't simply lie down together and forget their past antagonism and competition.

## A ROLE FOR EUROPE

There is reason to believe that the European community would be obliged to assist in the building of this model by bringing our peculiar animal into its herd, which of course would be a crucial incentive for both sides. This is not a subject of strong agreement among the participants in the project; and indeed, there are some who find it either not so important or even irrelevant (especially considering the difficulties currently being experienced by the European Union). But I believe that offering and encouraging the two states to join the European Union would be the cement that glued the whole process together in the long term, just as the European Union has served as the glue to keep its members together despite all the problems it has failed to address and perhaps even encouraged. Indeed, while leftists suspect that the plan is a right-wing conspiracy to prevent the partition of the country, and the right (as laid out by Naftali Bennett's Jewish Home party) plans ultimately to annex all the territory of "Area C" and grant the roughly 150,000 Palestinians living there full citizenship rights within Israel as its preferred solution, a Parallel States solution would ensure in a pragmatic way that all the inhabitants of the country enjoyed the fullest rights possible without having to dilute their core identities or put their basic security and future at risk.

That is the plan, in a nutshell. The chapters you have read are packed with details; if they demonstrate one thing, it's that at least we are not hallucinating. Surprisingly, in discussing the Parallel States solution with a range of people from the extremes of left and right in both communities, hardly anyone suggested sending us for psychiatric observation. All listened attentively. Sometimes their eyes lit up. Astonishingly, people from the right wing in Israel are more receptive to the idea than those from the left, precisely because it satisfies perhaps the most important core goal: to remain rooted as sovereign citizens in the biblical heartland of Eretz Yisrael, in a way that no other plan does.

Our Palestinian partners would, I hope, testify that they have rarely if ever reached the same level of understanding with Israelis as they have in the forum we've created and shared, usually intimately, sometimes publicly, for a good part of the past decade. What is important here is the lack of duplicity. Unlike our Oslo compatriots, the Israeli participants have not said one thing and meant another. There was no agenda of drawing out talks while creating facts on the ground. At any rate, we are not the creators of facts. We are trying, rather, to create a viable future.

I believe from my experience that rarely, if ever, have Palestinians been shown the same openness by Israelis, leftists or rightists, as in our meetings. There has developed an understanding between us that, above all, a separation into two states does not satisfy their true longings—an understanding that, they have said, the Palestinians do not have with most of the Israeli peace activists. The half (or really, rump) country supposedly waiting around the corner is not what they are dreaming of. The Palestinians with whom we collaborated declined to let go of their national childhood; of the good childhood and the bad childhood, of the memory of its ordeals and of the pain caused by their expulsion from it.

## PEACE AS A MIRROR IMAGE

Let's face it, no one really wants two half-states if there is a way we can both have it all. Neither of us will be whole with half the country—and such important halves! Jerusalem, Hebron, Jaffa, Haifa—permanently removed from our bodies.

The emphasis here is on a mirror image, and this is something many among us tend to repress. Not until we face squarely the joint trauma of the two nations can the deep scars be healed. I believe that the Parallel States plan copes precisely with this repression through the solutions it proposes. That is what makes it revolutionary in the deepest sense of the word.

I have no choice but to believe that if a leader arises who thinks in such terms, he or she will also be able to find a path to the bitterest of our enemies, including, from "our" side, the leaders of Hamas, whom at present we see largely through gun sights or rocket launchers. I have no choice but to believe, because if I do not have faith my life here will be unbearable. Masada is not the place I want to live, not even in a villa. It seems to me that this is also not the wish of the majority of the nation that is emerging here, for whom pampering and self-indulgence are the usual mantras. The leader I would like to see in my lifetime will be able to say to the Palestinian and Arabs more broadly without fear, "Let us live together here *(Bo'u nihiye kaan beyahad)*." Not only does it have a nice rhythm to it; we simply have no other choice.

The other day I joined a tour of villages in the Nablus area, arranged by a group called "Combatants for Peace" (young veterans from combat units in the Israeli army who have their counterparts, former Palestinian fighters, in the West Bank) and I was amazed to realize how close the situation is there to the Parallel States vision.

There were the Palestinian villages, pastoral, at one with the natural ancient landscape, and there were the Israeli settlements, bringing with them the Zionist landscape from inside the pre-1967 parts of Israel, with the artificial pine "forests" that surround them. Two cultures in all respects—architecture, way of life, aesthetic values—that exist side by side, sometimes entangled with each other, with no mutual recognition whatever. Without mutual recognition. Astonishing, really. But this state of affairs is made possible not only by the force of the stronger, not only by the IDF, but also thanks to the goodwill and cooperation of the Palestinian security forces.

This impossible-possible situation in the heart of Samaria, in the heart of Palestine, is a cause for hope, in spite of the numerous complaints and the everyday injustice. It is a proof that the mutual will of two different cultures to live together, side by side, can achieve the impossible, the unimaginable. The wrong can be made into right if only you believe and let go of superstitions, if only you show respect for the other's right to live as you yourself wish to live. Parallel lives in parallel states doesn't mean endless bloodshed. It could mean the opposite: endless vital forces making a dream come true.

NOTES

1. This chapter is adapted from a column originally published in *Haaretz* on November 24, 2012, in Hebrew (www.haaretz.co.il/magazine/1.1871620) and on November 29, 2012, in English (www.haaretz.com/weekend/magazine/parallel-lives-parallel-states-a-new-solution-to-our-age-old-conflict.premium-1.481408).

2. Quoted in Revital Hovel, "Lapid Reveals a Political Matter" (in Hebrew), *Haaretz,* October 30, 2012.

3. Quoted in Avi Shlaim, *The Iron Wall: Israel and the Arab World* (New York: W.W. Norton, 2001), 101.

4. Eyal Megged, "A Dream of One Land," *The Guardian,* January 5, 2005.

# Contributors

HUSSEIN AGHA is currently a senior associate member of St Antony's College, Oxford. He was publisher and editor, with Ahmad Samih Khalidi, of the London-based *Strategic Review* between 1980 and 1989. He served as adviser to the Lebanese Reconciliation Conference in Lausanne in 1984 and to the Palestinian delegation at the Madrid-Washington peace talks in 1991 and 1992. He has been active in Palestinian politics for four decades and a long-term participant in track II talks. He was a founding member of the core group of the Washington-based Search for Common Ground (Middle East) between 1989 and 2003. His books (cowritten with Ahmad Samih Khalidi) include *Syria and Iran: Rivalry and Cooperation* (1995), *Track-2 Diplomacy: Lessons from the Middle East* (2003), and *A Palestinian National Security Framework* (2006), and he writes on political and strategic affairs for many international publications.

RAPHAEL BAR-EL is a professor emeritus in the Department of Public Policy and Administration at Ben-Gurion University, which he founded and chaired from 1996 to 2002 and from 2008 to 2010. He was dean of the School of Economics and Business Administration at the Ruppin Academic Center between 2010 and 2012, and is today the chair of the Applied Economics Department at the Sapir Academic College. He has a doctorate in economics (dissertation: "The Role of Industrialization in Regional Development"). He was in charge of the Economic Development Plan within the team of the Long-Term Master Plan for Israel and of the economic master plans for a few cities in Israel. He collaborates with various academic institutions around the world in research projects related to regional economic growth and cooperation.

JENS BARTELSON is a professor of political science at Lund University, Sweden. His fields of interest include international political theory, the history of political thought, political philosophy, and social theory. He has written mainly about the concept of the sovereign state and the philosophy of world community. He is the author of *Visions of World Community* (2009), *The Critique of the State* (2001), and *A Genealogy of Sovereignty* (1995).

IRIS CANOR teaches European law, public international law, and private international law at the Haim Striks School of Law at the College of Management and Academic Studies in Rishon LeZion, Israel. She is adjunct professor at Europa Institute, Germany, and has held visiting positions at the Max Planck Institute for Comparative Public Law and International Law (Heidelberg), Columbia Law School, New York University, and the Center for Transnational Legal Studies (London). Her main research interests and publications focus on the relation between European law and international law, transnational law, international human rights, and law and globalization.

ANDREW CRAIG earned his bachelor of arts degree in economics from Marquette University and his juris doctorate from the University of Iowa College of Law, focusing on international humanitarian and human rights law. While completing his JD, Andrew contributed to Al Mustakbal Foundation's work as an intern and joined the foundation full-time in fall 2013.

ÁLVARO DE SOTO'S twenty-five years in the UN Secretariat spanned the terms of three secretaries-general, starting in 1982. He conducted the 1990–1991 negotiations leading to the comprehensive peace accords that ended the war in El Salvador. He was the UN special envoy for Myanmar from 1995 to 1999. He mediated the 1999–2004 negotiations on the Cyprus problem, which led to parallel referendums on the comprehensive Annan Plan for a settlement, and was special representative for the Western Sahara from 2003 to 2005. He left the United Nations in 2007 after two years in Jerusalem and Gaza as the chief UN envoy for the Arab-Israeli conflict. Among current affiliations he is a member of the Global Leadership Foundation and a senior fellow at the Ralph Bunche Institute in New York. Since 2011 he has led a master's-level seminar course on post–Cold War conflict resolution at the Paris School of International Affairs at Sciences Po, in Paris.

NIMROD HURVITZ received his doctorate from Princeton University in 1994 and currently teaches at Ben-Gurion University, Israel. He has written extensively about Islamic religious movements. His book *The Formation of Hanbalism* (2002) has been translated into Arabic (2011). Between 2004 and 2006 he was a visiting scholar at Harvard University Law School and a scholar-in-residence at Skidmore College. He lectures on the Middle East and contributes op-eds to leading Israeli newspapers such as *Haaretz* (English), *Yediot Ahronot, Maariv,* and *Makor Rishon,* as well as HNN (History News Network). He is also a contributor to the Web site CanThink.

HIBA HUSSEINI is the managing partner the law firm of Husseini and Husseini in Ramallah. Under her management the firm serves a large domestic and international client base on a wide range of business matters. Prior to returning to Palestine in 1994, she practiced law in Washington, D.C. Husseini chairs the legal committee of the Final-Status Negotiations between the Palestinians and Israelis and has served as a legal adviser to the peace process negotiations since

1994. She is a founding member of Al-Mustakbal Foundation, a nonpartisan organization aimed at promoting economic development and rule of law in Palestine. She has written widely on business law, rule of law, and economic development. Husseini holds a juris doctorate from Georgetown University (1992), master's degree in political science from the George Washington University (1986), master of science degree in corporate finance from the University of Sorbonne (2002), and a bachelor's degree in political science from the University of Tennessee (1982). She speaks three languages.

AHMAD SAMIH KHALIDI is currently senior associate member of St Antony's College, Oxford, and editor in chief of the *Journal of Palestine Studies* (Arabic edition). He was coeditor with Hussein Agha of the London-based Arabic-language bimonthly *Strategic Review* between 1980 and 1989. He served as adviser to the Palestinian delegation at the Madrid-Washington peace talks from 1991 to 1993 and as senior adviser on security to the Cairo-Taba PLO-Israeli talks in 1993. He was cochair of the American Academy of Arts and Sciences project on Israeli-Palestinian security from 1993 to 1995. He has been active in Palestinian politics and track II activities for more than thirty years. His books (cowritten with Hussein Agha) include *Syria and Iran: Rivalry and Cooperation* (1995), *Track-2 Diplomacy: Lessons from the Middle East* (2003), and *A Palestinian National Security Framework* (2006).

RAJA KHALIDI, whose family is originally from Jerusalem, has lived mainly in the Middle East and Europe. He was trained as a development economist, with a bachelor's degree (with honors) from Oxford University and master of science degree from the University of London (SOAS). He has conducted research and published widely on Palestinian economic conditions in Lebanon, in Israel, and in the Occupied Territory. He worked with the United Nations Conference on Trade and Development from 1985 to 2013, was coordinator of its Programme of Assistance to the Palestinian people, and a senior economist in its Division on Globalization and Development Strategies. He has been a member of the Arab Society for Economic Research, an advisory member of the Palestinian Welfare Association, a founding member of the Palestine Family Relief Fund (Geneva), and member of the board of trustees of the Palestine Economic Policy Research Institute, MAS (Ramallah).

MARK LEVINE is a professor of history at the University of California, Irvine, and distinguished visiting professor at the Center for Middle Eastern Studies, Lund University, Sweden. He is the author and editor of more than half a dozen books, many of them focused on Palestine-Israel, including *Overthrowing Geography: Jaffa, Tel Aviv, and the Struggle for Palestine* (2005), *Reapproaching Borders: New Perspectives on the Study of Israel-Palestine* (with Sandra Sufian, 2007), *Impossible Peace: Israel/Palestine since 1989* (2009), and *Struggle and Survival in Palestine/Israel* (with Gershon Shafir, 2012). He is a senior columnist at al-Jazeera's flagship English Web site and codirector of the project Research, Advocacy and Public Policy: Human Rights in the Arab World with Lund University and the Issam Fares Institute at the American University in Beirut.

EYAL MEGGED was born in New York in 1948, and grew up in Tel Aviv. He studied philosophy and art history at Tel Aviv University. A poet and novelist,

Megged has served as editor of a weekly *Voice of Israel* radio program and has written regular columns for Israel's leading newspapers on a wide range of subjects, including literature, culture, and sports. At present he writes regularly for *Haaretz*. Megged has been awarded the Macmillan Prize (1993); the Yedioth Ahronoth Prize for his short story, "Cup Final"; the Book Publishers Association's Gold and Platinum book prizes for his novels *Everlasting Life* (1999), *Saving Grace* (2001), and *The Kamikaze's Woman* (2013); and the Prime Minister's Prize twice (1990 and 2005).

MATHIAS MOSSBERG is a retired ambassador, president of the Swedish–North African Chamber of Commerce, and senior fellow at the Center for Middle Eastern Studies, Lund University, Sweden. Prior to joining Lund University, Ambassador Mossberg was adviser on dialogue with the Muslim world at the Swedish Ministry for Foreign Affairs, and before that vice president of the East-West Institute in New York and responsible for its Middle East program. He was Sweden's ambassador to Morocco (1994–96), and served in diplomatic posts in London, Amman, New York, Moscow, and Geneva. He has long experience with mediation and conflict management, both in the Caucasus and in the Middle East, where he was deeply involved in Sweden's efforts to promote the peace process, and often served as an envoy of the Swedish minister for Foreign Affairs. He has published books and articles about Swedish security policy, conflict management, and the Israeli-Palestinian conflict. He received his bachelor of law and of arts degree from Uppsala University and also studied at Collège d'Europe, Bruges, and Institut des Hautes Études Internationales, Geneva. In addition to his native Swedish, he speaks English, French, German, and Russian.

ABSAL NUSEIBEH read psychology and Middle Eastern studies at the University of Toronto before beginning clinical training in the Gaza Strip at the Gaza Mental Health Program. After completing an LLB at the University of Buckingham in 2005, he returned to Palestine to train in corporate law. Soon afterward he began to work as a legal consultant for the Palestine Liberation Organization's Negotiations Support Unit and later took on a full-time position advising on the legal side of final-status issues including Jerusalem, security, and other questions. He was also seconded to help establish the newly formed Higher Council for Youth and Sport. In January 2013 he opened his own law firm in East Jerusalem.

LIAM O'MARA IV is a doctoral candidate in Middle Eastern history at the University of California, Irvine. His dissertation explores the roots of, and commonalities within, popular protest movements from Israel, Egypt, and Turkey. He is an adjunct lecturer at Chapman University and at the California State University Dominguez Hills and San Bernardino campuses, where he teaches on the intersections of religion, nationalism, popular culture, and political protest.

SHARIF SILMI is an entrepreneur, consultant, and strategist; currently he is the managing principal of a wireless retail chain in California. A native of Jerusalem, Palestine, Sharif advocates issues important to the Palestinian cause, with a particular focus on youth and strengthening connections between Palestine and the diaspora. He completed his undergraduate studies at the California

State University, East Bay, and holds a juris doctorate from the University of the Pacific, McGeorge School of Law, where he was vice president of the International Law Society. Silmi is married with three young daughters.

PETER WALLENSTEEN has been senior professor of peace and conflict research since 2012 (and was holder of the Dag Hammarskjöld Chair of Peace and Conflict Research from 1985 to 2012) at Uppsala University, as well as the Richard G. Starmann Sr. Research Professor of Peace Studies at the Kroc Institute for International Peace Studies, University of Notre Dame, Indiana (since 2006). He directs the Uppsala Conflict Data Program, which publishes annual data on armed conflicts online, as well as in the SIPRI Yearbooks and the *Journal of Peace Research*. His book *Peace Research: Theory and Practice* (2011) brings together his writings and includes an account of his involvement with the Israel-PLO negotiations from 1990. His book *Understanding Conflict Resolution* (2012) is now in its third edition. It is used worldwide and has been translated into Arabic. With Isak Svensson he published *The Go-Between* (2010), on the mediation experiences of Ambassador Jan Eliasson. He is currently engaged in separate projects on Nordic mediation, on the concept of Quality Peace, and on regional organizations in peacemaking.

DROR ZEEVI teaches Ottoman and Turkish history at Ben-Gurion University of the Negev in the Department of Middle East Studies, which he helped found and chaired from 1995 to 1998 and from 2002 to 2004. He was also among the founders and chair of the Chaim Herzog Center for Middle East Studies and Diplomacy. His research and teaching interests include Ottoman and Middle Eastern society and culture. His book on Ottoman Jerusalem, *An Ottoman Century: The District of Jerusalem in the 1600s* (1996) was translated into Hebrew and Turkish. Another book, *Producing Desire: Changing Sexual Discourse in the Ottoman Middle East, 1500–1900* (2006) was recently translated into Turkish. His current research focuses on the Armenian massacres in the Ottoman Empire and Turkey, 1894–1924.

# Index

Israeli security strategy *(continued)*
for, 75–77; joint security system, 77–78;
multilayered network for, 82–83;
national interests, 115; power
asymmetries and, 113–15; PSP and,
68–69, 74–77, 91–92, 239–40; threat
perceptions, 73–74, 79–82; Zionist
historical narrative and, 69–73
Israeli settlements: Haredi-only, 215–16,
217–18, 230n38; as Israeli-Palestinian
conflict issue, 7; PSP and, 4, 7, 26–27,
75; PSP legal system and, 176, 190–91;
rightwing demand for, 3, 234
Israeli settler movement: political parties,
214; PSP and, 206–7; religious
grounding of, 214, 217–18
Israeli War of Independence (1948), 71,
130, 246
Israel-Palestine Parallel States economy:
benefits of, 155–58, 162–63, 242;
constraints/detriments of, 159–64;
cooperating parties, 164; current
structural imbalances and, 128–37,
153–55, 160–62, 166, 167, 170–71,
241; economic depolarization, 143–45;
economic development strategies,
138–43, 163; economic integration
theories and, 131–34; economic openess
assumed in, 155, 171; goals for, 142,
144, 154; high-tech collaboration,
166–68, 172; intervention measures in,
165, 168; labor-force mobility in,
164–66, 172; need for, 123–25, 153–55;
parameters assumed in, 125–28, 162,
164, 242; rebalancing efforts, 143–45;
regional cooperation projects, 168–70,
172; reterritorialization and, 241–42;
separation vs. union, 145–49; two-stage
agreement needed for, 164, 171; vision
for, 149–50
Israel-Palestine Parallel States legal system/
judiciary: civil/private law, 196–97,
204n46; complications involved in,
200–201; constitutional law, 195–96;
criminal law, 198–99; feasibility of,
175–80; harmonized legislation in, 5–7,
22–23; historical precedents for,
178–79; implementation realities, 7,
192–95; international recognition and,
182–84; land/property law, 197–98;
Palestinian legal history and, 184–87;
PSP basic assumptions and, 180–82,
187; social justice issues in, 189–92;
sovereignty/jurisdiction in, 187–88

Israel-Palestine Protocol on Economic
Relations (1994), 136

Jabari, Ahmed, 246
Japan, 50
Jaseem, A., 169
Jerusalem, 18; economy of, 131; Haredi
neighborhoods in, 223; holy places in,
97, 98, 102, 112, 243; Israeli control of,
94–95, 212; as Israeli-Palestinian
conflict issue, 7; Jewish access to biblical
heartland in, 24, 225; linkage plans with
West Bank, 214; Occupied Territories
isolated from, 104, 234, 240; Palestin-
ian capital in, 97, 98, 100, 112; Palestin-
ian claims to, 209; Palestinian
population of, 95; PSP and, 14, 23–24,
191; tourism projects proposed for, 170.
*See also* East Jerusalem
Jerusalem Old City Initiative (University of
Windsor, Canada), 24
Jewish Diaspora, 69, 70, 71, 72
Jewish Enlightenment, 69, 211
Jewish Home Party, 214, 252
Jewish identity: security and, 16–17;
Zionism and, 71–72, 176–77
Jewish law, 185
Jewish nationalism, 212–14, 224
jihadists, international, 76
Jordan: Hamas and, 207; Hashemite rule
in, 78; Israeli-Palestinian conflict impact
on, 95; Israeli relations with, 78, 156;
joint regional cooperation projects
with, 169, 170; Ottoman-era parallel
legal systems in, 179; Palestine ruled
by, 99; Palestinian refugees in, 121;
Palestinian statehood and, 103;
radical internal groups and strategic
weapons in, 76; West Bank claimed
by, 97, 207
Jordanian East Bank, 185
Jordanian Parliament, 185
Jordan River Valley, 80, 84, 87, 108, 145
Judaism: gender issues and, 221–22;
Ottoman-era legal jurisdictions and,
178–79; PSP and, 24, 75; social
justice as imperative in, 225–26;
ultra-Orthodox, 216 *(see also*
Haredim (ultra-Orthodox Jews));
Zionist movement and, 211–12, 213
Judt, Tony, 147
justice. *See* social justice
*Justice and Only Justice* (Ateek), 226–27
Jütersonke, Oliver, 10–11